M000188219

Community Planning

To My Parents

Community Planning

How to Solve Urban and Environmental Problems

Stephanie B. Kelly

ROWMAN & LITTLEFIELD PUBLISHERS, INC.
Lanham • *Boulder* • *New York* • *Toronto* • *Oxford*

ROWMAN & LITTLEFIELD PUBLISHERS, INC.

Published in the United States of America
by Rowman & Littlefield Publishers, Inc.
A wholly owned subsidiary of The Rowman & Littlefield Publishing Group, Inc.
4501 Forbes Boulevard, Suite 200, Lanham, Maryland 20706
www.rowmanlittlefield.com

PO Box 317
Oxford
OX2 9RU, UK

Copyright © 2004 by Rowman & Littlefield Publishers, Inc.

All rights reserved. No part of this publication may be reproduced,
stored in a retrieval system, or transmitted in any form or by any
means, electronic, mechanical, photocopying, recording, or otherwise,
without the prior permission of the publisher.

British Library Cataloguing in Publication Information Available

Library of Congress Cataloging-in-Publication Data

Kelly, Stephanie B., 1948–
  Community planning : how to solve urban and environmental problems / Stephanie B.
Kelly.
    p. cm.
  Includes bibliographical references and index.
  ISBN 0-7425-3519-3 (hardcover : alk. paper)—ISBN 0-7425-3520-7 (pbk. : alk.
paper)
  1. City planning—United States—Problems, exercises, etc. 2. City
planning—Environmental aspects—United States—Problems, exercises, etc. 3.
Land use, Urban—United States. 4. Urban ecology—United States. 5.
Sustainable development—United States. 6. Urban policy—United States. I.
Title.
  HT167.K46 2004
  307.1'216'0973—dc22
                                    2004007918

Printed in the United States of America

∞™ The paper used in this publication meets the minimum requirements of American
National Standard for Information Sciences—Permanence of Paper for Printed Library
Materials, ANSI/NISO Z39.48-1992.

Contents

Preface

Community planning in the United States has reached a critical juncture in many regions of the country. Blighted, urban areas need revitalization, small towns need to preserve their open space, and water and air quality issues need to be addressed. One day when I was explaining the state of planning to a Chinese friend, he told me a story about a Chinese character whose meaning clearly defines the problem-oriented approach in this book.

The Chinese character *weiji* symbolizes crisis and opportunity. *Wei* means danger, and *ji* implies chance, a pivot, or a crucial point in time. *Weiji* means that every crisis carries two elements—danger and opportunity—and that opportunity is inherently present in the midst of crisis. As the Chinese saying puts it, "No matter the difficulty of the circumstances, no matter how dangerous the situation. . . . At the heart of each crisis lies a tremendous opportunity. Great blessings lie ahead for the one who knows the secret of finding the opportunity within each crisis." This philosophy follows the Chinese Taoist worldview, which has the ying-yang balance at its core, and suggests that a curse can be a blessing in disguise and vice versa.[1]

Weiji signifies the dual nature of a crisis, which consists of recognizing peril and searching for potential. This philosophy can be applied to the community-planning process. Although the inner-city, rural, and pollution problems we face today seem insurmountable, we can search for inventive, cross-disciplinary solutions that set new directions and reshape our communities. To be effective players in community planning, we need to learn to respond to critical situations with a keen sense of the consequences of our actions on trends and events in the community in the future.

There are different layers of knowledge that support the problem-solving approach in this book. The geography and functional layout of the community, how the layout evolved, and the stakeholders in the planning process comprise the first layer. What is everyone thinking and what is the basis for their opinions? We need to learn the body of knowledge and necessary skills that define the field of community planning. After all the data are collected and analyzed, we recommend action plans that address the specific issues of concern of the residents and municipal and planning officials. We will, over time, need a mastery of all these perspectives to solve planning problems.

Problem solving is an integral part of the community-planning process. In actuality it is the vital force that drives the planning process. I first realized this when I taught a course called Special Topics in Affordable Housing. The objectives of the class were to identify areas of concern in housing availability and affordability and recommend solutions for the housing problems. During the course of the semester I observed that the students had difficulty making the leap from collecting and analyzing data to applying actions that would address the concerns. Clearly, the students needed strong problem-solving skills to achieve the goals for the class, as well as for future work and graduate school. They needed to analyze the situation theoretically and learn how to apply practical tools to solve the problem. Overall, problem solving is the essential link between conceptualizing the process of community planning and implementing community plans that work.

Ever since that semester, teaching problem-solving skills has been my primary goal. It is the creative problem solver who can address the tensions incumbent in planning efforts and match the appropriate tools with planning problems. As we struggle with budget deficits and competition for resources across the country, future planners will have to deal with the following urban and environmental situations that continue to challenge our communities:

- High vacancy rates and dilapidated conditions in many downtowns, creating the need for economic development and revitalization
- Severe blighted areas and lack of quality affordable housing, causing a dramatic rise in homelessness rates in many neighborhoods
- Business mergers and shutdowns, creating the need for job retraining
- High levels of toxins and hazardous materials, contaminating our atmosphere and water bodies and endangering our health
- Rapid migration shifts, creating increased demand on infrastructure in edge cities and suburban areas

To plan effectively, we need to learn to analyze data, prepare inventories and needs assessments, and apply practical tools to solve problems. The combination of readings, discussion topics, and exercises in this text provides the framework to develop action plans to solve problems.

ACKNOWLEDGMENTS

I am indebted to my family for their support and patience during the process of writing this book. A special thanks goes to my husband, Joseph, who helped me compile the bibliography. Inevitably in the field of planning it is not only computer time that interrupts family life but also travel time to collect data on current case studies. I also wish to thank Amy L. Audibert, my research assistant, for her diligent efforts in editing and her contributions to the section on smart growth. Finally, I am grateful to Monty Geer who added his artistic talents with the illustrations.

NOTE

1. *Art Print, Crisis and Opportunity by Seeds of Wisdom* (Galaxi Trading Company), retrieved May 15, 2004, from www.insight-books.com/ARTP/9991283056.html.

Introduction

One of the earliest examples of a critical planning situation occurred in the Southwest United States in our prehistoric stage of development. The Hohokam Indians, who migrated north from the area that is now Mexico into what is now the Tucson Basin in Arizona in 300 B.C., faced critical water and agricultural problems. With ingenious technological skill, the Hohokam constructed irrigation systems using only stone instruments and organized labor. The Hohokam used this complex system of canals to redirect water from rivers to fields above the floodplains, where they planted their crops. By A.D. 1200 the Indians had built hundreds of miles of canals in what is now the Phoenix area alone. The Hohokam practiced sustainable development, which maintains a balance between the use of natural resources and human needs. The Hohokam civilization vanished in A.D. 1400.

Civano, named after the Hohokam period of civilization, is a planned community that opened in Tucson in 1998. Civano is a traditional neighborhood development based on the Hohokam philosophy of sustainable development. The goals of the community are to promote economic growth while maintaining small-town values and ecological harmony. The plan for Civano, with a completion date of 2010, is a cluster design with commercial, cultural, and civic activities centered on the village square. Half of the residences and two-thirds of the jobs will be no more than a five-minute walk from the town center. The goal is to create one job for every two households and jobs in businesses engaged in solar power and other renewable-resource fields.

Whether the issues are life threatening as with the Hohokam or life adjusting as with Civano, there is a certain process we can follow to solve problems.

With a disciplined approach to assess the situation and the necessary skill set, effective plans can be developed. The plans may be for new planned communities to solve traffic, energy, and natural-resource problems or for older communities that need revitalization. The specific content and areas of research change over time, but the basic problem-solving approach is timeless.

PURPOSE OF THE TEXT AND EXERCISES

Community planning is consensus building, problem solving, and future setting. We make plans in order to be prepared and to avoid surprises down the line. Certainly, events such as the attacks of September 11, 2001, natural disasters, and the ongoing demands on federal and state funds have been a wake up call for all of us. Community awareness, preparedness, and protection have become priorities in planning practice. In response to the political and economic uncertainties, most major planning efforts begin with visioning, problem identification, and needs identification. Planning essentially has evolved into a proactive process, where planners project the needs of the residents and link them with specific action plans and programs for the future. This text provides a framework to support this emerging trend. Students are introduced to the theoretical aspects of planning, as well as a problem-oriented approach and planning exercises that reinforce the practical applications of problem solving. It is intended as the first text for planning majors, but it would aid any who want to learn about and plan for their community. Whether embarking on a career or community involvement, _community service planners_ hold the key to effective plan making in the future.

The text covers the basic theoretical principles of community planning and how planning has evolved in the United States.[1] The objectives are to define the interdisciplinary nature of the field, identify the forces that shape the planning process, and explain the field's subspecialities.[2] Throughout the text, connections are made between the theoretical principles of planning and the practical applications. This leads to an emphasis on problem solving, the essential skill that links theory to implementation and practice. At the end of the term students will have an understanding of the events that shaped community planning in the United States, the particular forces that impact the planning process, and the knowledge that is needed to link content areas to solve planning problems. After achieving an understanding of the dynamics of the components of planning and mastering the applications of problem solving, students are prepared to move on to the next stage of developing and managing the comprehensive plan.

FOCUS ON A PROBLEM-ORIENTED APPROACH

The community-planning process is constantly in a state of flux. The dynamics are such that all players involved come to the table with their own perspectives and their own morals, ethics, and values. Bringing together such a diverse group with their individual goals, while trying at the same time to meet common goals, is extremely challenging. Many push and pull factors contribute dynamic tension to the process. For example, certain groups might want to push ahead for industrial development, while other groups might want to pull back and maintain the rural character of the community. It is this dynamic tension that planners must meet head on before they can recommend an action plan or think about developing a comprehensive plan. Once a consensus about the priority goals for a community is reached and problem areas have been identified, the planner can begin the process of plan making.

The problem-solving approach presented in this text supports the direction in planning practice that many public agencies and consulting firms now follow. The visioning process, which identifies the issues of concern, sets the direction for a specific community plan. Controversies over zoning revisions, concerns about water and air contamination, or economic development issues may arise at any time during a consensus-building session. The problem-oriented approach is geared to address these specific issues, whether part of the comprehensive plan or not. The approach is similar to the type of planning Eric Kelly and Barbara Becker describe as issue driven.[3] The research and analysis components are determined based on the data concerning that one area of planning. Following this approach specific actions are recommended, grants and funding are matched to the problem, and the action plans are revised or implemented in a timely manner.

To solve problems in our communities, we need to link planning with real-world situations. Have you ever wondered how planning gets done in your community? Did you ever ask yourself: Why did they build that factory so close to the river? How did the developers of that office complex get a permit to expand when the traffic is already backed up downtown? This text is about learning how to apply tools that protect resources and special places while ensuring economic stability. The task is not easy because what one person wants, another will be against. The trick is to learn how to reach a consensus and come up with actions that will shape the community the way the majority wants it shaped while still recognizing the views of the minority. When the residents *own* the ideas about what they want or need for their community, they also *own* the responsibility to carry out realistic, commonsense plans that make their visions a reality.

The method that we will be learning to develop action plans for an area is a problem-oriented approach. This method teaches us to think analytically and intuitively about urban and environmental issues and the needs of the residents in an area. It teaches us to identify the resources in an area, analyze the needs of the people, and recommend how to allocate the resources. Solving community problems requires a certain set of skills. Clearly, planners must know a lot about physical geography, environmental issues, land-use regulations, and socioeconomic forces of a region. But beyond the background information, the planner also needs to know how to solve a particular problem.

The beauty of the problem-solving approach is that we address urban and environmental issues that need immediate attention yet may appear to have no easy answers. We learn how to solve urban revitalization, environmental pollution, affordable housing, and transportation problems. The approach works in any planning situation:

- Focus on the planning issue
- Follow the steps for the problem-solving approach
- Develop your action plans

Overall, you will learn to rethink how to deal with our resources and how to develop problem-oriented plans to protect and preserve what's left. You will learn a set of technical tools to apply to specific planning situations and research and communication skills for presentations. You will be prepared to use and reuse the problem-solving approach in graduate school and the workplace. In the end you will have new perspectives about resource allocation and the role you will play in your job and community.

PLANS OVER TIME

Planning trends in the United States have been linked to particular historic periods and political administrations in control at the time. Major historic events, such as war or economic decline, dictate the planning actions across the country. The following periods of history denote a defined planning emphasis: the period 1900–1929 was a prosperous, expansion era in planning and economic development; the depression years of the 1930s were marked by the struggle for economic survival; the postwar years into the 1960s were marked by social activism to revitalize our cities; and the modern era from the 1970s to the present is a period of constant balancing between economic development and resource protection.[4]

Throughout our history, planning professionals and officials have argued about the rights of the private property owner versus public control. Starting with President Franklin D. Roosevelt, who faced massive economic disaster with the Great Depression, administrations have differed on how to coordinate and fund government programs. Roosevelt responded to the depression by establishing major housing and construction projects to stimulate the economy. Placing these programs under the federal government caused much debate within his administration. The debate continued in the Kennedy–Johnson era with major social programs under federal control; the Nixon, Ford, and Reagan administrations with the focus on state control; and the Bush administrations (George W. Bush and his father, George H. W. Bush) with a push for more state control.[5]

The great debate over whether planning initiatives should be coordinated at the federal, state, or local level continues to this day. Major federal programs, such as urban renewal, which focused on clearing up blighted areas and providing housing for all Americans, and Department of Transportation (DOT) programs for highway improvement, have been criticized for years. The distribution of funding, in terms of who benefits from the final targeted action plans, has been questioned in many cases with these large-scale federal programs. Consequently, funding at the federal level for massive planning programs has been drastically reduced over the years.

The evolution of the comprehensive plan is described within the context of the historical highlights of planning in the United States. Basically, the term *comprehensive plan* denotes comprehensive, geographic coverage of the area under study, a complete overview of the physical development and long-range goals for the community. Comprehensive plans cover every aspect of planning, including land use, economic development, environmental issues, housing, urban design, and transportation. Although comprehensive plans also cover a long duration of time, usually twenty years, the plans are periodically updated and revised. Typically, every five years planners should review, reevaluate, and revise the comprehensive plan. Kelly and Becker define and explore the elements of the comprehensive plan and discuss the relationship of the comprehensive plan with other types of plans, including the general plan and the master plan.[6]

The goals of the comprehensive plan generally fall under the areas governed by police power—protection of the public's *health, safety, and welfare*. The following specific goals are frequently cited in comprehensive plans: land use, health, environmental protection, public safety, circulation, support services, fiscal health or budget, and economic goals. The comprehensive planning process is divided into the following stages: research, clarification of goals and objectives, plan formulation, plan implementation, and review and revision. These stages may overlap and over time may be revisited.[7] Since comprehensive planning involves all aspects of planning over such a long period, the plans are often filed away and not updated to reflect changing situations. Problem-oriented planning helps integrate specific issues into the comprehensive plan and keep the comprehensive plan a dynamic document in real time.

ELEMENTS OF THE TEXT

The most effective way to learn about community planning is to make your own plans. As we read each chapter and apply practical applications from the corresponding exercises, we learn to link the theoretical concepts with real-world planning problems on campus, downtown, and in our hometowns. Since the field of planning is constantly in flux, collect and share current data and updated statistics from local newspapers, journal articles, and fieldwork exercises to make decisions and solve problems. By the end of the term our planning materials will include relevant data and case studies that we can reference for problem solving.

At the end of each chapter a discussion box poses pertinent questions about particular concepts in the chapter. The purpose of the discussion questions is to reinforce how the concepts are related to the theoretical basis of planning, as well as planning practice. Notes and suggested readings about specific topics in the chapter are also found at the end of each chapter. At the end of each part of the book a learning challenge tests your level of mastery of the knowledge and skills covered in those chapters. A learning challenge is a pedagogical technique that helps you integrate the content and skills you need at each stage of the planning process. The chapter content, exercises, and discussion questions prepare you to respond to the challenge.

The text and supplementary materials are suitable for students in regional, environmental, city, and community planning. The interdisciplinary, problem-solving approach of the text is valuable for students in related fields including geography, sociology, criminal justice, public administration, and economics. The text is also suitable for students who are unsure of their major and express an interest in an innovative, emerging field. Finally, the content and problem-solving techniques are valuable for all students who wish to participate in community-service activities in the future. The concepts in the text reinforce the interdisciplinary nature of community planning by drawing together theories and resources from the related fields. The practical aspects of the text make it a suitable reference for professional planners and local planning board members.

OVERVIEW OF THE TEXT

Several major themes run throughout the text. The first is that an understanding of the theoretical principles of community planning leads to effective practical applications in problem solving. We will learn to integrate the appropriate content and apply specific tools to solve problems. The second theme is that the problem-oriented approach is an effective way of dealing with the immediate situations that confront us in community planning. This approach is focused and timely. While dealing with specific issues such as the development of low-income housing, the expansion of playground and recreational areas, and the revitalization of an old mill, the text shows how problem-oriented plans fit into the comprehensive plan for the community. The third theme is the political implications planners working in private and public planning firms must confront. Discussions about the role of federal, state, and local regulations in planning practice are woven into the text.

Part I, which focuses on connections between theories and practical applications, comprises the foundation for the rest of the book. Chapter 1 is an introduction to the basic theories that have shaped community planning. The interdisciplinary nature of planning is related to planning practice and problem solving. Chapter 2 is an introduction to the problem-oriented planning process, which is an innovative approach that is effective in identifying and solving planning problems. Chapter 3 prepares us to identify the land ethic of a community, which is essentially the value that the members of the community hold for the land. The land ethic of early settlers across the United States contrasts dramatically with current contemporary society, and conflicting land ethics between those retaining an earlier land ethic and those with a more progressive one may be the most fundamental cause of tension within a community.

Part II focuses on the political and legal aspects of planning practice in the United States. Chapter 4 introduces some historical highlights of city-planning history. Chapter 5 describes the legal issues that influence how planning and zoning are carried out across the country. Chapter 6 discusses the concept of growth management and the tools that can be used to address growth-management problems. The principles of the innovative concept of new urbanism, or smart growth, are introduced as potential solutions to growth-management problems across the country.

Part III concentrates on the subspecialty areas of community planning, which represent the content areas from which we draw data to solve problems. The specialized areas also represent the primary areas where planners work. We will learn how to connect content areas to solve problems. Chapter 7 is an overview of environmental planning, the site-planning process, and brownfields development. Site planning involves collecting data on the physical geographic features of the area and generating maps to show where development should and should not occur. Several mapping techniques that identify environmental constraints and suitability for development are explained.

Chapter 8 is an overview of the elements of urban design and capital-improvements programs (CIPs). The chapter explores how these elements are integrated into the community-planning process. Chapter 9 focuses on historic-site preservation and revitalization and includes sections on urban renewal and gentrification. In this stage we analyze data about demographic and socioeconomic trends and community-needs assessments.

Chapter 10 deals with transportation planning, energy planning, and alternative energy sources. Transportation-management principles and the basics of traffic-impact analysis studies are reviewed. Chapter 11 covers research methods, including geographic information systems (GIS) that analyze layers of data, and grant-proposal techniques that are used in the planning process. The chapter also ties together the themes of the text by reinforcing how the problem-oriented approach is integrated into the community-planning process. It gives us a kaleidoscope view of the region, with all the planning issues and the internal dynamic tensions, making up the big picture.

Discussion Box

What is the relationship between a problem-oriented plan and a comprehensive plan? Discuss why your community needs both types of plans.

NOTES

1. Mellier Scott, *American City Planning Since 1890* (Los Angeles: University of California Press, 1969). See chapter 1 for a historical overview of the beginnings of city planning in the United States.

2. Planning practice is based on tensions that relate to ways of solving problems. As the profession has evolved, the theories of physical scientists have collided with those of social scientists. These conflicts, or tensions, run throughout the field today. The approach to problem solving is based on what theories and applications are taken from which disciplines.

3. Eric Damian Kelly and Barbara Becker, *Community Planning: An Introduction to the Comprehensive Plan* (Washington, D.C.: Island Press, 2000). See chapter 1, where they discuss various alternatives to the comprehensive plan. One approach, called issue

driven, is similar in some respects to the problem-oriented approach in terms of focusing on specific issues of immediate concern to trigger the planning process.

4. Frank So, Irving Hand, and Bruce McDowell, *The Practice of State and Regional Planning* (Chicago: American Planning Association, 1986).

5. Scott, *American City Planning*, chapter 6.

6. Kelly and Becker, *Community Planning*. See chapter 2 for an overview of the elements of the comprehensive plan.

7. John Levy, *Contemporary Urban Planning* (Upper Saddle River, N.J.: Prentice Hall, 2003). In chapter 8, Levy presents an overview of the goals of comprehensive planning and the stages involved in the comprehensive planning process.

Part I

RESHAPING THE PLANNING PROCESS

Part I outlines a problem-solving approach that has evolved over the past several decades in planning agencies and firms across the country. To meet the political and economic uncertainties of our times and the ever increasing demands on resources, planners have become very creative in plan making. Specific issues are addressed in a timely manner, and resources are allocated in many instances across jurisdictional boundaries. The problem-oriented approach in this text focuses on a specific problem area, integrates the related research about the possible plan options, and identifies the most effective plan.

Chapter 1 introduces the fundamental theories of community planning and connections between planning principles and practical applications. Learning about the theories and the interdisciplinary makeup of planning prepares us for problem solving.

Chapter 2 is an introduction to the problem-oriented planning process. The steps involved in the process are outlined, and the methods that generate the data we need to solve problems are related to the various stages in the process.

In chapter 3 the factors that influence city form, basic spatial-analysis principles, and settlement or land-ethic issues in the United States are discussed to teach you how to develop a community overview. How have the geographic, cultural, and social forces of the past shaped your community? Historically, what events and trends influenced the circulation, business, and residential patterns of your community? Is the community profile of today still directly connected to the past, or have special-interest groups or major development trends completely changed the direction your community is headed? Addressing these issues is integral to the planning process today, because once we identify the issues of concern of the community, we can begin to formulate their view for the future.

Chapter One

Fundamental Theories
of Community Planning

It is important to realize from the beginning that understanding theories about the planning process must come before making plans. The reason for this is that asking theoretical questions about a planning issue, such as lack of affordable housing or traffic jams, helps us understand the present situation. Why and how did the current planning situation turn out the way it did? If there is a lack of affordable housing in a community, we begin our study by asking a series of theoretical questions. Is the low number of affordable housing units in the community due to the lack of multifamily zoning districts? Is it due to discriminatory building practices such as large-lot zoning that demands larger houses?

If a section of the community now faces traffic congestion problems, we ask a series of theoretical questions focused on circulation patterns. Did the planning process to approve new commercial and retail businesses take into account the impact on traffic flow in the area? Did planners follow a regional circulation plan when considering new strip mall development? As the theories evolved throughout the history of planning, tensions developed concerning the interdisciplinary nature of community planning and helped to create the generalist versus the specialist approach in solving planning problems.[1]

INTERDISCIPLINARY NATURE OF COMMUNITY PLANNING

The Association of Integrative Studies, founded in 1979, describes interdisciplinary studies as cross-discipline learning. The association can be traced back to the general systems movement of the 1950s, which was formed in response to what members felt was too much specialization in education. The systems approach involves looking at a field as a whole and analyzing how its respective

3

Does your town offer housing units for all income levels?

parts relate to each other.[2] In *Interdisciplinary Undergraduate Programs* William Newell notes that John Dewey and Alexander Meiklejohn are cited as the primary movers for contemporary interdisciplinary programs. Dealing specifically in practical applications to problem solving, both Dewey and Meiklejohn refer to taking concepts from several disciplines to solve problems.[3] According to Newell, education across disciplines means learning about related concepts from several disciplines that are integrated to form an interdisciplinary field. Throughout this text, theories and concepts that cut across disciplines related to planning form the building blocks to solve planning problems.

Community planning, which is made up of concepts and theories from several related disciplines including geography, sociology, economics, law, architecture, public administration, and biology, falls under the category of interdisciplinary studies.[4] The movement to create the planning profession began in the early 1900s, as cities struggled to solve environmental pollution, sanitation, housing, and transportation problems brought about by the Industrial Revolution. It became evident that an expert in solving urban and rural problems was needed. The sanitary-reform period marks the birth of city planning, and sanitation formed the initial criteria for the certification process for the planning professional. As city planning evolved throughout our history, academicians and professional planners would interchangeably use the terms *city*, *regional*, or *community planning*. Although city and regional planning also include public participation components, community planning is typically used to denote the local planning process with the greatest emphasis on public participation.

The debate about whether community planning is a hard-core science based in econometrics or a social science based in sociological theory is as evident in planning literature today as it was in the formative years of the field.[5] Along with this debate, however, most theorists agree that the planner has to integrate physical science data with social science data to solve complex problems. Starting with the earliest urban planners, theorists supported the notion that planning is an interdisciplinary field.[6] John Gaus states that city planning is made up of several related disciplines.

> City planning, it held, was not merely a special field for the application of the skill of any single profession, such as engineering or landscape architecture, but must draw upon the several arts and sciences, including architecture, political economy, the science of government, sociology, sanitary science, physical geography, and publicity, public movement and organizations.[7]

Solving community problems is challenging because of the complex overtones of inner city and rural issues. An environmental pollution issue may be related to a natural-resource issue, which in turn may be related to a business or employment issue. It is critical to recognize that we must draw from several related disciplines to identify the most effective action plans. In the end it is our skill in identifying relationships and interpreting impacts that determines to a great extent our ability to solve problems.

Muzafer Sherif and Carolyn Sherif argue that the primary reason to create interdisciplinary courses is that it is difficult, if not impossible, to delineate where one discipline ends and another begins. The overlap runs throughout the disciplines. Several methods have been proposed to combine concepts across disciplines to create an interdisciplinary approach.[8] Sherif and Sherif developed a method called insightful borrowing, the process of merging concepts from several disciplines. Insightful borrowing is based on learning and knowing where, what, and how to borrow from other disciplines. It is this cross-referencing that brings together the necessary content and skills to solve problems. For example, by analyzing a biologist's test results of levels of acid precipitation from a lake and a chemical engineer's emission-level measurements from a manufacturing plant, the planner can begin to consider relationships between air contaminants and pH levels to solve an environmental-planning problem. While combining concepts in this case, the planner must interpret the effect of certain chemical reactions on the organisms in the lake. This requires an understanding of fundamental chemical theories, consequent reactions on the organisms, and appropriate applications to solve the problem.

The key to problem solving is the ability to determine which theories and skills are necessary to address a particular planning situation. Robert

Dubin, in Sherif and Sherif, describes what he calls the contiguous-problem approach in interdisciplinary courses. This approach involves identifying and analyzing the relationships between separate research areas and applying tools to solve the problem. An illustration of this type of research in community planning is the simultaneous study of water quality in a city water system and a study of disease statistics across the city. In this case students from various disciplines can attempt to solve the water quality and health problems concurrently by relating pollutant types and levels to particular health impacts.

Harvey Perloff attempts to solve the problem of integrating material across disciplines by suggesting that dimensions from disciplines can be incorporated into a planning course. Perloff defines these dimensions as methodologies, substantive fields, or problem areas. The dimensions may be from the physical science or social science disciplines, depending on the opportunities for interdisciplinary structure. Perloff emphasizes that the dimensions taken from related disciplines should not be bits of knowledge but substantive disciplinary components.[9]

Historically, theorists have argued whether the generalist approach, which emphasizes a broad base of planning knowledge, is more effective than the specialist approach, which indicates a specific specialty area in planning. The current consensus in the field is that planning problems are so complex a planner needs to be a generalist with a specialty area of expertise to function effectively. Mellier Scott suggests that the areas of knowledge that the planner needs are not purely architecture, engineering, law, or environmental science. Somehow the knowledge base should share ties with all these fields, but in essence the planner has to have enough general education and enough specialization to be effective.[10] Perloff emphasizes that a balance should be found between the theoretical and the technical aspects of the coursework. The coursework should include systematic, creative techniques to address and resolve social, physical, and economic problems of neighborhoods, cities, suburbs, and metropolitan regions. It should pull concepts from related disciplines to analyze, synthesize, and evaluate data and offer alternatives for action.

PRINCIPLES OF PLANNING

The primary principles that guide the community-planning process are that planning is a prescriptive activity, planning should be intuitive, and planning can control future actions. Each one of these principles is part of the decision-making process in planning and directly linked to the actions we recommend for solving a problem. The first principle, thinking of planning as a prescriptive activity, helps us predict and anticipate chain reactions. Just as a physician administers a specific medicine to change the course of a disease and prevent complications, planners think of tactics to change situations and avoid chain reactions in community planning. In each planning situation, alternative actions to a problem are considered, and the planner recommends a series of actions that in the end will solve the problem. For example, the proposal for a new big-box store such as Wal-Mart creates several complex planning issues. Although the taxes and revenues for the community, as well as employment opportunities, increase, planners often have to address environmental issues and increased traffic. Throughout the process, alternatives that lessen the impacts on the environment must be considered. This balancing act is pivotal in developing effective problem-oriented plans.

The second principle, planning should be intuitive, helps us link recommended actions to final outcomes in planning. The interpretation of intuitive thinking from a planning perspective is that it formulates realistic, substantive insights for decision making. Intuitive thinking is realistic because the facts are considered as they show up in the data. It is substantive because the approach requires the planner to ask a series of thoughtful questions about the future events and trends in the area. Intuitive thinking involves interpreting the facts of a situation by recognizing connections between current conditions and future events. Intuitive planning is a way of rearranging the facts in several different scenarios to predict the outcome of each scenario. By following this process we can see how certain recommendations may cause certain outcomes.

Finally, it is critical that we recognize that planning can control future actions. John Friedmann supports a theoretical model that fuses actions and planning.[11] Whenever an action is proposed, it should be thought through with the end result in mind. Friedmann also suggests that an element of uncertainty is inherent in the planning process and that the decision maker should think about potential impacts from each proposed action. In the problem-oriented approach, the impacts of each alternative are considered in light of the results that may occur in the final plan.

Paul Davidoff considers the connections between alternatives and outcomes as major determinants in the decision-making process. Davidoff calls one element *the achievement of ends*. By this he means that throughout the planning process we need to analyze the connections between alternatives and final outcomes. Each alternative we choose has a specified impact on the way the final plan unfolds. Another element, *the exercise of choice*, indicates that planning is value laden. When we make choices we are influenced by our own system of values, as well as the values of others. The process is legitimate and ethical, as long as we recognize the values of everyone involved and to whom we are accountable. Is our client a private citizen, a community, or an agency? The final element states that planning is an *orientation to the future*. Planning is an end-directed process in which the future result is always kept in mind during the decision-making process. Davidoff is emphasizing that to develop effective final plans the end results must be part of the thinking from the beginning.[12]

David Braybrooke and Charles E. Lindblom question the principle of controlling future actions in planning through a comprehensive, long-range approach. They advocate a disjointed incremental approach to decision making. Instead of the all-encompassing, broad approach of the comprehensive, rational model, the disjointed incremental approach deals with *successive limited comparisons*. Throughout the process actions are considered in current situations and applied as necessary to address specific needs. The impacts of individual actions are related to other actions in the plan. Braybrooke and Lindblom call their evaluation technique in decision making *reconstructive treatment of data*. It is a retrospective process where evaluation is ongoing and constantly reassessing current conditions. We can draw a parallel here with the problem-oriented approach introduced in this text. The following questions are continually addressed during this retrospective process: Did our planning accomplish its goals? Did it work? What went wrong? How can we do better next time?[13]

DIFFERENT LEVELS OF THINKING
IN THE PLANNING PROCESS

The thinking that is involved in the planning process proceeds at four different levels. The first level of thinking in the process is intuitive thinking. As we discussed earlier, intuitive thinking is an underlying principle in planning. It is this fundamental level of thinking that integrates all the planning objectives. Throughout the planning process we have to be clear about how the planning issues we are studying are related to other disciplines and to each other. It is important that the plan we develop shows the interconnectedness of the issues involved.

The descriptive level is the second level of thinking in the planning process. This level of thinking is objective. It involves gathering facts from the related sources that will help solve the specific planning problem at hand. These sources include the physical geographic facts about the specific site, the demographic statistics of the region, and the socioeconomic trends of the region.

The third level of thinking is the evaluative level. This level involves analyzing all the data at the descriptive level, coming up with options that might solve the specific problem, and weighing those options. At the evaluative level, we learn to weigh what options and development alternatives are best for the community. The costs and benefits of each option are considered in order to determine the most appropriate option.

The fourth level of thinking involves subjective or normative thinking. This level requires the planner to consider the values or bias of each actor in the planning process. Planners should ask: What values or bias might the city officials, the townsfolk, the developers, or the planners themselves bring to the planning process? It is important to recognize how a certain bias might influence the final decisions that are made.

PROBLEM-SOLVING EXPERIENCES

Since planning problems are complex, we often need to cross-reference and learn techniques from several disciplines to solve problems. First, we need to determine the areas of background knowledge that are needed to address issues. Generally, these areas include geography, sociology, economics, law, architecture, public administration, biology, and public health. The skills and techniques associated with testing and analysis for specific tasks are identified and carried out and lead to recommended actions to solve problems.

The study of geography, which focuses on the description of the earth and the relationships between humans and the environment, is the foundation for how we develop the land. From the physical constraints and cultural geographic determinants derive the land use of an area. The process involved in analyzing a site to determine its suitability for a particular project is called *site-location analysis*. This process involves collecting data on the type of soil, elevation, and landform classification in a region to determine *what development should go where*. After the geographic site determinants have been considered, a conceptual plan showing the proposed project can be drawn.

Planners study sociological theories concerning the social organization and ethnic fabric of the community to develop needs assessments for future facilities and programs. Demographic studies, which include population projection figures and ethnicity, employment, and income level statistics, are conducted to determine the needs of the community. These studies identify migration patterns and mobility routes and business and housing trends in the community. With these data we can analyze the economic feasibility of proposals and predict the success or failure of a particular project. We can predict what types of projects will be a good *fit* for the downtown and the amount and types of housing that are needed in the community. Recommendations for economic development plans are based on the demographic projections and needs of the residents of the community.

Topics in law, such as the constitutional legalities of development, are related to planning. Land-use law issues frequently arise in planning when new or revised zoning ordinances are proposed. The legal aspects of eminent domain, just compensation, and the takings issue in particular come up frequently in planning. The planner needs to know how to reference the constitutionality of a particular project and the process involved in carrying out the development. Knowledge of regulatory statutes is another related area of law that directly influences the problem-solving process in planning. Statutes that impact planning practice include the antisnob zoning act, which controls for discrimination in housing, and the federal and state environmental-policy acts that regulate development within environmental constraints. Finally, the decisions that judges have handed down in a state or county may be critical in a planning decision. The pattern of court case law may indicate a particular philosophy or bias on the part of a state or county.

The field of architecture includes fundamental design theory and techniques that are very useful to the planner. Planners need to be educated in basic urban-design theory and techniques and have cartographic skills. These skills are valuable in solving urban-design problems that inevitably arise when architectural controls or zoning ordinances are proposed for city blocks or subdivisions. Both manual drawing techniques and up-to-date computer-aided cartography skills are needed.

Public administration includes the topics of governmental processes and controls that are essential for the planner. The planner needs to know how government works at the federal, state, and local levels. A project proposal will not be approved if suitable permits were not acquired and specified regulations followed for development. The planner needs to know the setup of the governing bodies in the municipality and county. When the governmental structure is clear, the planner can fit together the geographic layer of information with the governmental layer to identify feasible solutions to planning problems.

With the growing concern about air, water, and soil pollution on a global scale, the planner must frequently reference biological and public health principles. The planner needs to know how to access material and resources that deal with specific environmental health issues confronting a particular area. For example, if a subdivision is proposed for an area with vernal pools, the planner needs to consult a biologist or environmental scientist to delineate endangered areas. It has become essential for the planner to learn how to link any possible connections between air- and water-quality problems with natural resources in a given location and notify the appropriate experts to conduct studies.

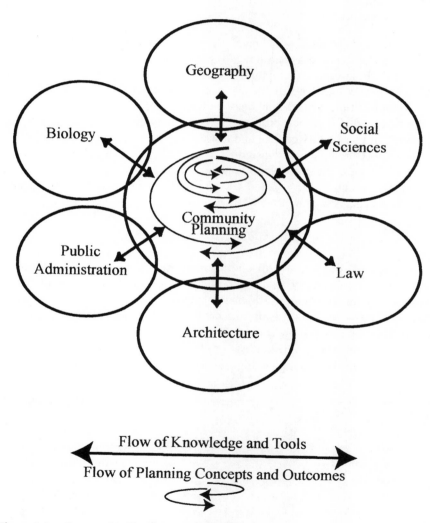

Figure 1.1.   Community Planning as Interdisciplinary Activity

SUBSPECIALIZED AREAS IN PLANNING

The specialization areas in planning include environmental planning, land use, urban design and community development, historic-site preservation and revitalization, economic development, transportation and energy planning, and GIS. Each planning situation requires specific data, concepts, and techniques from related disciplines to solve the problem. The following is a list of typical planning problems with related research areas that the planner would investigate in each case:

- A site-analysis problem would involve land-use and natural-resources research.
- A design problem in a central business district, subdivision, or mall would involve urban-design theory and guidelines research.
- Housing and social needs in the inner city would focus on community-development theory and grant applications.
- Environmental pollution problems would be studied within the context of water- and air-quality control and testing.
- Issues regarding the historic significance of a building or district would focus on historic-site-preservation planning.
- Circulation and traffic problems would involve transportation theory and traffic-impact research.

CONCLUSION

This chapter covers the interdisciplinary aspects of the field of community planning and the underlying theories and principles that define the planning process. By pointing out relationships between the principles and specific planning situations, the decision-making process becomes clearer. The disciplines from which we draw content and skills to solve planning problems are discussed. The subspecialized areas in planning are also introduced to show the relationships between planning research and problem solving.

Discussion Box
    What are the basic theories of community planning? Why do you need to think about planning theories before applying practical solutions? If you were collecting data to solve a problem, what level of thinking would you be using? If you were weighing the options among various alternatives, what level of thinking would you be using? If you were analyzing what all the stakeholders were bringing to the table, what level of thinking would you be using?

PLANNING EXERCISE 1: GATHERING
HOMETOWN MAPS, ORDINANCES, AND PLANS

Visit your local planning department to ask for the zoning map, land-use map, and zoning ordinance. The zoning ordinance contains the regulations and guidelines for development in a community. Also ask for a copy of the comprehensive or master plan for your community. We will be referring to these documents throughout the semester, and your final project will be based on specifics in these documents.

Read over the documents, and take note of the zoning districts and any special zoning overlays for your community. Are there any environmentally protected zones such as a water-supply district or an aquifer-protection bylaw? Are there any historic districts? Does the ordinance encourage a diversity of housing types? If there is a comprehensive plan for your community, what are the major sections of the plan? What are the goals, objectives, and action plans?

NOTES

1. William Newell, *The Interdisciplinary Undergraduate Programs—A Directory* (Chicago: Planners Press, 1986).

2. Heidi Jacobs, ed., *Interdisciplinary Curriculum: Design and Implementation* (Alexandria, Va.: Edwards Brothers, 1989).

3. Newell, *Interdisciplinary Programs*.

4. William Alonso, "Beyond the Interdisciplinary Approach to Planning," *Journal of the American Institute of Planners* (May 1971): 169–173, 169. In Alonso's definition, "The ordinary recipe for the interdisciplinary approach goes something like this—Take a physical planner, a sociologist, and economist; beat the mixture until it blends; pour and spread."

5. In planning practice, community planning is most often considered synonymous with city and regional planning. Some consider one difference to be that community planning always has an emphasis on community participation, while city and regional planning usually include this component, but not always. Theorists disagree, however, over whether regional planning belongs in the hard or soft social science camp. Alonso, in "Beyond the Interdisciplinary," argues that regional planning is a hard science. Michael Seelig, in "A Redefinition of the School's Role," *Journal of the American Planning Association* (September 1972): 178–184, maintains that regional planning is a soft social science.

6. Harvey Perloff, *Education for Planning: City, State and Regional* (Baltimore, Md.: Johns Hopkins Press, 1957). Andreas Faludi, *A Reader in Planning Theory* (Oxford: Pergamon Press, 1973). Faludi theorizes that a lot of the problems that have developed in decision making in planning stem from the focus on specialized education. He calls the dilemma the blueprint versus the process mode of planning. In the blueprint

mode, architects and engineers drew technical design plans to solve problems. John Friedmann, *Regional Policy: Readings in Theory and Applications* (Cambridge, Mass.: MIT Press, 1975). Friedmann's writings focus on regional theory and applications.

7. John Gaus in Mellier Scott, *American City Planning Since 1890* (Los Angeles: University of California Press, 1969), p. 266. John Gaus, *The Education of Planners* (Cambridge, Mass.: Harvard Graduate School of Design, 1943).

8. Muzafer Sherif and Carolyn Sherif, *Interdisciplinary Relationships in the Social Sciences* (Chicago: Aldine, 1969).

9. Perloff, *Education for Planning*.

10. Scott, *American City Planning*.

11. Friedmann, *Regional Policy*.

12. Paul Davidoff in Faludi, *A Reader in Planning Theory*.

13. David Braybrooke and Charles E. Lindblom, *A Strategy of Decision: Policy Evaluation as a Social Process* (New York: The Free Press, 1963).

Chapter Two

Problem-Oriented Planning and Problem Solving

Plans are something that we make everyday. Whether it is a simple plan to meet friends at the movies or a detailed project plan at work, we all spend a lot of time making plans. If you think about it for a minute, you could evaluate how effective your plan was on any given day by reflecting on how much effort you put into making connections between specific actions and your goals. Did you first ask yourself what you wanted to accomplish with your plan? Did you think of specific ways to reach the goals you set for an activity? This process of evaluation can tell you how effective your planning methods have been.

The community-planning process involves learning to develop problem-oriented plans that address issues and solve problems in our communities. Whether it is a plan to preserve open space and natural resources, improve water or air quality, revitalize a neighborhood, or develop social facilities, the recommendations should be specific and relevant to the concerns of the members of the community. Overall, the problem-oriented approach is based on steps that build on each other and prepare us to make the right decisions to solve a problem. To be effective, this planning approach should be idealistic in concept, realistic in scope, and dynamic and efficient in implementation.

It could be argued that problem-oriented planning is based on the corporate strategic-planning model used for years for internal organizational decision making at both public and private organizations. The paradigm shift occurred decades ago when planners started borrowing the strategic-planning model for use in planning practice. The ongoing paradigm has been evident over time as planning agencies adopted the model.

The strategic-planning model is now more defined and working its way into planning textbooks. It is essentially a paradigm that encourages retrospective, expansive thinking in real time, rather than the old paradigm that focuses on rigid, long-term thinking.[1] Considering the uncertainty of the availability of resources and funding in these fiscally constrained times, the problem-oriented method follows the reconstructive evaluation model of Braybrooke and Lindblom discussed in chapter 1. Under this model planners constantly monitor current situations and adjust action plans according to changing conditions.[2] It is a spiral approach, in which new problem areas are continuously integrated into the comprehensive plan, keeping the plan up-to-date. In the end, problem-oriented planning addresses the immediacy of needs in the community, while recognizing and facilitating the purpose of the comprehensive plan over time.[3]

PROBLEM-ORIENTED PLANNING PROCESS

What is different or innovative about a problem-oriented approach in planning? Don't planners practice problem solving in formulating the comprehensive or master plan for their communities? Yes, in fact, it would be impossible to bring such a diversity of stakeholders, opinions, and values of a community together without an interdisciplinary structured approach. How else could planners solve the most basic of problems: How do we decide where we want to go as a community? The process of deliberate problem identification, data gathering and analysis, and evaluation of best options results in a blueprint for future change in the community.[4] Planning, however, is more than making plans. It is about process, as well as formulation. Above all else, planning is about making plans happen.

Problem-oriented planning focuses on identifying and addressing issues that affect or alter an orderly planning process. It applies a structured approach to resolving these individual problems in a way that preserves the integrity of a comprehensive or master plan. In practical terms, it is what planners do on a daily basis to keep plans intact, yet dynamic, in the face of challenges and the demand for change. How do problem-oriented plans, then, differ from traditional comprehensive and master plans? Generally, problem-oriented plans are

- Dictated by a short time frame, with an acute or subacute deadline
- Surrounded by a sense of urgency that requires settling for the practical, not the ideal
- Driven by resource demands and priorities, either monetary or natural resources
- Conflict driven, rather than consensus driven
- Prompted by changes external to the community-planning process (for example, public policy, case law, natural disaster, public threats such as the September 11, 2001, attacks, and bioterrorism)

- Initiated by sudden internal community conflicts (demographic, socioeconomic, or political shifts)

Where do problems arise? The problem issues that will require formulation of a problem-oriented plan may be generated from within existing plans or may be entirely new and due to unanticipated circumstances. When a problem arises within an existing set of plans, it may be due to a need for updating the plans, a lack of progress in achieving the planned goal, or an adverse interaction with a related process. When problems arise that seem outside existing planning efforts, these may be

- Entirely new problems (for example, dealing with bioterrorism)
- Cross-boundary problems (an issue in an adjacent community that spills over)
- Temporary and self-limiting issues but needing accommodation

No matter where or how the problems arise, the planner must control the situation by having a structured problem-solving process in place. Although we must focus on the problem at hand, we must also consider the interdisciplinary and comprehensive context in which the problem must be solved. To do otherwise would fragment the planning process. Ultimately, problem-oriented plans must integrate with the greater planning goals of the community.

The need to address problems related to conflicts over the availability of resources has become particularly apparent lately. Due to the deteriorating economic situation and increasing social needs of many groups across the country, the emphasis in problem-oriented planning has become the distribution of resources. It is critical that resource allocation, the process of analyzing how funding and resources are shared across the landscape, should be based on the concept of social equity. Resources should be allocated according to the needs of groups across the community, regardless of geographic location or jurisdiction. For example, if an inner-city neighborhood needs recreational and educational facilities, a well-equipped regional high school in a suburb nearby could be opened for sports and job-training activities for the children in the surrounding area. The facility would provide services for the inner-city children, which may be instrumental in lowering crime rates, promoting educational opportunities, and encouraging racial understanding.

Problem-oriented planning introduces an innovative way to identify the primary issues of concern of a community, to link resources with neighborhood needs, and to make recommendations for action plans to solve planning problems. If we continually ask the questions that are included in the text and collect the pertinent data regarding the responses, we will learn how to make effective plans for cities and towns. After the data have been analyzed, we will draw conclusions and present the findings and results. The specific disciplines we draw from to support this approach reinforces the theory that planning is interdisciplinary.

The problem-oriented planning process is valuable and efficient, because the process can be used over and over to solve all types of planning problems. It is a creative process that encourages us to think about planning circles with focal points that form an integrated network. In this way boundaries within and between communities do not exist. Considering resources as shared commodities across the planning area creates very workable and effective plans. The problem-oriented planning process includes the following steps:

1. Define the problem
2. Articulate the goals and objectives
3. Analyze and evaluate
4. Implement action plans
5. Measure results

The steps should be conducted in the order given. However, the process is not rigid. Sometimes it is necessary to spend more time on one component or return to a component several times. The reason for this is that the data needed to solve planning problems may change with each new alternative. If, for example, we are creating a community development plan for a city that recently lost several manufacturing plants, we need to analyze the economic trends for the region. This requires a socioeconomic study. Updated economic and demographic projections for the region are required for this type of study. This means that each time we select a new alternative we have to change our projections.

The following outline explains each step in detail and provides illustrations along the way to understand what data are needed at each step. The problem-oriented approach is very flexible and adaptable to any planning situation.

1. Define the Problem: Ask Questions to Identify Issues of Concern

The first step involves stating the problem and indicating connected areas of planning concern. The problem statement is the focus for the plan and sets the stage for the investigation to follow. We identify the priority problems by soliciting public input and reaching a consensus about what are the most pressing issues in the community. Do we need a housing plan, due to the lack of affordable units in the community? Do we need an environmental plan, due to severe contamination of a river tributary that runs through the community?

Do we need a community-development plan, because everyone is tired of the blight and lack of commercial growth in the downtown? Or do we need an open-space and recreation plan, because so many people are voicing concerns about the lack of recreational areas and playing fields due to a large number of subdivisions being built? The key areas in which data should be collected in developing a plan include the physical elements of the region, the socio-economic factors of the region, and practical applications for problem solving. Every connected facet of the problem must be included to set up a logical series of action plans.

Gathering opinions from as many members and special-interest groups in the community as possible is the most effective way to achieve a consensus and set priorities about the immediate problems for the community. Most state grants, open-space and recreation plans, and community-development grants require evidence of public participation. Participants for public input include local government boards, government organizations, and special-interest groups such as civic and service organizations, the chamber of commerce, ethnic groups, religious organizations, professional affiliations, and neighborhood associations. The following strategies are used to reach specific individuals and groups:

Open public meetings—The traditional way to introduce issues to the public and gain input is through a well-publicized open meeting. Public meetings may involve the whole community or particular neighborhood groups. This approach works well in identifying issues for a neighborhood needs assessment. Public meetings must have a strong leader to keep the discussion focused. At the public meetings, questions asked are

- What changes do we need in the community?
- Why do we need this change?
- Whom will it help?
- Who should carry out each part of the problem-oriented plan?
- Where should planning actions take place?
- What funding plan and grants are available to pay for the actions that are recommended?
- When should each action of the plan take place?

More specific follow-up questions may be asked regarding controversial topics or new developments that arise during the course of gathering information.

Personal interviews—Interviews are an effective way to learn about the opinions and attitudes of citizens. A major drawback to this method, however, is that personal interviews are time consuming. And if the goal is to achieve a scientifically valid response, the questionnaire must be set up so that sound statistical analysis can be conducted. This requires formulating questions that may be analyzed statistically and training the interviewers to ask the questions in a consistent manner.

Opinion survey—If the population that needs to be polled is large and finances are sufficient, a mail or telephone survey should be considered. A survey can reach a majority of the population of a community or a statistically significant sample that represents the entire community. The format of the questionnaire or telephone interview must be clear and understandable to encourage participation.

Focus sessions—A focus session, or charrette, pulls together a small group of people to answer questions and discuss issues under the direction of a moderator or facilitator. Focus sessions are particularly helpful in defining the major topics of neighborhood concern. Different people from a variety of backgrounds and interests can be brought together to concentrate on each of the topics. The small group discussion format of focus sessions can lead to joint understanding and analysis that goes well beyond what would be possible in a personal interview, while allowing for more individual expression than may occur in large group meetings.

Workshops—When defining the needs of a neighborhood, it is helpful to hold workshops, or breakout sessions, on particular topics. Breakout sessions can cover a variety of topics and reach many divergent groups of people. For example, specific planning issues such as affordable housing or business improvement districts (BIDs) can be presented and explained to the groups. An understanding of these issues helps the residents of the neighborhood define their specific needs.

After we have prioritized the issues from the group sessions, we identify the highest priority issues as the problem statements. From here we determine which problem is the most pressing and which one offers the best opportunity for success considering the economic status and political climate of the community. The political feasibility of particular plans and actions is critical to the problem-identification phase, as well as throughout the planning process in determining which problem to choose. The success of each stage of the problem-oriented approach depends on the support of the various factions of the community.

2. Articulate the Goals and Objectives

At this stage formulate goals that are directly linked to the problem statement. The goals represent the ultimate solutions to the problem and where the community wants to be in the future. For example, if the community raises the

"I'm all for consensus, but what's in it for me?"

Cartoon 1.   The Dilemma of Planning

concern of lack of affordable housing, the goal is to provide a variety of housing types for all income levels. The objectives are the specific ways to achieve the goals. In the affordable-housing example, the objectives would be zoning more multifamily districts and building more multifamily homes. The goals and objectives should emphasize content material that is related to the problem statement.

3. Analyze and Evaluate

This step involves creating and evaluating alternatives to meet the needs of the targeted population. First, we identify and map all the sites that are related to the planning problem and may influence the alternatives we choose. These points on the map may include underutilized or blighted facilities, potential building sites, open-space parcels, contaminated areas, transportation centers, and social welfare facilities across the region. Throughout the analysis it should be understood that equity across the system means placing facilities and resources within reach of each particular group. We need to anticipate the impacts of each alternative to avoid any unintended consequences. For example, building affordable housing units in an area not connected to public transportation will create problems for low-income residents who more than likely do not own cars. This is not the case with programs aimed at moderate-income families, who often live outside large cities and own cars.

Next we define the geographic area for the study by drawing a circle around the points. When delineating the circle, consider bioregions, geographic areas similar in terrain and vegetation, and regional areas connected by telecommunications and support services. Keep in mind the concept of interdependence between towns, cities, and suburbs, and ignore jurisdictional boundaries. For example, if there is a need for a community health center in the inner city, why not renovate an underutilized office complex in a nearby suburb? The underserved in this case cross boundaries to gain access and the underutilized facility becomes an attraction for grants for which the community may be eligible.

It is at this point that developers submit various alternatives to meet the needs and concerns of the residents. Options may include new projects, alternatives for renovation of existent buildings, or redesign of facilities to meet the needs of residents. The following guidelines are useful in developing alternatives: negotiate with developers on a continual basis, conduct feasibility analysis, and determine if each option can be accomplished given the known constraints. Experts from related fields such as business and economic development, real estate, and transportation should be invited to attend meetings to offer recommendations on the alternatives. In the final analysis it is most beneficial to choose the options that are most feasible given the current fiscal and political status of the community. A plan seen as coming from the top down will never be as successful as a plan that was initiated and supported from the ground up.

Cost-benefit analyses should be conducted to determine the feasibility of development for each proposed option. The factors to consider include the social and economic costs and benefits of each option and environmental impacts. The data for the study include infrastructure costs for supporting services such as bridges, roads, water and sewer lines, and projected taxes from the project. Overall, the costs and benefits of construction, socioeconomic factors, and environmental impacts determine the best alternative to choose.

The following methods may be used to conduct prediction and projection studies: set up demographic models to project population, run economic models to predict tax base, and conduct cost-benefit analyses on infrastructure and support services for each alternative. The demographic and economic computer modeling programs manipulate data to predict growth in specified segments of the population and workforce. Future economic development projects can be based on a computer model that predicts the potential numbers of manufacturing, professional, and service-related jobs available in the community in the future. The projection figures allow the planners to match growth statistics with the type of facilities that will be needed. For example, if an increase in elementary-school-age children is predicted for a community, public school facilities can be planned.

Finally, we need to weigh the various options and choose the most appropriate one. Intuitively think about how each option will address the planning problem, and consider the results of the cost-benefit analyses. Which option answers the needs of the residents in the most effective, cost-beneficial way? Besides the fiscal data, also assess the political support for each option. After running each option through the process, choose the one that addresses the main concerns of the community. Unfortunately, the reality of the situation is that, due to political and resource constraints and sometimes the lack of clarity of needs, the planning process is often less quantitative than described. For this reason it is important to keep reevaluating and revising the alternatives throughout the planning process.

4. Implement Action Plans

Community problems are complex, and often one aspect of a problem may be related to another problem. As the planner makes the final decision to implement specific action plans, a final look at the relationships between actions is required. This approach is valuable because it continually points to new information that is needed and triggers new directions to follow to avoid chain reactions. For example, before a coal-fired power plant is approved, potential impacts of plant emissions on air quality and thermal discharge on water quality in the area should be researched. Although the intent in this case is to solve the electricity and employment problems, the related aspects of air and water pollution must be addressed. Under pressure to solve the serious job and related economic problems, environmental issues may go unnoticed.

At this stage the procedures for carrying out the action plans are clearly stated. The responsibilities and duties of those in charge of programs and activities and specific timelines for the scope of work and completion of projects should be noted. Changes should be made at any point in the process to accommodate staffing or supervisory issues related to the planning process. Finally, it must be underscored that the political waters must be tested. Will the community vote for the plan we chose? The most highly developed plan will not be successful if the plan does not have the political backing of the municipal officials, the residents, and special-interest groups in the community.

5. Measure Results

Even though the problem-oriented process is up-to-date and efficient, change is inevitable in planning. Plans must be monitored over time, with a structure in place to evaluate the effectiveness of current programs. The monitoring procedures should include criteria to assess programs and guidelines for the roles and responsibilities of the planners and municipal officials. The action plans that were established to achieve certain goals in the plan should be evaluated annually or as needed in case of an emergency situation. As new issues arise, a *feedback loop* is created and potential changes are evaluated. When changes are needed, a feedback loop triggers the planning process with its inclusive steps to start up again. For example, an affordable housing problem-oriented plan may need to be reviewed and new programs developed if homeless shelters reach capacity due to an economic downturn or severe weather conditions. Planners could quickly conduct a needs assessment at local shelters and develop a list of available facilities by referencing the planning map. Making changes and adopting new options become part of an ongoing process to check and recheck the effectiveness of the plan.

CONCLUSION

The problem-oriented approach is presented as a way to solve planning problems that demand immediate attention. By focusing on the planning issue and following the steps for the problem-oriented planning approach, effective action plans can be developed. Since the issues of concern were formulated within the broad areas of long-range planning, problem-oriented plans remain consistent with the comprehensive plan. The structure of the planning process is geared for retrospective changes along the way.

Discussion Box
What are the main aspects of a problem-oriented plan? How do problem-oriented plans differ from traditional comprehensive plans? How do problem-oriented plans relate to comprehensive plans? Analyzing various scenarios, or hypothetical situations, is a primary component of the problem-oriented planning process. Consider, for example, the following scenario: an incinerator for hazardous waste is being proposed for your community. What areas of study (what types of data) would you need to solve this problem?

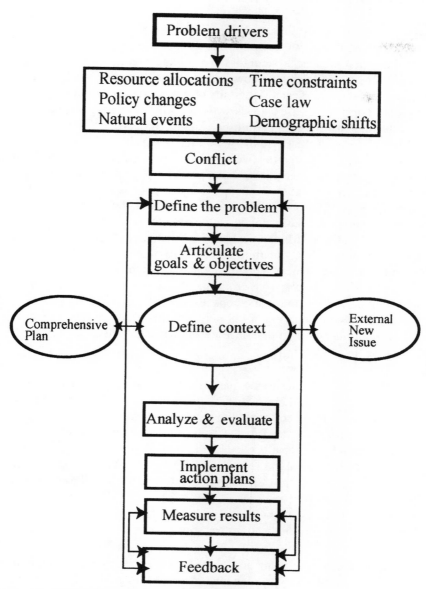

Figure 2.1. Problem-Oriented Planning Process

PLANNING EXERCISE 2: CAMPUS NEEDS ASSESSMENT

The second exercise involves applying the visioning process from this chapter to determine issues of concern on the campus. Issues may be as straightforward as a new pathway system for the quadrangle on campus or something as complex as the best site for a new student union. With your group you will be filling in the data for each step in the problem-oriented planning process. The purpose of this exercise is to show the parts of a campus plan and how to start collecting data for each part of the planning process.

First, read through the steps and with your group fill in the data for each section. We will discuss the fieldwork that is required and how to collect the appropriate data. Reference materials are available to provide background information and support data.

Step 1. Define the problem by asking questions to identify issues of concern for the campus. What, why, who, where, how, and when? For this exercise collect all the answers to the questions that your group comes up with in the discussions. Then, for fieldwork ask your roommates, friends, faculty, and staff what concerns them about the campus. Bring this list of concerns back to your planning group for discussion. As discussed in this chapter, public forums and workshops are part of the visioning process to determine issues of concern. For our purposes this small sampling of issues acts as a building block to demonstrate the data that are necessary to develop a plan.

- First, fill in the responses to the questions that your group collected. What issues do you feel should be addressed on our campus? How should the issues be addressed? When should the issues be addressed?
- Then, categorize the data. Did the college community indicate that new buildings should be recommended? Did circulation, traffic, or parking issues come up? Were natural-resource protection or environmental issues a concern? Identify the type of problems and the areas where the community feels improvement is necessary.
- Finally, prioritize the data by indicating which concerns came up the most. What are the political implications for your concerns?

Step 2. Articulate the goals and objectives for the campus community. Consult the college campus plan and discuss the goals and objectives that are listed in the plan. Does your group feel that the goals need to be updated?

Step 3. Analyze and evaluate the data that have been collected. Review the following data from the indicated reference materials:

- Geographic profile: soil types and characteristics (*source* Natural Resource Conservation Service)
- Elevation, slope, floodplain, wetlands, and other environmental data (*source* topographic maps, land-use maps)
- Demographic profile. Current and projected population of the college community with breakdown of groups by age, sex, and minority percentages (*source* college institutional research reports)

Next, map the environmentally sensitive campus areas and sites where new buildings are planned on a blank campus map. Draw circulation routes around the campus including parking lots, and indicate where any traffic problems exist. Then, locate and mark points of concern such as underutilized facilities, overcrowded facilities, transportation nodules, and sensitive receptors, for example, nearby schools or hospitals.

Discuss the alternatives that are outlined in the college campus plan. Do the alternatives need to be updated? What new projects are being proposed for the campus? What projects does your group recommend? Where are the projects located and what are the potential problems? What alternatives are being recommended for circulation patterns and parking facilities? Does your group agree with these recommendations? What cost-benefit and economic modeling tests would you run to determine the best option of the proposed projects for the campus? Evaluate the alternatives in the campus plan and weigh the options for new alternatives your group wants to recommend. What factors influence the alternatives?

Step 4. Implement action plans. The final part of the campus-planning process is developing action plans. Consider the alternatives and think about the proposals that would be feasible to develop. What proposals would solve the issues of concern of the campus community? It is critical to consider the environmental, social, and economic implications of any proposal you recommend.

Step 5. Measure results. Discuss and make suggestions regarding the monitoring process that the college has in place to review and update the college campus plan. Is there a mechanism in place to annually evaluate the success of programs? Are forums, focal groups, and surveys planned to update the plan? Who are the stakeholders involved in the college planning committees? Should there be changes made in the college planning process?

NOTES

1. David Braybrooke and Charles E. Lindblom, *A Strategy of Decision: Policy Evaluation as a Social Process* (New York: The Free Press, 1963). See chapter 2, "A Critique of the Classical Ideals."

2. Charles E. Lindblom, "The Science of 'Muddling Through,'" in Andreas Faludi, ed., *A Reader in Planning Theory*, Part III (Oxford: Pergamon Press, 1973).

3. Amitai Etzioni, "Mixed-Scanning: A Third Approach to Decision Making," in Faludi, *A Reader in Planning Theory*.

4. Edward J. Kaiser, David R. Godschalk, and F. Stuart Chapin, Jr., *Land Use Planning* (Urbana: University of Illinois Press, 1995).

Chapter Three

Community Overview and Land Ethic

A community overview is a composite of the impacts of historical and development trends on the design and function of the community and how the members of the community value their land. Understanding the major factors that influence the formation of cities, the basic principles of spatial analysis, and the classification of cities creates the context for problem solving in the planning process. Analysis of the settlement patterns in a region indicates the land ethic of the community.

FACTORS THAT INFLUENCE CITY FORM

Urban geographers and planners study the physical geographic setting of the city and relate this information to the technological stage of development of the society. The way that people are influenced by the following factors determines to a great extent the location and urban form of their cities:

- Physical geography influences settlement patterns
- Social organization and behavior influence urban design
- Technology and industrial development influence societal structure and urban form
- The level of trade influences urban form and design[1]

When these four key relationships in urban planning are applied to specific cities, it becomes clear why and how our cities are shaped the way they are today. Certain site-location influences develop into urban trends that set urban-design patterns for a region. The relationship between the physical environment and urban form may be researched by analyzing databases of geographic attributes, geomorphology data, meteorological factors, and environmental hazards. From this data it can be shown how the climate and physical geographic attributes of a region may entice or restrict growth.

Political and economic forces also influence the urban form of cities. Trends in population growth and economic development are directly related to the political stability of the government during a particular time in history. The evolution of cities through the Greek and Roman Empires and the Middle Ages directly followed periods of war, empire building, and peace. At the height of the Greek and Roman Empires, architectural design and urban growth rapidly advanced across Europe. Comparatively, the darkest hour in urban planning occurred during the feudal era of the Middle Ages, when society was struggling to survive political instability.

The classical civilizations of the Greeks and Romans influenced to a great extent how we designed and structured our cities in the United States. The Greeks contributed several key urban-design concepts to our Western culture. The architectural lines of Greek classicism dominate our buildings, and the Greek emphasis on monuments, landmarks, and open space is evident in many of our cities. Greek urban-design patterns, including organic design and the grid pattern, also appear in urban-design plans in the United States. The organic design pattern is a natural free-flow design, where paths are laid out according to the topography and existing landform barriers. Hippodamus, who is called the first city planner, designed several Greek cities around the grid pattern, which is a geometric, block design. His plans consisted of a central core of civic buildings with concentric zones of residential housing surrounding the core.

The design and symbolic value of the Greek agora, the central marketplace, and the stoa, the central administrative building, are also incorporated into many city designs in the United States. The town commons in communities across New England are patterned after the concept of the agora. In terms of governmental influence, Greek culture was distinctive in that it was not a monolithic empire. It was a collection of independent city-states with a common cultural bond. Each state maintained its own self-sustaining agricultural system and network of facilities. The town-meeting concept that is still practiced in some New England and mid-Atlantic states is based on the Greek city-state form of government.

Roman society also greatly influenced urban design in the United States. Roman civilization evolved simultaneously with Greek about 700 B.C. In fact, the two societies were closely connected, exchanging ideas and influencing one another. Although the Romans physically conquered the Greeks, Greek culture remained pervasive in the Roman mind. The greatest Roman legacy to urban planning was engineering skills. The Romans improved the semicircular arch, which was probably first integrated into urban design in the Middle East, and created the vault and the dome. The network of roads, which the Romans set up for military transport, was also an advanced engineering feat for the times.

As early Roman planners grappled with mounting urban problems, the need for regulations arose. In Julius Caesar's time, wheeled traffic was forbidden on Roman streets in daylight hours. Augustus attempted to create what we could call the first zoning ordinance when he set up restrictions on the height of buildings, because of fire hazards. The Roman author and architect Vitruvius focused on solar orientation and energy efficiency and is credited with practicing solar architecture.[2] Urban planning in the United States was directly influenced by the Greek aesthetic sense and the Roman calculating, technical sense. Along with the influences of language, philosophy, and military strategy, our artistic foundation is based on Greek and Roman cultures.

By studying the urban-design and planning trends that occurred over time, we can discover why certain trends occur today. In the United States the evolution of distinct urban-design patterns has been based on site-location factors. The regions of the Southwest and Southeast with moderate, sunny climates have developed into the high-growth Sun Belt. Demographics in these regions show great increases in population, whereas the industrial northeast and mid-Atlantic regions, with colder climates, have shown decreases in population. These areas, sometimes referred to as the Frost Belt or Rust Belt, have lost a considerable amount of manufacturing jobs over the past few decades. Site-location factors are instrumental in determining what type of city will develop at a specific site and what role that city will play in the region.

BASICS OF SPATIAL ANALYSIS

As human beings we have a certain way of looking at the land around us. We have particular ideas about what we do in certain places, and we plan our daily activities based on these ideas. In effect we place symbolic value on the different activities we take part in and the places where we do these activities. This symbolic value creates a sense of order about the land around us. The set of images we have of where we live, work, worship, and socialize makes up our mental map of our surroundings. It is this mental map that dictates our behavior patterns.

At the fundamental level, we organize space according to the particular needs we have. There are several spatial organization concepts that are basic to understanding social behavior. Two sets of symbolic spatial concepts are sacred and profane space and secular and private space. The major difference between sacred and profane space involves the concept of reverence. Sacred space generally means holy, sanctified space, which would include religious or meditative activities, with access limited to a select group of people. The prominence of sacred spaces is shown in the cathedrals in Europe and the Buddhist temples in China and across Southeast Asia, where places of worship are built on hills or in central areas of communities.

Profane space, on the other hand, is usually thought of as space appropriate for a necessary, but disdained, use such as a prison or landfill. Profane areas are limited to people who are shunned by society, in the case of prisons, or the wastes of society, in the case of landfills. The intent in both cases is to put aside, or hide, these particular land uses. The term *NIMBY* (not in my backyard) is used to denote those land uses that people do not want to be near. Many neighborhoods across the country have banded together under the NIMBY rallying cry to fight such developments as an affordable-housing project or halfway house.

The major difference between secular space and private space is accessibility. Secular space includes public spaces, or areas that are not restricted to particular activities, such as the ancient gardens and public baths of Babylonia. The purpose of these public areas was to create a place of relaxation and free flow of ideas. It could be said that our modern Disneyland answers the need for a fantasy environment, except that the expense of the park limits access for all. Comparatively speaking, private space is an area designated for a specific use by its owner, a person or group, who controls the access and type of use of the private space. In some societies, such as the United States, private property rights are fundamental rights in the federal and state constitutions. As William Blackstone defined property rights in Great Britain in the mid-1700s, the settlers to the new republic would own the whole *bundle of sticks*, or total development rights, for a piece of property in the New World.

The symbolic value that the people hold for the land determines how they will use the land and to a great extent how the community will develop. The land ethic, which is the set of values that a group collectively shares for their community, is evident when decisions are made about the preservation of fragile areas of the community, the design of settlement patterns, and the quality of development. The group has a land ethic dominated by sustainable development if the majority is concerned with preserving natural resources and protecting the land from environmental degradation. We can study the urban designs of cities and determine the land ethic of the people. We can also speculate about the social organization of the space. Are the patterns haphazard or rigid? Do they follow some ideal? Where are the sacred spaces, the profane spaces, and the secular spaces? What does all this tell us about the society we are studying?

TYPOLOGY OF CITIES

After considering the influence of physical geography and social and cultural attributes on specific cities, the cities can be placed in categories. The following typology classifies cities based on their urban-design patterns. The patterns are based on why and how space is organized the way it is in a city and region. Some cities clearly belong in one category, while other cities may have characteristics of two or more categories. Another factor that is relevant in determining the type of city is whether the city acts as a break-of-bulk point. Many cities developed because cargo had to be converted from one form of shipping to another, typically ocean-going boats to various means of inland travel or a break from one type of inland travel to another. Certainly many, if not most, of the major cities in this country and in the world initially developed as break-of-bulk points. When categorizing cities in the United States—from Boston to Philadelphia and Pittsburgh and west to St. Louis, Wichita, and San Francisco—it is evident that all these cities developed as break-of-bulk points.

Cities Set Up Politically

Traditionally, political cities follow a rigid pattern based on the political, governmental structure of the nation. The prototype for these cities is a layout with concentric zones, with each zone specifically designated for a particular governmental use or class of people. The central zone is generally where the governmental capital buildings are located. Xi'an, China, surrounded by a wall and a moat, is an example of an ancient city set up for political, defensive purposes. Modern-day political cities include Brasilia, Brazil; Canberra, Australia; and Washington, D.C.

Cities Set Up for Economic Purposes

Generally, cities set up for economic purposes follow Walter Christaller's central-place theory, which states that across the countryside there will be a number of large towns that act as central places for smaller towns in the region.[3] In this hierarchy of communities, the central places have a higher quality and greater diversity of goods than the small towns. This type of settlement pattern in many cases is the organizational pattern for an entire region. New

England in the United States and the Bavarian region in southern Germany are examples of areas patterned after the central-place theory.

Cities Set Up for Trade

Cities set up for trade are based on the central business district (CBD) concept that developed throughout northern Europe and the Northeast and Midwest in the United States in the early 1900s. The CBD concept is based on the concentric zonal model of the industrial city.[4] A series of concentric rings emanates around a functional center and continues to the periphery of the city. The rings are differentiated by commercial and business functions, as well as distinctive ethnic neighborhoods. Prototypical examples of CBD cities include Chicago, Boston, and New York City. CBD cities also serve as central places in the region.[5] In some cases a city such as New York acts as a primate city, which is a major international trade and cultural center.

Cities Set Up for Agriculture

Agricultural cities are set up in regions best suited for large-scale food production and distribution. The division of land in agricultural cities is based on the productivity of the soils and the type of crops that can be grown. In the United States the Midwest was divided according to large-scale development and rotation of crops to feed the nation. The division of the land and the location of farms are related to distribution networks set up to deliver the products to other parts of the country. The original survey for the Midwest was based on an imposed grid system overlaid across the Wheat Belt.[6]

Cities Set Up for Religious Centers

The life of the people in a religious city focuses on the philosophies and practices of a particular religion. In the United States, Salt Lake City, Utah, was founded as a religious city that followed the teachings of the Mormon faith. Originally settled by Joseph Smith, who is known for his calling to found the city in the name of the Mormon religion, Salt Lake City today remains a major center for people practicing that faith. The Mormon temple is a central focus for the physical landscape of the city, as well as the social and cultural lifestyle of the people. In Southeast Asia the Buddhist temple is the central religious focus for people, and in Arab nations the mosque is the center of spiritual life for Muslims. In many cases the mosque in the Islam religion offers educational and medical services, in addition to spiritual and religious support.

The typology may be used to classify ancient as well as modern cities. It creates a point of reference in dealing with the reasons cities developed in certain ways.

LAND ETHIC AND SETTLEMENT PATTERNS IN THE UNITED STATES

The symbolic value that people place on land, as we discussed earlier, is the basis for the attitudes that people hold about developing the land. As the land is being settled, questions about buildings and space arise: What type of development will be allowed? How many projects will be approved? Where will the development be located? The answers to these questions form the settlement patterns of an area.

According to Lewis Mumford, four major migration patterns defined the settlement of the United States. These four migrations are Plymouth Rock, the mill towns, metropolitan development, and suburbanization.[7] In the following analysis two migrations are added: the early Indian settlements as the migration preceding Mumford's first migration and the exurb, as the last migration. The last migration is a contemporary pattern that has recently become apparent. As we consider Mumford's theory on U.S. migration, it is important to think about the land ethic of the people during each era of migration. Each specific pattern of migration is related to how the people valued the land. Drawing connections between the settlement patterns and land ethic of the past helps us to identify current land ethics.

Early Indian Settlement Patterns in the United States

The Indian settlements in the United States mark the beginnings of civilization in our country. As we discussed in the introduction, the Hohokam built an extensive irrigation system and practiced sustainable development. The Hopi and Anasazi Indians in what is now northern Arizona also made major contributions to urban planning. These Indians, who lived in pueblos that date from 500 B.C., practiced subsistence agriculture, in which only crops that are needed are grown. The well-preserved ruins of these tribes show an advanced understanding of the physical environment. The White House ruins in northeast Arizona and the Anasazi ruins just north of Phoenix show a remarkable understanding of solar orientation. The apartment-like buildings of these Indian cliff dwellers face south to gain maximum exposure to the sun in winter and have overhangs for protection from the sun in summer. When we explore the ruins of these prehistoric

Indians, we can make connections between how they thought about the land and the settlement patterns.

The land ethic of the Indians was dominated by a sense of the spiritual value they placed on natural objects such as rivers, rocks, and elements of weather. Their goal was to reach environmental homeostasis, which is a balance between what is taken out of nature and what is put back into the system. Their knowledge of the natural order of species and vegetation dictated their hunting and survival techniques. Indians believed that humans are part of the whole system, sharing the land equally with all its inhabitants. We are actually borrowing the land and preserving it for our children. This is why Indians had no conception of private property rights.

First Migration Wave: Plimouth Plantation

Fleeing British persecution, the Pilgrims landed in the New World at what is now Plymouth, Massachusetts, in 1620. They learned to cope with New England winters, plant crops, and deal with the Indians. Plimouth Plantation was based on a defensive, fortified layout, with a lookout tower and surrounding walls. The village was divided into segments for crops, with a common garden area; housing, which consisted of clustered, attached units; and sport and play, which consisted of open fields. The areas of public space for agriculture, defense, and play epitomized a sense of communal property, rather than private property.

The Pilgrims had a strong farming, or agrarian, work ethic. Their sense of value of the land was based on a communal feeling that what one did affected the whole group. Out of necessity, or as spiritual partners, they committed themselves to the *common good*. The way they used the land and arranged their buildings and spaces was based on this sense of what was necessary and good for the group. The early settlements in Virginia, the Carolinas, and Georgia, which were also based on the agrarian land ethic, were large-scale plantations divided into areas for various crops. Since many owners of these plantations owned slaves, the plantation included a manor for the main house and outlying huts for the slaves.

Second Migration Wave: The Mill Towns

During the Industrial Revolution in the late 1800s, the United States was experiencing rapid development of factory expansion across the northeast and mid-Atlantic states. An influx of immigrants added to the surge in population in developing mill towns. Communities such as Chicopee and Holyoke, Massachusetts, and Cleveland, Ohio, developed workingmen's housing around the mills. The sense of responsibility to maintain communal property during this period gave way to a sense of independence. With the emphasis on the long hours of the factory job, the land ethic of the American people changed from concerns for the communal group to concerns for the family unit.

Third Migration Wave: Metropolitan Development

During the early 1900s a major population movement to urban areas in the United States created many major cities across the country. New York City reached a population of more than 3 million people during this time, with Manhattan itself with a population of 2.2 million and a density of one hundred thousand people per square mile. Along with the escalation in urbanization came the development of the steel girder, which prompted the construction of skyscrapers. Architects capitalized on this new form of design in cities such as New York and Chicago. During this era, exploration west of the Mississippi River also occurred. Since the Midwest was earmarked for agriculture, the plan for dividing up the land was carried out according to crop production. Deeded parcels and titles were given to farmers to plant particular crops.

As urbanization spread across the country, the development of the CBD began to occur in metropolitan areas. Geographically, the CBD is the most efficient place for a large-scale transportation network, which is required for the movement and distribution of goods and other economic activities. The central transportation network with links to population areas and support services is most easily accessed from the central core. Since water access is a major criterion in the distribution of goods, it was beneficial for regions with port access to locate the major trading city at the port area. During this time many port cities such as New York, Boston, Baltimore, and Philadelphia became important access cities for international trade routes. The introduction of railroad technology in the United States spurred the development of central terminals in the CBD. As manufacturers and wholesalers began locating at specified rail-serviced sites, the population surrounding these sites naturally increased.

The land ethic of centralized, inner-city life predominated in this migration wave of rapid urbanization. The American people began to believe that the heart of the city was the most exciting place to live. With their economic advantages, cultural diversity, and job opportunities, the urban areas offered the most favored and progressive life-style during the era of city forming in the country. As the settlement patterns of this time reveal, the population of port and major rail-trade cities grew exponentially.

The other land-ethic perspective that can be attributed to this period is the development of economic concerns with the land. It is at this time that Americans first begin to value the land for large-scale, agribusiness purposes. The concept of cooperative land use, in which large farms are joined with other farms to form joint farming ventures, was coming to the forefront in terms of economic value. The thinking was that, to serve the growing population, which had spread from coast to coast by this time, the government would have to encourage and sponsor the development of a major agribusiness network in the Midwest. This complex, efficient distribution routing system would eventually serve what came to be known as the breadbasket region in the United States.

Fourth Migration Wave: Suburbanization

As the inner cities became overcrowded in the early twentieth century, Americans began realizing that their houses were becoming dilapidated and pollution was threatening their air and water. By the mid 1940s World War II had ended, income levels were rising, and automobiles were being mass produced. With the expansion of commuter rail to peripheral areas and the development of the interstate highway system, under the National Defense Highway Act of 1956, the journey to work was considerably extended. Built in the name of military defense by the Eisenhower administration, the highway system provided the network for new single-family housing subdivisions on a large scale across the country. Veterans returning home from World War II were given special low-interest rates to buy homes. This decentralizing movement, suburbanization, has come to define the urban form of many modern cities in the United States.[8]

The land ethic that was fostered by the movement to the suburbs is based on mobility and the American dream of owning your own home. Our society in fact became very transient with the access to highways and new opportunities to change jobs. The cities that developed in the Southwest and the Southeast, including Los Angeles, Phoenix, Denver, and Miami, epitomize the decentralized design that encourages a transient society.[9] Lacking traditional CBDs, these cities became miles and miles of urban sprawl, with few landmarks to demarcate neighborhoods. For example, the Phoenix Plan 2000, which was developed in the late 1980s, divided the city into nine urban villages. The mall was chosen as the central core for most of the villages, and neighborhoods were delineated around the malls.

Americans during this period began to covet the life-style of working in the inner city and commuting home to suburbs at the outskirts of the city. John Levitt envisioned a subdivision where Americans would fulfill their dream of owning a single-family house with the opportunity to commute to work. Levitt built his subdivision, called Levittown, in Long Island, New York, during the 1940s. The ranch- and Cape Cod–style tract development influenced the direction housing design would take across the country as people began realizing that they could work in the inner city and retreat at night to their homes with their private yards in the suburbs. The picket fences surrounding their houses provided privacy and demarcated their expanse of land.

As new areas of the country were approved for development, either by local board review in New England or county review in the West, builders looked to this new form of subdivision development. In the West builders would often get approval to develop an area near the city, usually county lands that bordered the city, after it had been annexed. The annexation process is a legal tool used extensively in the West to expand city boundaries. It is this process that has accounted for the rapid growth in area and population of many Western cities. Phoenix, for example, grew from a mid-size town of fifty thousand in the early 1950s to more than one million today. The Phoenix area has expanded through annexation, particularly to the west to Glendale and north to Scottsdale, to more than three hundred square miles.

The suburb became the ideal urban form for America from the 1950s to the 1980s. Americans enjoyed this newfound life-style, which offered a stimulating work environment in the inner city and at the same time a peaceful home environment away from the city. Most importantly, the American people coveted the freedom to choose where they worked and lived. The restrictions on development and land-use controls that eventually would come into play with the introduction of zoning and other regulations would cause much disagreement and unrest in many segments of the American population. To this day the imposition of zoning regulations still causes much dissension, as we will see in the following chapters.

Last Migration Wave: The Exurb

Due to rising costs of energy, traffic problems, air pollution, and the lack of affordable housing, Americans are beginning to question urban-sprawl development. In many cases designers and homeowners are now rethinking the value of the inner-city life-style and the land ethic of cultural diversity and communal sustenance. A new migration wave back to the inner cities has begun, with incentives to revitalize the central cores and re-create an increase in dense areas in the inner cities for housing and business. At the same time many planners believe that we have to redesign our decentralized cities and create new exurbs, which contain housing, business, commercial, and recreational opportunities for mid-size population centers.

CONCLUSION

Clearly, the sanitation and pollution problems of the Industrial Revolution were dramatic, but many modern cities and suburbs have also deteriorated recently to critical levels. As we developed into a suburbanized society, we created severe housing, energy, transportation, and environmental problems. It is the role of the planner to develop the community overview and work with the public to refine and reshape the direction for the future. When the people of the community realize where they have evolved from and where they have to go, we hope they will be receptive to new ideas.

Discussion Box
   Do you see evidence of the various types of settlement patterns in your community today? Discuss the specific type of settlement and how aspects of the planning layouts impact current planning practices in the community.

Learning Challenge: Land Ethic and Cultural Landscape
   Identify the push and pull factors that have influenced the way your community has evolved. How would you articulate the land ethic of your community, and your own land ethic? How have the dynamics of planning shaped the set of values the people hold for the land? Analyze the relationship between current land use and the past planning practices in your community.

PLANNING EXERCISE 3: YOUR HOMETOWN

Think about how you would describe certain places and types of land use in your hometown. Where are the sacred spaces and the profane spaces? What places are open to the public and which are bounded and privately owned? As we discussed in the chapter we place a certain value on particular sections of land in our neighborhood and in our community. Think about what space in your hometown should be left undeveloped. Projects should be approved only in areas that are suitable for development and where they do not add excessive pollution to the environment in order to maintain the stability of the land and the surrounding area.

   Meet with your group to discuss your hometown. Respond to the following questions based on your memories and knowledge of your hometown.

- Spatially, what is the layout of your hometown?
- Where did you play as a child? List favorite haunts.
- List places you were not allowed to go. Why not?
- List places you didn't want to go. Why not?
- Where did you socialize with your friends in high school? What places were off limits?
- Now think about the *special places* in your hometown. Write about and discuss why these places have such great value to your community. Do you know of ways that the special places are or should be protected?

NOTES

1. Rodolphe El-Khoury and Edward Robbins, *Shaping the City: Studies in History, Theory and Urban Design* (New York: Routledge, 2004).

2. Mark Wilson Jones, *Principles of Roman Architecture* (New Haven, Conn.: Yale University Press, 2000).

3. Arthur Getis, Judith Getis, and Jerome Fellmann, chapter 11 in *Introduction to Geography*, 2nd ed. (Dubuque, Iowa: Wm. C. Brown, 1981).

4. Getis, Getis, and Fellmann, *Introduction to Geography*.

5. H. J. de Blij and Peter O. Muller, chapter 3 in *Geography: Realms, Regions, and Concepts* (New York: J. Wiley & Sons, 2002).

6. Rutherford H. Platt, chapter 5 in *Land Use Control, Geography, Law, and Public Policy* (Englewood Cliffs, N.J.: Prentice Hall, 1991).

7. Lewis Mumford, "The Fourth Migration," *Survey LIV* (May 1, 1925): 130–133.

8. Dolores Hayden, *Building Suburbia: Greenfields and Urban Growth, 1820–2000* (New York: Pantheon Books, 2003).

9. Phoenix in fact is named for a bird in Egyptian mythology that consumed itself by fire and sprang from its ashes.

Part II

POLITICS OF PLANNING

It can be said that planning evolves in the political arena. Planning issues are politically charged, and the planning process at the local or regional level is directly related to federal and state regulations. The problem is this: the way we govern, and therefore the way we plan, varies across the nation. For this reason it is crucial to know how planning is accomplished at the local level in home-rule states, as well as at the regional level in states governed by county controls. Chapter 4 describes the historical events and trends that shaped community planning in the United States. Case-study comparisons of local and county board planning reveal the differences in how planning is carried out across the country.

Chapter 5 covers the legal issues that impact planning and the influence of Euclidean zoning on planning. Many planning problems we currently face are the result of inappropriate zoning practices of the past. Chapter 6 introduces the concept of growth management and how to develop a plan to shape the community for the future. New urbanism and smart-growth principles are also introduced in the chapter.

Chapter Four

Historical and Political Aspects of Planning in the United States

The planning structure in a country dictates how funding is allocated in communities and how land-use controls and regulations are implemented. Community planning in the United States is not based on a centralized, national planning structure, such as in many unitary European and Asian countries. In countries with centralized governments, planning is carried out primarily from a national level and funding is distributed through federal programs. The planning process in the United States varies across the country, from local jurisdictional control in many New England and mid-Atlantic states to more county, regional control in states such as Arizona and California. Overall, however, the trend across the country is to concentrate more on state and local grants than large-scale federal grants.

PERIODS OF CITY PLANNING

Urban theorists and planners refer to the history of planning in the United States as the evolution of city planning. Melville Branch divides city planning in the United States into several distinct periods.

- Reform in housing and public health standards during the mid to late 1800s
- Idealism in the creation of magnificent, beautiful cities in the late 1800s to the early 1900s
- Stagnation and diversion to war during the late 1930s to the mid 1940s
- Funding boom followed by funding drain from the 1960s to the present[1]

The period of reform in city planning in the United States in the mid to late 1800s dealt with problems created by the Industrial Revolution. Planners during

45

this period concentrated on solving water and air pollution problems, decreasing transportation congestion, and upgrading housing conditions. The period of idealism began with the Columbian Exposition in 1893 and the city-beautiful movement that followed. With the period's emphasis on European Renaissance design and innovative park-planning techniques, the focus in urban design shifted to the aesthetic aspects of planning. During the war years, the planning focus was on economic and social programs to support the military efforts. Branch concludes that the end of the world wars and the development of the interstate highway system created the momentum for the development of large-scale subdivisions. There was abundant funding for public housing, redevelopment, and environmental controls throughout the 1960s. The major federally funded programs, including urban renewal, dominated the planning arena.

In contrast to the period of national planning in the 1960s and 1970s, our current period is based more on a problem-oriented approach. The 1960s were still part of the era of the comprehensive plan, especially plans funded with monies from the amended Housing Act of 1954. Arguably, we have gone from an era of the comprehensive plan, which implied that we could foresee all eventualities and solutions, to an era where we acknowledge that we are muddling through and practicing more strategic planning. We now reject solutions requiring massive, urban-renewal-inspired demolition and focus on local publicly generated solutions. Although we still do a great deal of comprehensive planning, these plans are much more community-vision driven than older plans.

RESPONSE TO THE INDUSTRIAL REVOLUTION: THE SANITARY-REFORM MOVEMENT

James Watt's invention of the steam engine in Great Britain in 1769 was the catalyst that sparked the Industrial Revolution. Up until this point in history, manual labor predominated in cottage industries and guilds, where items were locally produced with the help of wind and water power to operate mills and primitive machinery. The transformation to a mechanized society, where goods could be mass produced, had dramatic, large-scale implications for land-use settlement patterns across the globe. Factory owners began to build large factories where they had access to coal and other raw materials and rail lines for distribution. As the population shifted to these industrialized cities, the central cores became overcrowded and congested. Water and air contamination in many cases reached hazardous levels and the incidence of infectious diseases was extremely high. The industrial city became a patchwork of haphazard factories surrounded by districts of squalid, densely packed multifamily housing.

This factory has been converted to an office complex.

The spirit of reform in response to the Industrial Revolution was based on reactive planning to the environmental conditions of the period. As Anthony Sutcliffe maintains, planners had to learn to respond to the impacts of large-scale industrial development. As unsanitary conditions worsened, national-policy administrators and city officials, as well as the public, began to recognize the extent of the degradation. As a result, a call for improvements in housing conditions and living standards was heard at both the national and local levels of planning. Movements to develop clean water supplies, install effective sewage systems, control contagious diseases, and create parks gained support across the country. The attempts of local authorities to implement controls to improve these conditions were the first steps toward modern city planning.[2] With the drive for controls came opposition from citizens demanding full use of their private property rights. The issue of governmental control versus private development rights, which originated in this era, would become the basis for the rules and regulations of land-use controls at the various levels of government.

Several reformers began writing about ways to solve city problems in the early 1900s, to gain support for city improvements. Charles Mulford Robinson, in *The Improvement of Cities and Towns*, and the publications of J. Horace McFarland drew attention to the problems of urbanization. The articles of the muckrakers Ida M. Turbell, Lincoln Steffens, Ray Stannard Baker, Upton Sinclair, and others disclosed alliances between corrupt political machines and big business.[3] Besides reforms, the reformers called for commissions and professionals to take charge of the planning for cities. Robinson, in particular, cited the need for a new type of specialist to help other experts and to coordinate efforts to make plans. Robinson called the specialized study the general science and art of city building. Many city leaders convened at a conference called the First National Conference on City Planning and Problems of Congestion, in Washington, D.C., in 1909 to discuss the issues of comprehensive planning. In the years just after this first planning conference, leading planners began to join other progressive movements to develop more practical and functional goals.

According to Lawrence Susskind, the drive to institutionalize planning at the professional and administrative levels formally began at this time. As planners began to formulate goals for programs, a debate ensued over whether city planning is based in the social, economic, and political realms or in the quantitative scientific realm. The sanitary-reform movement, or city-planning movement, by 1912 was a blend of the city-beautiful and the city-efficient movements.[4] According to Harvey Perloff, the themes of both movements were integrated and called the city functional.[5]

During this time European philanthropists such as Robert Owen and George Cadbury built model settlements for their factory workers. Their main objectives were to provide safe buildings, fresh air, and recreational space to create a contented, productive workforce. This type of settlement was developed in the United States to provide housing for immigrants in such factory cities as Chicopee and Holyoke, Massachusetts. Although many of the mills are now abandoned, many of the workingmen's homes, which are located along the canals, have been preserved and protected in these cities.

COLUMBIAN EXPOSITION AND THE CITY-BEAUTIFUL MOVEMENT

In response to the problems created by the Industrial Revolution, many architects and planners began to think about ways to solve the serious housing and transportation problems the nation faced. To commemorate the four-hundredth anniversary of Columbus's arrival in America, the Columbian Exposition of 1893 was organized to focus on planning issues and showcase the American city. As Mellier Scott maintains, the goal of the exposition was to promote aesthetic design.[6] In a competition to choose the city where the celebration would be held, Chicago was chosen.

These workingmen's homes are located along the canals in Holyoke, Massachusetts.

In 1893 a year after the four-hundredth anniversary, millions flocked to Chicago to see the elaborate boulevards, civic centers, monuments, and parks that were built from designs by noted architects such as Daniel Burnham and landscape architect Frederick Olmsted. The architects' designs stretched from the Chicago River to Jackson Park. Called the Chicago Plan, the plan featured an integrated design of classic buildings, exhibition halls, promenades, and open-space areas. It was Burnham's vision to display this magnificent city plan to the nation and the world as a model for cities across the country to follow. He met with planners, architects, and engineers at the exposition who exchanged ideas about how to create effective urban designs and implement the designs in their own cities. Burnham emerged from the Columbian Exposition with a tremendous amount of prominence in the field of architecture and influenced the urban-design plans for many cities in the United States.

The city-beautiful movement is noted for three major urban-planning trends: (1) municipal art, including outdoor sculpture and fountains; (2) civic improvement; and (3) planning commissions.[7] These trends are shown in the development of civic centers, public libraries, monumental city halls, union stations, banks, and college buildings in the grand-classic design. Planning commissions were established to deal with site-location problems with the projects that were being planned. Several books that were based on discussions from the Columbian Exposition about regulations for land use were used as the basis for zoning codes and subdivision rules and regulations in communities across the country.

The influence of the city-beautiful movement can be seen in many cities across the United States. Imposing, elaborate city halls, civic centers, and municipal buildings dominate many downtown areas built during this era. Washington, D.C., epitomizes the city-beautiful movement with its formal Mall of historic buildings and monuments and its radial design of paths leading from the central Mall. Both in design and function, the urban form of Washington represents the ideas of urban planners at the turn of the century.

GARDEN CITY CONCEPT

Ebenezer Howard, a British writer and progressive urban planner, wrote extensively about the problems of the industrial city and how to solve them. Howard presents the garden city as an alternative to the factory city. He describes the garden city as a clean, self-contained community with housing in designated areas, separated from streets for motor vehicle traffic. The cities are small in population and located a safe distance from the factories. The following components describe the model for the garden city, which created much debate in British urban-planning circles in the late 1800s:

- Land owned in public trust
- Maximum population of thirty thousand for each city
- Greenbelt to surround the city
- Mixture of land use

The British used the garden city concept to create New Towns, which they felt would control urban growth. Letchworth Garden City, built by designers Parker and Unwin under Howard's supervision, is the prototypical example of the garden city.[8] Located near London, its layout consists of residential areas with small central areas for business and commercial use. Pedestrian paths are integrated within the housing areas, while motorized traffic is routed outside the ring of the city. The British government did not develop extensive plans for more New Towns, and consequently, the projects began to blend in with other new semidetached housing projects around London. The genteel middle-class Londoners began buying these homes, rather than the industrial poor for whom Howard intended the homes. Howard's writings influenced the urban-planning movement in the early 1900s. He visited the United States for several years and tried to influence planners to follow his garden city model. Several planners did follow his design and developed planned communities in Radburn, New Jersey; Columbia, Maryland; and Reston, Virginia.

The garden city concept did not materialize in the United States on a grand scale, mainly because of the concept of private property rights. As immigrants who had fled governments dominated by central national planning, the American settlers would not support the concept of land in public trust or a population cap. During the great era of expansion of the West, the pioneers saw vast open spaces and an abundance of minerals and natural resources. Many urban planners contend that the Western spirit of adventure and individualism has turned in many cases into an attitude of domination over the land.

Pioneers such as Max Weber, a German, and Patrick Geddes, a Scot, discussed the problems caused by the Industrial Revolution from a sociological perspective. Weber and Geddes believed that many city problems stemmed from issues of social class and domination of some classes over others. Geddes, often called a forerunner of comprehensive planning, emphasized the need to identify social-welfare issues and environmental concerns in formulating plans. He advocated the integration of physical planning with socioeconomic planning to solve problems.[9]

Several European architects strongly influenced the urban design of American cities. The writings of Charles Edouard Jeanneret (1885–1965), who adopted the name Le Corbusier, inspired a whole generation of architects and urban planners. Corbusier's powerful vision of the modern city with skyscrapers surrounded by parks was imitated across the United States in many high-rise public housing projects. The Bauhaus School, founded in Weimar Germany in 1919, also influenced urban design in the United States. The Bauhaus School, which emphasized rigid geometric lines and the glass curtain wall, existed for a decade before being closed by the Nazis. The glass wall became the archetypal symbol of international modernism. Leading designers of the school fled Germany, going mainly to the United States, when the Nazis took power. By the 1950s the Bauhaus School set the tone for modernistic architecture. In some cases architects in Europe were hired to design cities in the United States. Pierre L'Enfant, a Frenchman, designed Washington, D.C., which was based on the design of Versailles, France. Both the radial layout with the grid pattern of streets in the central area and the baroque architecture are reminiscent of the European Renaissance era.

The most dramatic response to the unsanitary conditions created by the Industrial Revolution in the United States was the park movement initiated by Frederick Law Olmsted (1822–1903). Considered the first landscape architect in the United States, Olmsted designed many large public parks across the United States and Canada and hundreds of smaller public and semipublic parks. The design for New York's Central Park, whose original name was

Greensward, launched Olmsted's career as a renowned landscape architect. Along with his partner Calvert Vaux, Olmsted collaborated on a plan for the park, which they submitted and won approval for in 1858. Olmsted was chief architect and supervisor of the twenty-year project.[10]

Olmsted's other major parks include the Olmsted Park System in Buffalo, New York; Jackson Park and Riverside in Chicago; the grounds of the U.S. Capitol in Washington, D.C.; the Emerald Necklace System in Boston; Stanford University; and Mount Royal Park in Montreal, Canada. Olmsted and Vaux developed the Olmsted Park System in Buffalo, New York, beginning in 1868. The Olmsted Park System is the oldest coordinated system of public parks and parkways in the United States. Olmsted and Vaux's vision was to create islands of tranquility in an expanding metropolitan area. They designed three parks and connected them with wide pedestrian parkways and avenues, which excluded commercial traffic and extended the park throughout the city. The Olmsted-designed parks of the Buffalo Park System are listed on the National Register of Historic Places. Olmsted continued to design public grounds for the Board of Park Commissioners in Buffalo during the remainder of his career.[11]

Olmsted's Jackson Park is located in Chicago and the General Plan of Riverside was designed for a suburban community near Chicago. The General Plan of Riverside, which Olmsted developed in 1869, is the best example of Olmsted's idea of how suburbs should be designed. The sixteen-hundred-acre community along the Des Plaines River west of Chicago took two years to complete. Olmsted's vision was to have enough space for recreation and scenic areas for all the residents. He incorporated preservation techniques to protect floodplain areas and riverbanks, as well as two areas of uplands on the site.

Olmsted was commissioned in 1873 to supervise the planning for the grounds of the U.S. Capitol in Washington, D.C. Olmsted designed marble terraces, footwalks, and an iron trellis for the Capitol grounds. He retired as superintendent of the terrace project in 1885, although he continued to work on the project until 1889. In late 1875 the park commissioners in Boston asked Olmsted to design a park system for the city. Olmsted developed the Emerald Necklace, including the Boston Public Garden, the Commons, and the Back Bay Fens, strung together with a series of parkways and other parks.

In the western United States and in Canada, Olmsted drew on indigenous plants and materials to develop his plans. In 1888 Olmsted developed the campus plan for Stanford University in Palo Alto, California. For this plan he incorporated the California mission style of architecture and vegetation natural to the Mediterranean region in Europe, which is similar to the climate in California. In his plan for Mount Royal Park in Montreal, Olmsted blended the sections of the park within the natural topography of the central part of the city. Olmsted compared the sections of the park to stanzas in a poem. He believed that his plans were works of art, representing elements of landscape paintings and poetic expression.

Olmsted's park plans went beyond the layout of the park for recreational activities, trails for hiking, and water sports. He based his plans on the topography of the site and addressed drainage, water supply, and light and ventilation problems in his designs. He focused on the regional aspects in his plans, considering entire watershed areas in relation to future city plans and development projects. Many landscape architects speculate that if the planners in Buffalo had followed Olmsted's plans for the three-park system he devised, they might have prevented Lake Erie's current pollution. Similarly, Olmsted's green-ribbon, emerald plan for Boston included proposals to integrate the arm of Back Bay basin with the head of the tidewater in Muddy River. Irving Fisher contends that Olmsted's focus on flood control, water-quality cleanup, and beautification of the area might have prevented many of the contamination issues that Boston planners face today.[12]

The park movement came at a time in U.S. history when our society was changing from agrarian to industrial. With the ending of the Civil War in 1865, the country in the late 1800s faced the prospects of rapid industrialization and urbanization. For Olmsted it marked a time to capitalize on the progressive movement to plan cities in a comprehensive way, integrating all aspects of physical, social, and economic planning.

SEPARATION OF POWER

Although city planning in the United States incorporated planning approaches from the Greeks, Romans, and European Renaissance, it has evolved predominately into its own unique form of planning that favors the concept of private property rights. The U.S. Constitution and Bill of Rights were written to protect the individual rights of U.S. citizens. In fact the primary goal of the framers of the constitution who met in Philadelphia in 1787 was to create a system of government that separated power in the United States. The main reason for the separation of power was to have a government with a checks-and-balances system. The citizen in this type of democratic, fragmented government would always have recourse to contest unfair or unreasonable treatment under the law. The political structure of the government was divided into three branches—executive, legislative, and judicial.

The executive branch of government is the administrative level, including the president and presidential cabinet appointments at the federal level and state governors at the state level. The main function of the federal and state executive branches is to enforce laws. They also initiate and administer policy guidelines, or regulations. Since this type of policy planning is initiated at the national level, it is called *top-down* planning. Guidelines and policies in top-down planning are initiated and overseen by the central administration. The legislative branch of government is in charge of making statutory laws. This branch also allocates funding and oversees and levies tax controls and measures. The legislative bodies at the national and state levels are made up of the House of Representatives and the Senate.

The judicial branch of government in the United States is the court system. It is divided into superior and district court systems, and each state has guidelines for checks and balances that lead to the U.S. Supreme Court if necessary.[13] In terms of planning, some states also rely on a land court to determine land-dispute cases. It is important to review court case decisions in a specific state to identify patterns in the way development decisions are handed down. Some states, for example, show strict environmental-protection court decision patterns, while other states show more lenient building-practice patterns.

Over the course of our history, there have been particular instances when the federal government would oversee major regional planning projects. The Tennessee Valley Authority (TVA) was the brainchild of Franklin D. Roosevelt in 1933. The project was one of several regional planning projects under the New Deal national-planning movement that Roosevelt initiated to resolve urban problems. Proposed as a series of dams to provide flood control for the Tennessee Valley area, this project also included plans for natural-resource protection, recreational management, power generation, and job creation. Roosevelt's intent was a plan that would control for flooding, as well as encourage economic development in the Tennessee Valley area. The allocation of funds to build the dams and related projects was directly controlled at the federal level. Considered one of the most extensive regional plans in U.S. history, Roosevelt in fact had visions of initiating several other regional authorities across the country. The authorities would oversee the management of watershed projects that could generate sufficient power, create jobs, and boost related economic development for the surrounding area.[14] Three other major regional projects considered by Roosevelt were the Colorado River Basin Compact, the Pacific Northwest Regional Planning Commission, and the New England Regional Commission. The first two plans materialized with the construction of the Boulder, Bonneville, and Grand Coulee dams.

The second illustration of national planning is the interstate highway system initiated by Dwight D. Eisenhower in 1956. Proposed as a project to protect the country militarily from coast to coast, the National Defense Highway Act of 1956 was a national plan issued directly from the executive branch.

The funding for the project was distributed from the national level to the states involved in the highway development. Linking states by a network of highways, this transportation plan demanded centralized administration.

The implementation of the interstate system had profound effects on American city design. The layout of cities and the type and placement of development were directly related to the interstate system. The new freedom of mobility and opportunity to commute long distances to work impacted the design of cities in the United States, particularly in the West and Southwest. As the plan for the interstate highway system progressed across the country in the 1960s, a new type of development pattern followed suit. Commercial strip development, including motels and automobile support services, began to dominant the landscape. Along with the commercial development, single-family subdivisions were planned and constructed farther and farther away from central business districts. As access to the highway became more available, the commute to work could be expanded. In the end the patchwork of housing tracts that were built next to each other, forming suburbs across the country, was the direct result of the construction of the interstate. It is interesting to think about what the West and Southwest would look like today if the vast expanses of land were not opened up by the interstate system.

The centralized, top-down planning approach of the TVA and interstate highway examples is unique in U.S. city-planning history. Generally, regional planning projects of this scale are not evident throughout our history. Unlike Great Britain, for example, which has had a town planning act in effect since the early 1800s, the United States has not established a centralized planning agency to oversee community and regional planning across the country. As the New Deal programs of Franklin Roosevelt faded from currency, few attempts have been made to establish centralized planning projects. Each successive administration has handed more and more autonomy to the states to conduct community and regional planning.

The emphasis on state-level planning in the United States becomes evident right after each world war. With the focus on economic recovery and development, federal grants were distributed to the states to subsidize massive sewer and water infrastructure projects. A national housing program also distributed funds to the states for low-interest loans for veterans returning from the war. The postwar growth era from the late 1940s to the 1950s actually set the pattern for suburbanization in the United States. The tremendous growth in the housing and business sectors, particularly in the Southwest, created competition among the states for funds. As the Sun Belt cities began to urbanize rapidly after the construction of the interstate highway system, governmental officials began to think in terms of controlling major infrastructure and transportation projects at the state level.

With the exception of several major social programs, including the War on Poverty program and the Model Cities Program during the administration of Lyndon B. Johnson, each administration since the late 1950s has concentrated on giving more power and controls to state governments. The focus on central planning in the United States generally occurs in wartime, or postwartime, as was the case with John F. Kennedy and Johnson. Along with the intense radicalism and activism during the Vietnam War and right after the war, Kennedy and Johnson proposed massive funding for social and redevelopment programs. Federal urban renewal programs to revitalize large parts of cities were sponsored during this era, because the public mood supported social and welfare reform at the national level. As the federal debt grew and the recession hit in the early 1970s, the public mood shifted to favor less control on the part of government.

Richard M. Nixon in the 1970s ushered in the era of *realistic* urban planning. Nixon set up a grant program that distributed funds to cities for specific city projects. Community Development Block Grants (CDBGs) were awarded to applicants who proposed site-specific, realistic projects. Based on the concept of strategic planning, which focuses on a specific planning problem in a targeted area, the grant monies come from revenue-sharing programs. Revenue-sharing funds are clearly earmarked for the specified project, and often the city has to match a percentage of the grant. With the failure of many urban-renewal projects across the country, particularly the large-scale projects that covered extensive areas, the CDBGs offered an efficient way to solve city problems. Since the grants were targeted at a specific site, city planners and officials could closely monitor the allocation of funds and the implementation of action plans for the programs.

With increasing federal debt and recession throughout the Ronald Reagan and George H. W. Bush administrations, more and more of the electorate clamored for less government intervention. Government programs began to be labeled entitlement programs and viewed with distaste by the public. Legislative actions to give more controls for land-use planning to the states gained favor among political groups into the 2000s. The emphasis is definitely on state and local controls for land-use planning, rather than national or centralized planning controls as in nations in Europe and Asia and other parts of the world.

CONTROVERSIAL NATURE OF PLANNING

Planning by its very nature is controversial in the United States. The issues that involve development projects in controversy are generally focused on private property disputes over the right to develop a particular project. The public in many cases distrusts the planning process due to media coverage of politically charged issues such as locating affordable housing and siting landfills. Open space has been depleted in many regions of the country, and projects are often proposed for parcels that seem inappropriate for development to residents. The NIMBY (not in my backyard) syndrome affects more and more residents, and they are fighting development such as multifamily housing, landfills, and jails near their property.

Because the government of the United States is a participatory democracy, each citizen has the right to contest a proposed development. Throughout the decision-making process in locating development, the political overtones can become very intense. Planners must play several roles in overseeing the planning process: coordinate the legal aspects of public forums and hearings for projects, act as liaisons between developers and boards, and act as mediators between landowners and developers. Because of the controversial nature of projects and the bias that each player brings to the planning process, the role of mediator is usually the most difficult one for the planner.

Mediation in planning is difficult because of the ethical issues that often arise in the planning arena. Since special-interest groups involved in a proposed development bring vested interests to the table, conflicts between players often arise. Sometimes a city official, lawyer, or developer in the community has a vested interest that creates a conflict. The planner must sort out the bias of each player in the planning process, determine whether there are any unethical issues related to a particular project, and encourage the most appropriate development. All of this is accomplished while serving the public interest. This is the most challenging task for the planner.

CONCLUSION

As we struggle to allocate necessary resources for our communities and regions, planning remains more controversial than ever. Who gets what is the main topic of many public meetings and hearings. If support systems are preplanned from a regional perspective and with demographics in mind, the infrastructure is ready when the projects are approved. Everything is lined up according to the most efficient delivery systems. History and political forces challenge how we might allocate community resources. The integrity of the planning process at the local level determines how well a community meets these challenges.

Discussion Box

Who is in charge in your community and does the political system support social needs? What are the political issues and social trends that have created controversy in your community? Have you had to vote recently on low-income housing or a new school or converting an old downtown building to a school or boutiques? Who has addressed the political controversies and social issues over the years? Would you say that your community is currently experiencing overwhelming political conflict among the constituencies? Or is there currently a balance within the various political subsets? Explain how Howard's garden city concept is linked to planning practice today to create new-urbanism communities.

PLANNING EXERCISE 4:
DEVELOPING A COMMUNITY OVERVIEW

This exercise consists of four worksheets that together make up the community overview for your town or city. As you discuss and fill in information for the worksheets with your group, you are learning to collect, analyze, and synthesize data that are needed in the problem-oriented planning process. The first worksheet is a statistical profile, which identifies the latest population, employment, and support-services statistics for the community. The second worksheet is a fact-finding trip to city hall, in which you learn where and how to find pertinent data in each municipal department. The third worksheet is a downtown survey analysis, in which you come to a consensus with your group about ways to improve the downtown in your college community. The fourth worksheet involves a topographic exercise, which shows you what data you need to solve land-suitability issues in planning.

Statistical Profile of the Community

You need to analyze current and projected demographic, employment, and housing and commercial-property statistics to develop problem-oriented plans. The purpose of this worksheet is to introduce you to the statistics that are needed and identify where you can find the statistics for your community. With your group, respond to the following questions by searching the official state government website (yourstate.gov) and any available community-profile documents.

- What year was your community incorporated?
- What is the statistical breakdown of men, women, and minorities in your community?

- How many hospitals, schools, and recreational facilities are there in your community?
- Who is the largest employer in your community?
- How many persons in your community live below the poverty level?
- How many violent crimes per one thousand people were committed in your community last year?

Fact-Finding Trip to City Hall

The purpose of this worksheet is to find out what data you can collect in each department in city hall. Although working with your group in class is productive, it is also beneficial to consider attending a planning board, city council, or planning commission meeting during the semester. Watching these meetings shows you city or town government in action. Since planning is so controversial, there usually will be a politically charged item on the agenda. The sources for the data for this worksheet are planning and development documents describing specific roles of each department in city hall or the official government website for your state (yourstate.gov). List the information you would get from each of the following departments:

- Assessor's office
- City auditor
- Building department
- City clerk's office
- Planning or community development department
- Conservation commission
- Engineering department
- City health department
- Historical commission
- City's law department
- Personnel department
- Purchasing department
- Water department
- Zoning board of appeals
- Parks and recreation department

Downtown Survey

The purpose of this worksheet is to familiarize you with the downtown in your college community. Discuss the following situations with your group, and respond to the questions. The data sources needed here are recent downtown surveys that have been conducted in the community and updated business-inventory data.

- Review the results from a recent downtown survey. What issues of concern for the downtown are identified in the survey? What issues does your group identify as concerns?
- Come up with several ideas for shops, entertainment, and recreation that would improve the downtown. Consider the market, motor and pedestrian circulation patterns, and access for the particular business to determine the optimal location for each proposal.
- Analyze and evaluate the alternatives your group identified to revitalize the downtown. Considering cost-benefit analysis, what proposals are the most feasible?
- Describe several action plans that you would put in place to carry out the best option for the downtown. Think of some innovative, yet feasible programs to support your plans, such as parking or traffic alternatives, cultural events to draw people together, or volunteer programs to beautify the downtown.

Topographic Map Analysis

As we have discussed, there is a direct relationship between physical geographic features, including soil types, slope, drainage patterns, and landforms, and the type of development that should be approved in an area. This exercise involves learning how to read the elevation and natural features of the land on a topographic map to make sound decisions about the appropriate type of development and where to locate it. As a group discuss and respond to the following questions. Pay attention to the predominate landforms in this quadrangle and the human-settlement patterns. The source for this data is the topographic map and accompanying land-use pamphlet for the region.

- What quadrangle, or quad, is this? What quads border this one?
- What is the scale of this map?
- Find the highest point of elevation on the topographic map. What is it?
- Find and name the other predominate land features on the map. Are there any hilly terrain areas? Note any areas of close contour lines or ridgelines that would indicate steep slopes.
- Find and name water bodies such as rivers and tributaries, ponds, lakes, or coastal areas. Note the buffer between watershed areas and development.
- Discuss the overall settlement pattern, and find where new development has occurred by consulting the land-use pamphlet. Note specifically the

housing, commercial, and industrial development that has occurred in the past ten years. Where are the most populated areas? How much change has occurred?

NOTES

1. Melville Branch, *Planning Aspects and Applications* (New York: J. Wiley & Sons, 1966).

2. Anthony Sutcliffe, *The Rise of Modern Urban Planning 1800–1914* (New York: St. Martin's Press, 1980).

3. Sutcliffe, *The Rise*.

4. Lawrence Susskind, *Guide to Graduate Education in Urban and Regional Planning* (East Lansing, Mich.: East Lansing Association of Collegiate Schools of Planning, 1974).

5. Harvey Perloff, *Planning and the Urban Community: Essays on Urbanism and City Planning* (Pittsburgh, Pa.: Carnegie Institute and University of Pittsburg Press, 1961).

6. Mellier Scott, *American City Planning Since 1890* (Los Angeles: University of California Press, 1969).

7. Jon A. Peterson, *The Birth of City Planning in the United States, 1840–1917* (Baltimore, Md.: Johns Hopkins University Press, 2003).

8. Ebenezer Howard and Frederic James Osborne, *Garden Cities of To-morrow* (London: Faber and Faber, 1945).

9. Sutcliffe, *The Rise*.

10. Irving D. Fisher, *Frederick Law Olmsted and the City Planning Movement in the United States* (Ann Arbor, Mich.: UMI Research Press, 1986).

11. Retrieved May 14, 2004, from www.fredericklawolmsted.com.

12. Fisher, *Frederick Law Olmsted*.

13. Frank So, Irving Hand, and Bruce McDowell, *The Practice of State and Regional Planning* (Chicago: American Planning Association, 1986).

14. John Friedmann, *The Spatial Structure of Economic Development in the Tennessee Valley* (Chicago: University of Chicago Press, 1955).

Chapter Five

Process of Zoning and Legal Issues in the United States

Zoning is the process of dividing land into different land-use districts. The zoning ordinance dictates how the land-use districts of a community are laid out and what may or may not be built in each area of the community. The way zoning ordinances are written to a great extent determines what type of development is put where in a community. In some cases ordinances may prohibit particular land uses, or classes of people, from moving into the community. Shaping the communities in this way may be considered exclusionary. For example, if the zoning for a community is mostly one-acre, single-family residential lots with no multifamily lots, a low-income family wishing to move to the community might claim discrimination.

DEFINING ZONING AND ITS IMPLICATIONS

Zoning is a restrictive planning tool with regulatory police power that defines the permitted uses of land, dimensions of lots, and the location of buildings on lots for different districts. The power of zoning as a tool in the planning process is limited. Zoning regulations must be reasonable and bear a substantial relationship to public good, safety, health, welfare, and convenience. Therefore, whether a regulation is arbitrary or capricious is often argued in state land courts across the country. Court cases regarding private property rights may be argued in a state court or the U.S. Supreme Court. Usually, arguments center on the fact that zoning should shape, not prohibit, development.

The authority to zone land comes from governmental police powers, which allow municipalities to exercise reasonable controls on the use of land to protect the public health, safety, and welfare. Police powers are a powerful and necessary part of our system of government. The government may take private property, with compensation, to promote the public interest. For many years, the broad dicta, or authoritative pronouncement, was that no one may claim damages due to a police regulation developed to secure the public welfare, particularly in the area of health, and safety regulations.[1] The distinguishing characteristic between eminent domain and the police power is that the former involves the taking of property because of its need for the public use, while the latter involves the regulation of such property to prevent the use thereof in a manner that is detrimental to the public interest.[2]

The three constitutional amendments that are related to the legalities of zoning are the First, Fifth, and Fourteenth Amendments. These three amendments serve as protections when land-use regulations affect property owners. The language in these amendments specifically points to clauses that protect private property owners when they are acting legally in property disputes.

The First Amendment deals with the rights of association and privacy, which are related to freedom of expression in private property rights issues. The amendment states: "Congress shall make no law respecting an establishment of religion, or prohibiting the free exercise thereof; or abridging the freedom of speech, or of the press; or the right of the people peaceably to assemble, and to petition the Government for a redress of grievances." The relevant clause "or abridging the freedom of speech" is most often argued in land-use regulation cases involving signage disputes. Traditionally, prohibiting or restricting signage content is the most significant point of legal entanglements under the First Amendment. For example, a dispute may arise if an owner of a business requests a permit for a sign and residents in a nearby neighborhood complain that the sign is offensive. The owner would argue that his freedom of speech is being violated, whereas the residents would argue that the sign is a nuisance.

The Fifth Amendment deals with the takings issue. The amendment states: "No person shall be . . . deprived of life, liberty, or property, without due process of law; nor shall private property be taken for public use, without just compensation." The governmental taking of land by eminent domain is clearly allowable but only if "just compensation" is paid. Eminent domain is the power of government, an attribute of sovereignty, to condemn, or take, property for public use. In the past there was a perception that regulation was not a taking, but now we understand that regulations that go too far are also a taking, which we now call a regulatory taking. It is worth noting, however, that dramatic diminution of value is *not* necessarily a taking absent some type of physical intrusion. If the property owner is not satisfied with the compensation offered by the government, he or she may sue the government for unjust *tak-*

"Sometimes the American Dream
turns into the American nightmare."

Cartoon 2.   Seized by Eminent Domain

ing. The *takings clause* is used by private property owners to contest the amount of compensation offered by the government to seize their property. The Fifth Amendment essentially limits the power of government by requiring that the government pay just compensation when it takes private property by eminent domain.

The Fourteenth Amendment deals with police power. Section 1 of the amendment states: "All persons born or naturalized in the United States, and subject to the jurisdiction thereof, are citizens of the United States and of the State wherein they reside. No State shall make or enforce any law, which shall abridge the privileges or immunities of citizens of the United States; nor shall any State deprive any person of life, liberty, or property, without due process of law; nor deny to any person within its jurisdiction the equal protection of the laws." "Due process of law" means that individual rights are protected under the Fourteenth Amendment. Equal protection under the law refers to the statement in the amendment that "the right of all persons under like circumstances to enjoy equal treatment and security in their life, their liberty and their property and to bear no greater burdens than are imposed on others under like circumstances." In the land-use context there must be a legitimate governmental purpose for the classifications and use restrictions that are applied to properties. People and properties similarly situated must be treated similarly.

The "without due process" clause as it relates to the federal government was spelled out earlier, as noted, in the Fifth Amendment. The Fourteenth Amendment extends those rights to cover state government, and therefore local government, as a subdivision of state government actions. Due process disputes in land-use-regulation court cases fall under substantive due process and procedural due process. Substantive due process refers to the legitimacy of the government's purpose such as specific ordinance requirements. For example, a property owner could sue under the Fourteenth Amendment claiming unreasonable width of roads and sidewalks under the subdivision rules and regulations for the community. If the property owner feels the government purpose is not reasonable, there is recourse under the Fourteenth Amendment. Procedural due process specifically refers to the process and hearings that are required by federal and state law to publicize governmental intention to seize property. If a property owner claims public notice was not given or hearings were not held according to state statutes, the owner may sue under the Fourteenth Amendment.[3]

Sometimes state constitutions have different constitutional clauses that limit local authority. In one such example, Massachusetts refers to its state constitution to interpret search and seizure law, rather than the U.S. Constitution. The Fourth Amendment to the Constitution limits unreasonable searches and seizures. At the federal level, this amendment covers areas where one has a reasonable expectation of privacy, for example, your house and homestead. Back land, which is generally open, does not fall under this category of protection. Under this open-fields doctrine, police and regulatory officials can enter back land without a warrant to make searches, as long as there are sufficient grounds to enter. Typically, legitimate reasons for a search include crime-related issues, such as illegal drugs, or civil-related issues, such as zoning or wetlands enforcement. The Massachusetts Supreme Judicial Court has expressed a reluctance to apply the open-fields doctrine. Court rulings have cited the state constitution in restricting searches, making enforcement more difficult.

Home-rule authority is another aspect of state law that influences the amount of control the individual communities in the state have to exercise police power. In states without home-rule authority, local governments have only the authority expressly granted them by the state government. In home-rule-authority states, such as Massachusetts, the state constitution grants to local

Failed to Post Public Hearing Notice 14 Days in Advance

MONTY GEER

"I thought I'd have property rights, not property obligations."

Cartoon 3. Procedural Due Process

government any police power consistent with the constitution except where the state has prohibited this authority or covered the field so completely that it is clear they do not intend local authority. Overall, local communities in states without home-rule authority must follow more rigid police-power guidelines than communities in states with home-rule authority.

HISTORICAL PERSPECTIVES OF ZONING

The first settlers to migrate to the United States from Great Britain in the early 1600s had a land ethic based on agrarian principles. The colonists regarded land as a community resource to be used in the public interest. The Virginia House of Burgesses passed an act in 1631 requiring every adult male to grow two acres of corn. Other laws were passed regulating the production of flax and hemp in 1642 and mulberry trees in 1656. Over time as development spread across the country, there was a shift away from the agricultural focus to metropolitan development. Urban planners began developing plans for large geographic areas, which emphasized in many cases the grid design. Two examples of grid-pattern cities are William Penn's 1686 checkerboard plan for Philadelphia and James Oglethorpe's 1733 plan for Savannah.[4]

With the escalation of urbanization and the diffusion of the Industrial Revolution from Great Britain in the late 1800s, officials began to recognize the need for ordinances to protect the health, safety, and welfare of the public. Due to safety concerns about the proximity of garment factories to homes, New York City passed the first ordinance in the country in 1916. The highest court in New York upheld the ordinance in 1920. The New York ordinance was all inclusive, covering all the boroughs in the city. Regulatory controls included building height restrictions and building setbacks. The ordinance divided the city into the following zones: residential, commercial, *unrestricted*, and *undetermined*.[5]

The establishment of the New York City ordinance influenced the federal government to develop zoning-enabling legislation for the entire country. Herbert Hoover, then commerce secretary and later president, appointed a Department of Commerce advisory committee to develop a zoning-enabling act. The committee released various drafts and versions of the legislation between 1922 and 1926. The final version, the Standard State Zoning Enabling Act (SSZEA), was established in 1926. The act serves as a model for states to enact their own zoning-enabling legislation. Throughout the history of zoning in this country, the majority of municipalities have enacted some form of zoning ordinance. Most state zoning-enabling acts were similar to begin with but over the years have diverged. For example, different states have different procedures regarding the process of granting variances.

In 1926 Euclid, Ohio, became the test case to determine the legality of zoning. With the decision by the U.S. Supreme Court that upheld the Euclid ordinance, in *Village of Euclid v Ambler Realty Company* 272 US 365 (1926), the court case became the landmark case for zoning. The decision in the case confirmed the concept and use of zoning for future development in our country. Overall, traditional zoning has two components—classification of land uses, such as residential, commercial, and industrial, and regulation of development density, such as size, height, area, location, and land coverage. Known as Euclidean zoning, communities across the country have followed this zoning model since its inception to design ordinances and land-use regulations to control development.[6] It is interesting to note the double entendre of *Euclidean* coming from the village of Euclid and from Euclidean geometry. Some speculate that the Supreme Court took the case only because they were amused by the double meaning.

The arguments in the *Euclid* case focused on private property rights versus public control. The municipal officials had divided Euclid into various zones for residential, commercial, and industrial uses. The division was based on creating areas of single-family housing to maintain the character of the community. The goal was to develop an ordinance that would fulfill the American dream of owning home ownership, with a picket fence and backyard.

In the process of zoning the village, a parcel of vacant land owned by Ambler Realty Company was divided by Euclid's zoning ordinance into two zones with a buffer strip between them. Rail lines on the north and a major arterial roadway on the south bordered the land. Euclid officials zoned the northern portion for industry. Ambler Realty Company contested the decision when the southern portion was classified residential. The residential classification had a much lower value for Ambler, which intended to develop the whole parcel for industrial use. Ambler Realty challenged the ordinance, claiming that parcels the company owned had previously been zoned industrial. Ambler's suit stated that Euclid had violated its due process under the Fourteenth Amendment. The state supreme court found in favor of Ambler Realty Company. The U.S. Supreme Court found in favor of Euclid. The Euclid ordinance was upheld, setting the precedent for other communities to follow suit and develop ordinances.

SCOPE AND CONTENT OF A ZONING ORDINANCE

A zoning ordinance has two components: the map, which delineates the zoning districts, and the text, which defines the regulations. The zoning map shows how a community is divided into different land-use districts, or zones. Most zoning ordinances include, at the very least, residential, commercial, and industrial zones. The zoning map depicts each land-use district, with streets or property lines used as boundaries between districts. Zoning boundary lines must be easy to distinguish from other lines and information on the map. The map must be large enough to permit positive identification of individual parcels. A larger community may need more than one map for complete coverage, because of the details required. The official zoning map should include a title, including the name of the community and the date of adoption of the map; a north arrow; a scale and a legend listing each zoning district and showing how it may be identified on the zoning map; clearly identified zoning districts; and a space to make notations and to record dates of amendments.

The zoning text establishes land-use standards and regulations pertaining to districts shown on the zoning map. Traditionally, a zoning ordinance contains the following elements:

- Purpose, scope, and authority
- Definitions of terms used
- Descriptions of zoning districts
- Uses of land, water, and buildings permitted, prohibited, or permitted by special permit
- Characteristics of use, such as intensity of vehicles on arterial roadways
- Lot sizes, usually the minimum, but occasionally the maximum permitted size or density (units per acre)
- Dimensional and density control obtained through requirements for lot street frontage, width, and depth; setbacks, or distance of buildings from lot lines; proximity of a lot's buildings; and the percentage of the lot that may be covered by buildings, or floor-area ratio (FAR) (Many communities use minimum setbacks and some use maximum setbacks. FAR and maximum lot coverage are only two examples of many methods for regulating allowable intensity of uses.)
- Height of buildings and special features in feet and stories
- Changes in preexisting nonconforming uses and buildings
- Accessory or subordinate uses and buildings
- Parking and loading areas required on lots
- Regulation of signs and advertising devices
- Buffer strips at district boundaries, landscaping
- Earth-materials excavation, mining, and filling
- Site-plan referral and review provisions
- Administration of amendments, building and occupancy permits, enforcement and penalties, special permits, variances, and appeals

The zoning text lists permitted uses, specifies minimum standards that apply in each zoning district, and establishes the rules for administration and other concerns. The zoning ordinance text is usually divided into articles and sections that are numbered for easy reference. Each article has a particular purpose in the ordinance.[7]

The value of a zoning ordinance depends on how effectively it is administered and enforced. The zoning administrator may order the correction of any condition found in violation of the ordinance and may bring legal action to ensure compliance, including injunction, abatement, or other appropriate action or proceeding. The local planning board or commission is required to hold a public hearing on a proposed zoning ordinance. At the hearing citizens have an opportunity to express their views about the ordinance and its application to individual properties. The planning board may hold more than one public hearing if necessary. Following the required hearings, the governing body may adopt the zoning ordinance after making appropriate changes or corrections. If changes are made that would result in a more intensive land-use classification than was advertised in the public hearing notice, an additional public hearing is required before the ordinance may be adopted.

There will be occasions when an amendment to the zoning ordinance is necessary. Amendments may be substantive or procedural. Substantive amendments change the permitted use of land within a district or change a district boundary. Procedural amendments change, for example, the number of days to act upon a matter. When properly thought out and prepared, zoning amendments enable a locality to adjust to changing circumstances and needs. However, a zoning ordinance should not be amended needlessly or for inappropriate reasons. Too many substantive amendments may defeat the purpose of the zoning ordinance. Proposed amendments must be referred to the planning board for its recommendation before final action by the governing body. Public notice must be given and public hearings held before zoning amendments may be adopted.

Zoning ordinances cannot be written to address every issue that might arise in enforcing land regulations. Inevitably, landowners come forward with grievances against specific controls. The role of a zoning board of appeals (ZBA) is to adjudicate situations and grant variances for hardships. A ZBA should be created when the zoning ordinance is adopted. The board may be elected or appointed by the mayor. In communities without mayors, the legislative body or town manager, subject to local legislative approval, may appoint the ZBA.

The criteria that must be followed in granting variances are established in state law. When an ordinance causes undue hardship to a particular landowner, the ZBA may grant a variance. The hardship incurred by the landowner should relate to the dimensions, shape, or topography of the land or other extraordinary situation. The hardship should be unique to the property and should not be shared generally by other properties in the same zoning district. When a variance is granted, the ZBA may impose conditions on the location and features of a proposed structure or use. In granting a variance the ZBA must ensure that the change measures up to the intended spirit and purpose of the ordinance. The variance procedure must not be used to rezone land or to grant special privilege to the applicant. Let us reinforce here, as noted previously, that different states have different enabling laws and procedures, even down to the details of how hard it is to get a variance.

In most cases communities have rules and regulations that govern the development of subdivisions. Subdivision authority is typically not part of zoning or zoning-enabling acts. Some jurisdictions, and at least one model, use a unified development code that incorporates zoning, subdivision, and other regulations. Although these are the exceptions, not the rule, many planners support unified development codes in states that allow them. Historically, subdivision planning in the United States involves dividing parcels into individual allotments for development. The major issues included in subdivision review are hydrology and drainage, traffic-flow design, pedestrian ways, services, infrastructure, landscaping, environmental mitigation, housing and allotment design, and effective site layout and orientation.[8]

The first step in the development of a subdivision is approving the boundaries of the entire project area. The official map of the community is reviewed, and the parcels are aligned in the appropriate residential zoning district. The deeds and title are then passed. At this stage the developer may begin to delineate the boundaries for each housing site within the subdivision. The developer submits a preliminary site plan to the planning commission, or planning board, for approval. The developer will have a certain number of days to submit a definitive plan for the subdivision, based on the legal procedural process for the state where the subdivision is submitted.

The site plans for the subdivision will have to meet criteria that depend on the specific subdivision rules and regulations for the community. Generally, the lot size, house setback from the road, and side-yard setbacks are specifically listed in the rules and regulations. A traffic-circulation and access plan for public transport, private and emergency vehicles, and pedestrians may be required. Routes and alignment of primary access roads and minor roads, road widths, and traffic-management principles may be required. Other requirements under rules and regulations for subdivisions may include an open-space plan, areas for playgrounds, pedestrian pathways linking open-space areas, location of services, a landscape master plan, and a stormwater drainage plan for detention and absorption of stormwater on the site.

Typically, developers divide the parcel into the maximum number of buildable lots designated by the zoning. Each lot must meet the standard zoning requirement. If the subdivision meets all the requirements for the rules and regulations for the community, the planning commission or governing board of subdivision review traditionally has had to approve the plan. This method of subdividing land has been termed *cookie cutter* design by many planners and city officials. This practice has created problems with wetlands and other natural-resource areas within subdivisions that are unsuitable for development.

In response to cookie cutter design, Randall Arendt developed a subdivision planning process that considers the suitability of the parcel for development.[9]

The first step in Arendt's process is to identify the parts of the parcel that are unsuitable for development because of, for example, soils, slope, or drainage issues. Next, the site's infrastructure and roads are designed. In the last stage the houses and buildings are sited. In this way the areas of the parcel that are unsuitable for development are protected.

PROBLEMS RESULTING FROM TRADITIONAL ZONING METHODS

In many communities, traditional zoning techniques have proved to be ineffective land-management tools. Since traditional zoning is based on the concept of assigning uses to various districts, many problems arise when land is categorized by use without regard for the impact of projects across the community and region. In communities experiencing rapid land development, inflexible development regulations have proved to be ineffective in preserving environmentally sensitive areas. In urban areas, traditional zoning in many cases has not encouraged mixed use, despite mixed use often being the lifeblood of a community. Many downtown revitalization plans have been effective because mixed-use projects act as catalysts to promote commercial success and social and cultural interaction.

Many land-use problems have developed from traditional zoning, because in many cases the methods to control development are too rigid or do not support the policies and goals outlined in the comprehensive plan. When communities use zoning primarily to control development, the future vision may be lost. Zoning should be a tool in land-use development, not the overriding planning document. For example, under zoning regulations a parcel might be rezoned for industrial use, although industrial use previously was not allowed near a residential area. The zoning revision in this case is inconsistent with the comprehensive plan, and the incompatible use creates many problems for the surrounding neighborhood. The following are some of the reasons traditional zoning has caused so many problems in communities:

- Many zoning ordinances are not based on a clear policy of coordinated land development.
- Amendments for zoning ordinances and district boundaries are often made on a piecemeal basis, leading to an illogical intermixing of zoning districts.
- Physical separation of land uses has not always succeeded in protecting one use from the harmful impacts of another.
- Rigid zoning requirements often have been cited as a factor in the high cost of housing.

- Inflexible requirements have prevented innovative land development, failed to protect valuable historical and natural resources, and created monotonous suburban landscapes.

Problems with traditional zoning also arise due to exclusionary practices in zoning enforcement. Many communities have evolved into middle-income to high-income, single-family residential areas. Whether intentionally through large-lot zoning or design review or unintentionally through the absence of clauses to include multifamily housing, many communities have squeezed out affordable housing.

Finally, depletion of open space can be directly linked to traditional zoning practices. Under subdivision rules and regulations as they are usually written across the country, developers have been able to carve out the maximum number of lots possible for development. Open-space requirements and natural-resource protection clauses are missing from standard subdivision rules and regulations. It was not until the late 1980s that planners began to think about reviewing development plans based on a specified listing of site location and environmental criteria. This process is called *site-plan review* and has been adopted in many communities to solve problems of depletion of open space and natural resources and building within environmentally sensitive areas.

INNOVATIVE ZONING METHODS

Innovative zoning techniques create flexibility in the development process. Contrary to conventional Euclidean zoning that is restrictive, these techniques allow for consideration of the development of each site. Innovative zoning methods may take into account as many as four additional components of development.

- Locational analysis: the relation of the project to existing infrastructure including roads, schools, and sewer and water lines
- Composition: arrangement of proposed land uses on the site
- Timing: the amount of time it takes to finish the project
- Design: the architectural features of the project

When the preceding factors are analyzed, the costs and benefits of the development to the surrounding environment and economy can be predicted. Since so much flexibility is built into the innovative zoning process, negotiations that take place between planning representatives and developers must be fair and open. It is crucial that players in the process adhere to specified guidelines. Conflicts of interest must be avoided. The American Planning Association recommends three procedural guidelines to follow throughout the negotiation process.

- Public hearings should be called for substantive public participation. The hearings should be organized and conducted in a manner that assures the public that decisions will not be made without public input.
- The negotiation process should be separate from the decision-making process. Decision makers should not take part in negotiations, and they should not meet individually with developers. The result of negotiations should be recommendations to the decision-making body or officials, with the recommendations available for public review.
- Negotiation sessions should be as public as possible, and regular documentation of sessions should occur.

Zoning decisions can be made by either the legislative or administrative authorities of a local government. The legislative authority generally rules on matters requiring rezoning, such as planned unit developments and floating zones. Decision making can be delegated to an administrative authority, a zoning official, for specific issues such as reviewing development plans, overlay zones, and incentive zoning when rezoning is not required. The following innovative zoning techniques have been developed to create more flexibility in zoning:

- Traditional-neighborhood development zoning efforts: Based on the concept of re-creating diverse, community-oriented villages, traditional-neighborhood zoning has been instituted in many parts of the country. In Portland, Oregon, traditional-neighborhood zoning has been used for in-fill projects in urban areas, and in Florida zoning efforts to re-create traditional neighborhoods have been instituted in Celebration and Seaside. The intent of these projects is to create residential and commercial diversity with a communal feeling for past values.
- Performance standards: Instead of enumerating the permitted uses, any use is permitted if it complies with performance standards for the district. Performance standards are the threshold limits for a piece of property. Standards can include maximum permitted noise, smoke, glare, vibration, use of water, and parking and traffic generation. Enforcement of performance standards must be carefully carried out and monitored.[10]
- Impact zoning: Defines the maximum permitted impact on the neighborhood and uses the concept of land-carrying capacity, for example, how much impact can be absorbed without harm.

- Cluster zoning: Allowing buildings on smaller lots or even attached dwellings, while the land saved is set aside for open space and recreation. Shorter streets reduce the costs of construction and maintenance.
- Planned-unit development (PUD): An overall plan for a large tract that locates various uses in set percentages, from open space or a golf course to neighborhood stores, and is given a special permit as a unified development.
- Transfer of development rights (TDR): Where the level of intensity of development is not desired, the owner may be given approval to transfer, or sell, development rights to another location where extra intensity of development is appropriate. TDR can be used to preserve a historical site or a farm.
- Incentive zoning: Establishes specific public concessions, such as increased building height or density, which can be granted to a developer in return for specific contributions such as a plaza or other open space.
- Phased growth: Used primarily in new subdivisions, it limits construction to a certain percentage or number of lots annually, so as not to overload the local capacity to provide the needed services, such as schools and water supply.
- Building moratoria: Imposed through zoning for a specified time period (one or two years), to allow the planners to develop updated plans and programs.
- Overlay districts: A well-established approach to protection of floodplains, wetlands, or aquifers (to allow groundwater recharge) by superimposing over parts of conventional zoning districts an overlay district that incorporates additional restrictions and regulations, such as a prohibition of certain uses with a high potential for water contamination.[11]

Members of the planning board need to be educated about the impacts traditional zoning may have had on development problems in their community and how these problems may be solved. Once they are aware of the potential use of innovative zoning, they have the option to choose and implement the most appropriate techniques for their situation.

CONCLUSION

A zoning ordinance serves a dual purpose. It regulates new growth, and it provides minimum standards for development. The text of the ordinance should contain reasonable regulations designed to control land development and to provide standards for new and existing land uses. Likewise, the zoning map should be reasonably consistent with the comprehensive plan for the community. The map should show areas that are suitable for development, as well as areas that are unsuitable. The connections between how zoning is carried out and the problems that develop from traditional zoning are analyzed in terms of suggesting innovative techniques to solve zoning problems.

Case Study: Large-Lot Zoning, a United States Tradition

Contrary to the claim that communities across the United States are encouraging the development of denser housing projects, called cluster development, data from new housing developments show otherwise. According to Joseph Molinaro, director of land development services for the National Association of Home Builders in Washington, D.C., one acre or more is still the predominate rule in most parts of the country. The Department of Housing and Urban Development (HUD) Advisory Commission on Barriers to Affordable Housing cited large lot size as a significant cost booster and exclusionary tactic. One acre seems to be part of the American dream, according to the Lincoln Institute of Land Policy in Cambridge, Massachusetts. The Lincoln Institute is currently conducting research on the influence of lot size on growth management programs.

Historically, since the passage in 1785 of the Northwest Ordinance, which divided the U.S. territory into 640-acre sections, the one-acre standard has generally been implemented. As rail lines spread across the country early in this century, movement to the outskirts of major urban areas increased. According to Harvard landscape historian John Stilgoe, affluent Americans began buying property in the newly built subdivisions to have room for families to tend gardens. This land ethic of owning a single-family house with a large backyard in the suburbs has continued to the present.

The arguments that have consistently been used to support large-lot zoning are (1) large lots preserve farmland and open space, (2) large lots provide more land to support septic systems, and (3) large lots limit the number of individual wells for water. Recently, however, much of the planning literature is pointing to the discriminatory nature of large-lot zoning. Data show that in many cases large-lot zoning is enforced to keep out *undesirables*, by increasing the cost of the housing in a community. Many communities now recognize exclusionary practices and lack of affordable housing as major issues.

Planners in many cases are recommending changes in the zoning code to include cluster development districts and incentives for developers to build cluster projects. In Southern California's Orange County, for example, designers are experimenting with a variety of lot configurations to increase density and decrease house prices. The angled Z-lot and the zipper lot are refinements of the zero-lot-line houses first introduced in this area in the early 1960s. The zero lot line eliminated side and back lot lines in developments by siting two or more houses on each lot. The density of these projects is up to ten units per acre, considerably lowering the cost of each house compared with the typical one-acre lot size. Other new zoning options include the squat lot and the wide-shallow lot, both wider than they are deep, giving the perception of the traditional single-family lot. In Bridgeport, Connecticut, architect Zane Yost has designed a *not lot*, in which easements separate each house.

Zoning districts of increased density may also be incorporated into communities to increase affordable housing. Wallkill, New York, has set up a district where the minimum lot size has been lowered to six thousand square feet. In Arlington, Texas, districts have been set up where zero-lot-line houses are built on five-thousand-square-foot lots. Fairfax, Virginia, allows forty-two-hundred-square-foot lots in certain districts, a 20 percent density increase over single-family districts in the county.

Discussion Box

What aspects of traditional, Euclidean zoning have created controversies and problems in communities across the United States? Has your community experienced these problems? How? Discuss the specific zoning issues that have created controversy in your community. Have you had a zoning dispute about a new multifamily district or industrial park? Have different constituencies supported new economic development while others who may represent a land trust, for example, supported preservation of particular parcels slated for business projects? Has there been controversy over revising zoning to protect aquifers or watershed areas?

PLANNING EXERCISE 5: COLORING A ZONING MAP

Color the different zones in the assigned section of the zoning map for your hometown or college community. Follow the legend on the zoning map, which indicates the color for each zoning district.

NOTES

1. *Mugler v. Kansas*, 123 U.S. 623, 668-69 (1887).
2. Nichols's *The Law of Eminent Domain*, Sec.1.42 (J. Sackman, 3d rev. ed.1973), retrieved May 10, 2004, from http://caselaw.lp.findlaw.com/data/constitution/amendment05/16.html#1.

3. Charles Hoch, Linda Dalton, and Frank S. So, eds., chapter 14 in *The Practice of Local Government Planning* (Washington, D.C.: International City/County Management Association, 2000).

4. Rutherford H. Platt, *Land Use Control, Geography, Law, and Public Policy* (Englewood Cliffs, N.J.: Prentice Hall, 1991).

5. Hoch, Dalton, and So, *The Practice*.

6. Robert H. Nelson, *Zoning and Property Rights: An Analysis of the American System of Land-Use Regulation* (Cambridge, Mass.: MIT Press, 1977).

7. Richard F. Babcock and Charles Siemon, *The Zoning Game Revisited* (Boston: Oelgeschlager Gunn & Hain, 1985).

8. Babcock and Siemon, *The Zoning Game*.

9. Randall G. Arendt, *Conservation Design for Subdivisions: A Practical Guide to Creating Open Space Networks* (Washington, D.C.: Island Press, 1996).

10. Lane Kendig, *Performance Zoning* (Washington, D.C.: Planners Press, 1980).

11. David Listokin, *Land Use Controls: Present Problems and Future Reform* (New Brunswick, N.J.: Center for Urban Policy Research, Rutgers University, 1974).

Chapter Six

Growth Management

Growth management is the balance between protection of natural resources and development. The purpose of the growth-management plan is to show what kind of community will develop and what it will look like. From the beginning of the process, it is important to realize that political support for growth management often comes from public concerns about the character of the community. Many regions across the country, particularly suburbs in the Southwest and Southeast, are experiencing tremendous increases in population and runaway development. Communities are facing issues related to urban sprawl including traffic, infrastructure, and environmental problems while also trying to meet fiscal needs in uncertain economic times. A growth-management plan is the key factor in protecting and conserving resources while determining future economic development. Tools and techniques should be in place to guide development in suitable locations and prohibit development in unsuitable ones. New urbanism and smart-growth techniques that create more compact development should be considered in growth-management plans to solve urban sprawl problems.

WHAT IS THE GROWTH-MANAGEMENT PROCESS?

Growth management regulates the amount, timing, location, and character of development. Planners should consider the following issues in the growth-management process: environmental concerns, such as the suitability of soils for development; character and exclusionary issues; and fiscal concerns. Decisions that planners make about zoning districts, infrastructure, and the type of housing and lot sizes determine the land-use patterns. The land-use controls, or regulations for development, dictate what types of development will

81

be allowed or prohibited. It is critical to consider the aspects of due process and equal protection when developing public control measures that affect the use of privately owned land.[1]

Planners must understand how federal, state, and regional land-use law and regulations impact local growth-management planning. The court decisions that are handed down at the federal and state levels show urban and environmental-planning priorities and trends. Judicial court case review is the process of researching the patterns of land-use law decisions to help predict the outcome of a current planning situation. For example, judicial review of coastal management cases would indicate the direction the court takes in deciding coastal development issues.

The first landmark court case that dealt with growth-management planning is *Golden v Township of Ramapo* 285 NE 2d 291 (1972). The *Ramapo* case involved phased growth, which is correlating development with the construction of capital improvement. Ramapo's plan to control development included a capital-improvements program (CIP) to provide infrastructure and public service for the town with a goal for completion in eighteen years. Proposals for residential development, exempting individual homes, were evaluated in relation to the proximity of support services, including roads, fire and police, sewers, water mains, and park and recreational facilities. Points were given to each project based on its location to services. The Ramapo plan also granted permits to construct projects that at the time could not be built due to insufficient services. These projects would be built at a later date when infrastructure was in place. The court found in favor of the town of Ramapo, upholding the enforcement of the CIP-management-planning system. The court claimed that allowing construction in the future was a temporary restraint on the development process.

Another court case that dealt directly with the issue of growth management is *Construction Industry Association of Sonoma County v City of Petaluma* 375 F Supp 574 (1974) and 522 F2d 897 (1975). Petaluma, thirty-five miles north of San Francisco, developed a Petaluma Plan in response to runaway development in 1970–1971. Concerned about growth, Petaluma created a zoning ordinance that required developers to submit plans for development before approval. The Petaluma Plan established a building-permit cap of five hundred per year, a moratorium on extension of services, and limitation of sewer and water capacity to the population of fifty-five thousand.

The Petaluma review process used a point system in which proposed projects were rated in several areas and assigned a total number of points. The overall rating of a project would indicate its suitability for development and projects with the highest ratings would be approved. The criteria reviewed included access to sewer connection, drainage impacts, recreational facilities improvement, roads improvement, and support services improvement.

The federal district court found the Petaluma Plan to be invalid on the grounds that it prohibited the constitutional right to travel, or freedom of mobility. On an appeal from district court, the federal court of appeals reached contrary conclusions on the validity of the Petaluma Plan. The Court of Appeals viewed the issue strictly within the geographic confines of Petaluma. This court found that there was no deliberate intent to exclude. This set a precedent for the *right to travel* argument across the country. Another factor critical in the court decision was whether projections for water usage for the incoming development were accurate.

Using this court case as a precedent, many communities across the country have developed growth-management-system plans to control growth. Boulder, Colorado, and Davis, California, established ordinances and growth-management systems to regulate the type of development allowed in their communities. In these cases, judicial decisions upheld the right of communities to approve only energy-efficient projects. Ratings for solar orientation, solar heating and cooling, and energy efficiency were used in the approval process.

The Mount Laurel, New Jersey, case, *Southern Burlington County NAACP v Township of Mount Laurel* 456 A2d 390 (1983) is another case that has influenced the validity of growth-management plans. In this case the majority opinion stated that the city must revise the zoning and incorporate a variety of lot sizes to increase low-income housing. Since the size of the lot generally dictates the type and size of house that is constructed, lot size is often noted as the cause of lack of affordable housing in a community.[2] Another critical factor in this case was the question of racial bias. The National Association for the Advancement of Colored People (NAACP) contended that the underlying issue in the growth-management plan was racial discrimination. It is important to note that the findings in this case would not apply outside New Jersey, since the case was heard in a New Jersey court. Some other states are moving toward the same type of findings, however, including a recent case in Yonkers, New York.

Community ordinances and controls are directly related to the land-use-planning policies at the state level. Florida, for example, has a mandated state legislative act that requires every community in the state to develop a comprehensive plan. In Vermont, Act 250 establishes criteria for permit approval and construction that developers must meet for particular projects. When a development corporation applied for a permit to expand the ski trails at Sugarbush Mountain, a major ski resort in the southern part of the state, the construction process was delayed several times due to changes that were required under Act 250. The developers had to incorporate mitigation measures, which are ways to lessen environmental impacts, before the project could continue. In this case the measures included techniques to protect the forest and prevent erosion. Generally, planning problems associated with growth management on a regional scale involve land- and house-price speculation.[3] For example, when a community enforces a cap on development, the supply of housing units decreases and house prices increase. Land values also escalate, forcing developers to build on less expensive property in surrounding communities.

GROWTH-MANAGEMENT PROBLEM-ORIENTED PLAN

A community develops a growth-management problem-oriented plan to influence the characteristics of growth and achieve land-use goals, objectives, and policies. The process involves designing a set of zoning regulations, development incentives, and land-use policies that work together to encourage beneficial uses and discourage unwanted or damaging effects. In areas experiencing minimal growth, the plan should encourage beneficial industrial, commercial, and residential development. In a rapidly developing area, the plan should indicate where and when development can take place. It should be noted that this is the typical approach in developing a growth-management plan. As in every area of planning, the specifics for the plan are based on the site studies for the particular community.

The key element in the growth-management process is that development is managed within the constraints of the natural resources of the community while maintaining a healthy economic base. Extensive natural-resource inventory and mapping are conducted to show the location of environmentally fragile areas, including groundwater supply and aquifer-recharge areas, agricultural lands, and wetlands. Parcels slated for development are rated according to criteria that indicate the suitability of development of each parcel. The criteria, often referred to as performance standards, are based on the carrying capacity of the land, which indicates the development potential of each parcel. The criteria include such factors as the amount of drainage a parcel can handle based on the type of soil, the amount and type of development based on the slope of the area, and the air and water pollution that the area can handle without surpassing the threshold limits.[4] The primary goal in applying performance standards is to evaluate each parcel in terms of the impact a certain type of development will have on it. In some cases, one standard may apply, in other cases several standards may apply. After the parcel is rated according to each standard, a composite of all the impacts is calculated. The composite shows the environmental impact for each proposed project for the site.

Unfortunately, there is not one universal growth-management problem-oriented plan that fits every community. As noted previously, goals and objectives and existing physical, social, economic, and political conditions vary from place to place and make each community unique. While existing plans can be useful guides, to be effective the plan must adhere to the constraints of local conditions. Follow the steps in chapter 2 to develop an effective growth-management problem-oriented plan.

Define the Problem: Identify Local Land-Use Concerns

Identify which of the following issues may be of concern to the community:

- Sprawling suburban residential lots and transportation gridlock. Does the development lack a sense of place? Does the development build a sense of isolation?
- Lack of affordable housing due to high housing prices, exclusionary practices, high rental rates or lack of rental units, or imbalance between commercial and housing redevelopment.
- Loss of community character due to too much strip development occurring across the community or open space and recreational areas being depleted. Are nonconforming uses or incremental development along the country roads a problem?
- Environmental quality concerns arising from groundwater contamination, soil erosion, loss of vegetation or wildlife, or air and water contamination.
- Loss of economic base due to manufacturing firms closing and relocating or declining tourism.

Through public forums the community will come to a consensus on the concerns of the highest priority. The priorities are then analyzed in terms of those that need immediate attention and those that can be addressed later in the planning process.

Articulate the Goals and Objectives

The priorities indicate the overall goals for the plan. A lack of affordable housing calls for a goal to create a variety of housing types for the community. A depletion of open space calls for a goal to create measures to preserve open space, recreational areas, and farmland. Air or water quality contamination calls for a goal to require protection measures to address the issues. A decline in the manufacturing base calls for a goal to create an industrial park. The tools and techniques are the objectives to reach these goals.

Analyze and Evaluate

Changing the boundaries of zoning districts or creating new districts often provides opportunities to implement tools. For example, adjusting for density in central cores versus peripheral areas can encourage housing alternatives. Adopting overlays that allow flexible development alternatives such as open-space residential or cluster can save open space. Adopting restrictive overlay zones, such as aquifer protection, floodplain, and wetlands zones, can protect environmental and cultural resources. Considering boundary changes when support services are overburdened can create more effective infrastructure and transport networks. Clear guidelines should be drawn regarding who administers and enforces zoning bylaws and regulations in conformance with the long-range growth-management objectives.

Choose the appropriate tools from the following categories to address each prioritized issue: affordable housing, preservation of community character and open space, regulation of the rate of growth, regulation of aesthetics, protection of natural resources and environmental quality, and promotion of quality commercial and industrial development. Review the tool in relation to the technical expertise available to the community, the legality of the tool in reference to state and local statutes, the local politics of the community, and the available fiscal resources. Although various tools may meet the criteria to accomplish a goal, it is more effective to choose tools that each accomplish several goals. It is more efficient to implement, administer, and monitor a plan with fewer tools.

Tools that supplement and complement each other should be chosen. However, tools that affect the same characteristic of growth in the same manner should be avoided to reduce fiscal and administrative burdens for the community. Once a growth-management problem-oriented plan is implemented, a monitoring system should be established to evaluate the effectiveness of the program. When unintended consequences occur, corrections can be made to ensure intended results.

The order of the tools is not based on any emphasis of importance or on chronological order. The following guidelines are helpful when considering techniques for communities: choose tools for problems that you know a majority of the community want addressed and make sure you relate the tool to the problem.

Goal: Encourage Variety

If a community does not offer an adequate variety of housing types to meet the needs of all income levels, one or more of the following tools should be considered:

- Multifamily residential zoning: This type of zoning sets up districts in the community for multifamily, or two or more, dwelling units in appropriate sections of town. Use housing data to determine the needs of the residents in terms of housing prices and number of rental units. Multifamily projects should be located near public transportation and support services such as shopping, schools, and medical facilities.
- Inclusionary zoning for affordable housing: Inclusionary zoning encourages or requires affordable housing districts across the community. Percentages of subsidized housing units that are goals for the community may also be included in the ordinance. When enforced, inclusionary zoning helps to eliminate discriminatory practices in housing ordinances such as high-priced, single-family, large-lot subdivisions.
- Elderly and handicapped congregate zoning: Housing for the elderly and handicapped includes specified zoning districts for specialized units meeting their needs. Recent trends in elderly housing include developments that offer various levels of support services. Elders who are independent but want yard maintenance provided are choosing attached townhouses with a common meetinghouse for activities. Usually these projects offer some type of life lease. Due to demographic statistics showing increasing numbers of seniors

Multifamily districts provide low-income, affordable housing.

in the 80s–90s age group in the 2000s, elderly housing projects with full service including meals and nursing care are being proposed across the country.
Scattered site developments, or small projects in several sites across communities rather than large-scale projects in one area, may be proposed.

- Accessory-apartment zoning: Accessory-apartment zoning provides guidelines to divide large homes or lofts into smaller units to increase rental
  options in a town. This type of zoning is often established in college communities or other communities requiring more rental units.[5]
- Mixed-use zoning: Zoning that allows mixing commercial and residential
  uses in one development.

Goal: Preserve Community Character and Open Space

If a community is losing open space to development, one or more of the following tools should be considered:

- Open-space and cluster zoning: Open-space and cluster zoning involve
  grouping buildings, including housing or communal recreational facilities,
  into compact areas, and leaving open land throughout the development for
  passive recreational use. This zoning usually sets a certain percentage of
  open space as a requirement for approval of the project. Planned-unit development (PUD) is cluster zoning on a larger scale, generally covering
  larger acreage and including mixed-use development such as commercial,
  business, or recreational facilities. Figure 6.1 shows a traditional, cookie
  cutter design, in which similar architecturally styled houses are placed in
  uniform lots across the subdivision. The open-space or cluster zoning map
  shows the houses grouped in suitable areas across the plat, with unsuitable
  areas such as wetlands, agricultural, and open space left undeveloped.
- Preserving open space and conservation areas: Conservation deed restrictions are an effective way of preserving open space for the community and
  decreasing property taxes for the property owner. With a deed restriction,
  the owner keeps the title to the property but gives up the rights to develop
  it. In exchange for the development rights, instead of being taxed at the
  higher tax rate for developable land, the property owner receives a tax
  abatement.[6]
- Agricultural-preservation zoning: Agricultural-preservation zoning is a special
  form of tax assessment for preserving farmland. Farmers under this form of
  zoning may petition the state to obtain a lower tax rate on the condition they
  keep their land in farming. The program for agricultural preservation has
  guidelines that the farmer must follow to qualify for the special tax assessment. Massachusetts has an Agricultural Preservation Restriction (APR) program for which funding cannot keep up with the demand for restriction deeds.

Traditional Subdivision

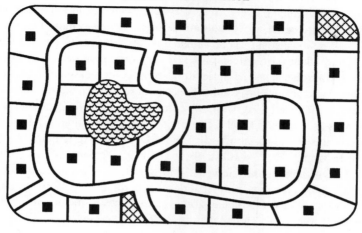

Open-Space/Cluster Zoning

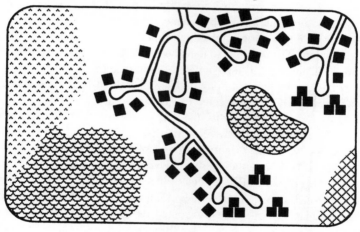

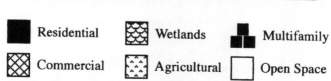

Figure 6.1. **Traditional Subdivision: Open-Space/Cluster Zoning**

Pennsylvania, which is the national leader in total number of farms protected and the rate at which parcels are preserved, has several agricultural programs to protect farmland. The Agricultural Conservation Easement Purchase Program was established in 1988. Under this law easements are purchased to protect individual farm parcels. In 2001 the Agricultural Area Security Law was signed, further defining agricultural conservation easements and providing for agricultural security areas and purchase of agricultural conservation easements. The Model Agricultural Zoning Ordinance in Lancaster County, which was established in 1994, encourages the continuation of farming in areas where it is already established.[7] The Berks County Agricultural Zoning Incentive Program (AZIP) was established in 1995. The goal of this program is to implement agricultural elements into the Berks County Comprehensive Plan. The county rewards municipalities that participate in AZIP by reimbursing them for expenses to amend zoning ordinances to include incentives for agricultural zoning. The municipalities that are interested in AZIP must have a comprehensive plan that clearly supports effective agricultural zoning.[8]

- Land trust and land bank: The purpose of a land trust is to buy and preserve open-space land and farms that are potential parcels for development. Traditionally, land trusts are formed by businesses or private interests in a community who donate funds for purchasing property that is or might be threatened by development. The donators to the land trust are given tax write-offs for their donations. A land bank is a designated funding source that acts as a bank in terms of having the power to buy and sell parcels of land that the bank's directors believe should be protected from development.

- Transfer of development rights (TDR), transit-oriented development, and traditional-neighborhood development: TDR deals with moving a landowner's development rights in an area of the community where development is not suitable to an area where development would be more suitable. More suitable areas include sections of the community that are already built-out (and rezoned to allow further development), have infrastructure, or have access to transportation. Transit-oriented development places development near transportation access points. Traditional-neighborhood development encourages a diverse variety of housing, commercial, and employment types in a high-density, village-center design.

- Historic-site-preservation zoning: Areas of a community that have historic properties may apply for historic-site-preservation zoning, which grants tax incentives for maintaining the historic integrity of the property. Communities in many states may also apply for historic-site-preservation district zoning, which designates an area of the community as a historic district, eligible for tax credits. Historic-site-preservation zoning often involves design review, or architectural criteria, of the properties. Design review is the process of overseeing the restoration or replication of a building, or group of buildings, in a district.

- Site-plan review: Site-plan review is based on a set of performance standards for a parcel of land. The governing planning board or agency performs a site-plan review. If the board decides that the project meets the criteria for the site and will not adversely impact the environment, the project will likely be approved. Site-plan review is structured to include criteria that are specifically related to the environmental attributes of the site.
- Flexible zoning: Flexible zoning is less rigid than traditional Euclidean zoning, in that a second zone may be superimposed on an area. Sometimes called overlays, or floating zones, this type of zoning allows for the placement of a specified type of usage over an area of a community. For example, zones for commercial strip malls may be overlays. Each overlay area would indicate the placement of a commercial development.

Goal: Regulate Growth Rate

If a community is experiencing growth in areas where sufficient infrastructure, such as water mains and sewer lines, is not available, one or more of the following tools should be considered:

- Major residential-development controls: Residential-control zoning includes standards and guidelines for the development of residential subdivisions. If a proposed development will overload the support services or infrastructure in the region, controls to stop the development or introduce the development in phases may be put into place.
- Phased-growth controls: Phased-growth controls are guidelines that allow only one portion of a development at a time. This procedure is followed to have the support services and infrastructure in place for each phase of the project. These controls, also called development scheduling, are particularly effective when new development is coordinated with the planned construction of trunk lines for sewer and water.
- Adequate-facilities ordinance and concurrency: Both of these tools deal with making sure necessary infrastructure and facilities are in place before projects are approved and built. The adequate-facilities ordinance is the generic approach, the one used typically in communities across the country. Concurrency is Florida's term for planning for adequate facilities to support development.

Goal: Regulate Aesthetics

If a community has concerns about the architectural design of buildings, signage, or the type of buildings proposed for the town such as fast-food chains, the following tools are the most effective:

Lack of signage controls create confusion and an unsightly streetscape.

- Design review: A design-review board made up of architects, urban designers, and urban planners oversees the approval process of pending projects in the community. Specific guidelines and standards must be clearly set
out and approved before the review process takes place. For its decisions to
be legally binding, the design-review board must be appointed or elected
under specified legal guidelines for enforcement in the state.
- Historic districts and architectural-conservation districts: Both of these
tools require strict design review and preservation techniques to conserve
buildings. Historic districts include buildings and sites that have architectural, archeological, or cultural significance. Architectural-conservation
districts focus on the architectural value of the building.

Goal: Protect Natural Resources and Environmental Quality

If a community is experiencing environmental problems in terms of providing clean water and air for the residents, the following tools should be considered:

- Water-supply-protection zoning: Water-supply-protection zoning protects
water bodies that supply clean water to a community. The water-supply area

must be delineated through a natural-resource-inventory mapping procedure using hydrology tests. Controls to protect the area such as curtailment of salt applications on roads during inclement weather or the elimination of pesticide spraying on crops located in the watershed must be specifically stated.

- Floodplain management: Floodplain management is for areas designated as floodplain by the Federal Emergency Management Agency (FEMA). Maps of floodplain areas including corridors along rivers and inland water bodies, as well as coastal areas, should be superimposed over a community to delineate those areas in need of floodplain protection. Maps should be field-tested and monitored to validate technical accuracy.
- Wetlands-protection bylaw: Wetlands protection is covered in many states by the Wetlands Act. This act sets forth the administration and enforcement of regulations to protect those lands that fall under the definition of wetlands. States vary in how closely they adhere to the Wetlands Act, which typically includes ways to identify wetlands such as type of soils, vegetation, and water-table characteristics. The administration and enforcement of the act is directly related to the type of development allowed within wetlands areas in a particular state.
- Stormwater regulations: Stormwater regulations prevent effluent from overflowing during storms. This tool is applicable to areas that combine sewage and stormwater runoff in the same line.
- Hazardous-materials bylaw: Hazardous-materials bylaws are enforced in areas where a known hazardous material contaminates an area. A listing of the hazardous materials considered a threat or harmful to health is published by the Environmental Protection Agency (EPA).

Goal: Promote Quality Commercial and Industrial Development

Consider using the following tools if a community has lost its manufacturing base and industrial projects should be approved to increase the tax base:

- Commercial-corridor standards: Commercial-corridor standards set out specific, appropriate guidelines for the urban design and placement of commercial buildings in an area. The advantage of commercial-corridor planning is the long-range impact it has on the community. Future goals in terms of commercial needs for the community and the surrounding region may be considered in this process.
- Sign standards: Sign standards provide aesthetic controls and opportunities for design review for commercial and industrial areas. Uniformity in signage may be planned for future implementation under this tool.
- Planned industrial development: Planned industrial development is a tool where a large-scale industrial-park zone is established. Requirements can

be incorporated into the initial park plan to control the design of the park over time. This tool is particularly effective in communities that are experiencing piecemeal development, which causes infrastructure problems. Many companies prefer to locate new facilities in industrial parks because it allows proximal warehousing, shipping, and packing buildings. Also, most industries require access to larger water and sewer lines, making it advantageous to be located in an industrial park.

• Mixed-use development, commercial and industrial district expansion, and transit-oriented development: Encouraging mixed-use development and adding more commercial and industrial districts promote the business and industrial base of the community. Placing development near transit lines creates higher density of use and improves access for shipping and distribution.

The tools that are chosen to solve problems must be complementary. Consider a community experiencing loss of open space, as well as lack of tax base. An industrial park could be planned for an area of town that is located near rail and shipping lines, in the outskirts of the community. Protected open space could be zoned in suitable areas across the community.

A municipal-services assessment, which is an overview of the facility needs of the community and the costs, helps to determine the cost-effectiveness of each alternative. An effective approach is to assess the fiscal status of the community. Hold a meeting of town officials and discuss the financial appropriations of each department. What is the current departmental allotment and what are future expenses? What are the tax revenues for the town and how are they allocated for each type of service? What municipal department is in charge of each problem?

Next, develop an inventory of existent municipal facilities, what improvements will be needed in the next three- to five-year interval, and potential funding sources. Throughout the planning process for capital facilities, the primary question is: What is the relationship between current land-use regulations and administrative procedures in the town? Are services adequate now and for the future? Is there enough planning for municipal services or is the process a reactive approach, in which only crises are solved and no real long-term planning is accomplished.

A community may have more than one problem, but the tools that are chosen to solve the problems must be compatible. It is critical to think through what effect one tool in an area might have on another tool in another area. For example, a community may be experiencing the depletion of open space, so deed restrictions for open space are encouraged. At the same time, however, the town may need more tax base. For this reason the incentives to encourage industrial development in the community are also a priority.

Implement Action Plans

The planner needs to determine whether the chosen tools will work effectively and whether community residents will accept and support the plan. Will the community have the resources and knowledge needed to implement the plan effectively? Is the plan reasonable and will it work? Do all the pieces fit together and complement one another, and will they accomplish the growth objectives desired by the community? Do some tools duplicate the effects of others, making the plan more complex and confusing that it needs to be? Do some tools cancel out the effects of other tools? Before submitting a final plan for a vote, the plan should be evaluated carefully to determine whether it will accomplish the goals of the community. Growth-management techniques can be complex, and it is not unusual for communities to encounter difficulties in coordinating and managing the process.

Measure Results

An effective way to measure the results of the growth-management plan is to construct a build-out scenario for the community and update it over time. The exercise involves figuring out what the community would look like if every remaining developable parcel were developed. The build-out shows the total capacity of development for a community based on the current zoning ordinance. Communities differ in the amount of land that is developed. Some are close to build-out, where almost all developable land has been used. The methods to control development in these communities involve increased density and reuse or razing, tearing down, and rebuilding.

The build-out shows how much a town could grow and what long-range effects are possible. It also shows how the present ordinance affects development in certain parts of the town. The effects of typical subdivisions on the landscape can be compared with innovative alternatives in growth management, such as open-space and cluster development. The following questions are guidelines that can be used to measure the results of the action plans: What municipal services have been impacted by the new tools and action plans? What is the financial cost since the tools were implemented? Have there been unwanted effects, including environmental and financial, on surrounding communities? Has the rate of development in the community changed? Have the goals been met? Have any unforeseen or unexpected effects arisen? Has the plan been too rigid or too flexible?

NEW URBANISM AND SMART-GROWTH TECHNIQUES

New urbanism seeks to replicate the traditional New England village of a hundred years ago, modernized to current needs. Even though urban planners coined the terms *new urbanism* and *smart growth* barely twenty years ago, the basis for the theories can be traced to the early 1900s with the garden city concept of Ebenezer Howard. The philosophy and principles of new urbanism mirror Howard's concept, but the impetus for the movement comes from the problems from suburban development rather than pollution from factories in the inner cities. According to two of the pioneering new-urbanist designers and planners, Andres Duany and Elizabeth Plater-Zyberk, Americans across the country are voicing their concerns about growth that is out of control and searching for solutions to problems in the suburbs.[9]

The goal of new-urbanism planners is to convert or transform suburban or urban areas into compact village settings. There are several techniques that planners are using to create mixed-use, compact, pedestrian-friendly places. New urbanism may begin with a greenfield or brownfield project, where a contaminated site is redeveloped. Urban in fill is another method, in which an abandoned mill or warehouse is revitalized by converting it into affordable housing or commercial or retail space. Suburban retrofitting is an effective technique in which high-density projects such as apartments or condominiums or conversion of single-family homes to multifamily are approved for low-density areas.[10] Smart-growth principles specify that services and destinations such as small grocery stores, banking, places of employment, and schools are within walking distance. Access to public transportation is also a high priority in designing new-urbanism areas.

The following outline introduces the general concepts of new urbanism, along with specific smart-growth principles that designers use to develop action plans:

Citizen participation

- Stakeholders and citizens should be involved in the planning process from the beginning. Public forums and charrettes should be held to identify concerns and reach consensus.
- Decisions and approval for projects should be predictable, fair, and cost-effective. Developers who propose smart-growth projects should be treated equitably and not face more obstacles than developers following traditional designs. Several states have smart-growth legislation, and many communities provide incentives for smart growth in local ordinances.
- A monitoring system should be in place as plans are approved and implemented. Consistency and continuous input reinforce effective planning.

Compact and mixed-use design

- New, clustered development works more efficiently if there is a mix of commercial and business, employment opportunities, and residential units. Sprawl areas with single-use districts force a dependency on the auto.
- Communities should offer a range of housing options: single-family houses, condominiums, affordable homes for low-income families, and in-law or granny-flat units.
- Some communities are setting up urban-growth boundaries, which are city boundary limits beyond which no development can occur.

Community character

- Distinctive, attractive communities with a strong sense of place should be promoted. The preservation and rehabilitation of historic buildings should be a high priority.
- An inventory of existing community assets such as parks, schools, and municipal buildings should be conducted to protect these public investments.
- Existent open space, farmland, and scenic and environmentally fragile areas should be protected. Protecting farms, waterways, ecosystems, and wildlife will maintain connections to nature.
- Growth should be encouraged in areas that are already built out. We should look for opportunities to fill in these areas.

Pedestrian-friendly areas

- Close-knit neighborhoods in which the corner store, transit stop, and schools are within walking distance should be the goal. Since neighbors are encouraged to interact, a pedestrian-friendly neighborhood contributes to a sense of community.
- Access to public transportation.
- A variety of transportation choices should be provided. The most effective way to eliminate automobile traffic is to provide other modes of transportation.
- Communities need safe and reliable public transportation, sidewalks, and bike paths. Plans to improve current circulation patterns and infrastructure should be in place.[11]

New Urbanism in Practice

Kentlands, Maryland, and Celebration, Florida, are two planned communities based on the philosophy and design principles of the new-urbanism movement.

Kentlands, encompassing 352 acres, broke ground in 1989 and Celebration, 4,900 acres, in 1995. Both communities function within new-urbanist criteria, yet their conception and day-to-day operational methods are very different. Kentlands was designed by the new-urbanist design firm of Duany Plater-Zyberk and built by a private developer, who eventually conceded managerial duties to elected residents. Celebration, however, is an entity of the Walt Disney Company and remained totally under Disney control until recently. On January 21, 2004, the Walt Disney Company sold the town center of Celebration to Lexin Capital, a private real estate investment firm. Disney will maintain a presence in the town of eight thousand for several years while focusing on selling the remaining commercial land.

The primary goal of Joseph Alfrandre, the developer of Kentlands Farm, was to adapt the organized layout of the old farm to meet the lifestyle requirements of a modern community. For Alfrandre, the beauty and order of the rather formal Kentlands Farm complex was his inspiration. Alfrandre and Duany Plater-Zyberk held charrettes to solicit ideas from residents, city officials, and urban planners and incorporated the input into the Kentlands Master Plan, thus increasing support for their plan. Kentlands, built out to capacity, contains a diverse choice of residences and civic and commercial buildings replicating a federal colonial-style brick village. The housing includes single-family residences, urban cottages, townhouses, rental and accessory apartments, and condominiums. Due to the new-urbanist pedestrian-friendly narrow-street design, all parking is off street, with garages located behind residences and accessed by alleys. Kentlands also includes one million square feet of commercial and retail space in the town's center and within walking distance of surrounding neighborhoods.[12]

Overall, Kentlands has achieved its goal as a new-urbanist community. Kentlands meets its mixed land-use criteria with its built-out residential, retail, and commercial areas and recreational and open-space areas. Capitalizing on its efforts to create public transportation opportunities, Kentlands will soon have a subway station within walking distance for residents. Citizen-stakeholder participation is also encouraged on a continuous basis by notifications about meetings, summary of minutes, amendments to codes or restrictions, and upcoming events.

In 1966 Walt Disney dreamed of designing a town where the way of life would reflect the spirit of the past, as well as a vision for the future. Disney's dream was realized with the development of Celebration, Florida, a planned community on 5,000 acres near Orlando, Florida, in northwest Osceola County. Based on the fundamental principles of place, community, health, technology, and education, Celebration would represent the utopian small-town America for the future. When totally built out the mixed-use town will have twenty thousand residents; commercial, business, and retail zones; and health, recreational, and educational facilities. A focal point of the town is the Celebration School and Teaching Academy. Disney's goal was to create an educational center that would provide opportunities for all ages to participate. He believed his ideas would revolutionize education and transform the community.

Disney spared no costs in the development of Celebration, hiring three separate design firms to oversee conceptual architectural and landscaping planning: Cooper, Robertson & Partners, Robert A. M. Stern Architects, and UDA Architects. Intending to re-create the main street of yesteryear, Disney contracted internationally renowned architects to design downtown civic and commercial structures, an architectural fantasy comprising Cesar Pelli's movie theater, Robert Venturi's bank, Michael Graves's post office, and Philip Johnson's fifty-two-column town hall. Celebration offers six styles of housing: classical, Victorian, colonial revival, coastal, Mediterranean, and French. Lot sizes range from estate or manor to cottage, townhouse, garden, bungalow, and terrace. The price range of the housing is also diverse, from rental units and accessory apartments to million-dollar homes a mere walk from the golf course's fairways.

The intent of the Celebration planners was to create a diverse, multi-income community made up of seniors and young families. As the demographics from the recent 2000 census show, Celebration has not reached this goal. Of the total population (2,736), the median age is 36.9 years; 48.6% are male and 51.4% are female. Of the total, 15% are 55 or older. Racially, 94.6% are white; 1.9% are black or African American; 2.6% are Asian; 0.4% American Indian or Alaskan Native; 7.6% are Hispanic or Latino. The median household income is $74,231. The number of families below poverty level is 30, or 4.3%. The median house price is $380,900.[13]

Both the residents of Kentlands and Celebration acknowledge and agree to uphold the laws, codes, or covenants stated in the contracts they sign as residents of their chosen community. Mandatory design-review criteria exist both in Celebration and Kentlands. The most significant difference between Kentlands, a private development venture, and Celebration, an entity of a major corporation, is the function of the management body that governs each community. The Kentlands Citizens Assembly Board of Trustees, which is the chief governing body, oversees the Community Charter of Kentlands. Although citizens were not included in the original board, in January 2000 an election among the residents chose the board's president and by June of the same year residents filled all five seats on the board.

The story of citizen participation in Celebration is different. The Walt Disney Company controls all aspects of life through covenants and rules and regulations. Citizen input is not actively solicited or encouraged. A prime example of this is the education controversy that erupted between the Walt Disney Company and the residents. In 1966 Walt Disney stated: "I'd love to be part of building a school of tomorrow. . . . This might be a pilot operation for the teaching age—to go out across the country and across the world." The Celebration school is a unique public-private collaboration of the School District of Osceola County, Stetson University, and Disney. Barely a year into operation, parents began to have concerns regarding the state-of-the-art school, which Disney marketed as the strongest selling point of the town. The matter received national attention as parents sought an audience with the Walt Disney Company to voice their concerns over the liberal teaching methods in the school. Disney executives responded that the school was a public school, not a private one, and did not encourage citizen participation by creating a school committee.[14]

Disney should consider adopting the type of citizen-stakeholder participation that Kentlands did. Although Celebration meets the smart-growth criteria of pedestrian-friendly areas, mixed use, and open-space and greenbelt areas and opportunities for interaction, the citizen-stakeholder participation is not met. The sense of community may exist, but not in a governing and decision-making role. For Celebration to fulfill the criteria of a new-urbanist community, Disney must evolve from an ownership role into a partnership role with the residents. It will be interesting to see what develops with the new ownership of Celebration. Will the sale to Lexin Capital change the way business is conducted in Celebration? Will more participation by the residents be encouraged in formulating policy and developing plans? While Disney still faces resident dissension over public school issues and rigid covenants, property values are among the highest in the Orlando area. The majority of the residents call Celebration a success story.

CONCLUSION

In this chapter we have discussed the concept of growth management and learned to develop a growth-management problem-oriented plan. The tools that are chosen for a community to solve the identified planning problems must be tailor-made for that community. We make adjustments and fit the tools and techniques to the unique situation. We also explored the case studies of two new-urbanism communities, Kentlands and Celebration. By comparing the smart-growth principles that each community follows, we learned to apply the techniques to local development projects.

Discussion Box

Is your community a candidate for a growth-management plan? Why or why not? What local land-use concerns would indicate the need for a growth-management plan? What tools would you use if your community were experiencing a lack of a variety of housing for all income levels? If your community were losing open space to development? If your community needs to protect its natural resources? If your community needs commercial or industrial development? What smart-growth techniques would improve the low-density problems your community or a neighboring community is facing?

Learning Challenge: Political Climate and Social-Planning Awareness
Read about local planning issues in your newspaper, attend a public meeting or forum, and identify primary issues of concern. Does the community feel that municipal officials and planners are dealing with the concerns? What role have the various political factions in the community played in shaping the physical design and social underpinnings of the community? Identify the social-awareness level by analyzing the type and location of support services in reference to demographic statistics and the needs of particular groups that reside in the community.

PLANNING EXERCISE 6: HOUSING-CONDITION SURVEY

Each group will be given a *work map*, which is a map showing the building footings and placement for a specific section of the community in figure 6.2. The *work map* is blank, as is the top portion of the condition survey map. Your assignment is to fill in the appropriate symbols that are indicated in the legend in the condition survey map for the housing units in your group study area. The bottom map in figure 6.2 shows a section of the community that has been surveyed, with the appropriate symbols for the designated buildings.

The following steps are involved in a housing-condition survey:

- First, review the zoning for your designated area and look up the specifics about this zoning district in the zoning ordinance for the community. What is its zone designation? What are the dimensions and other details for this zone?

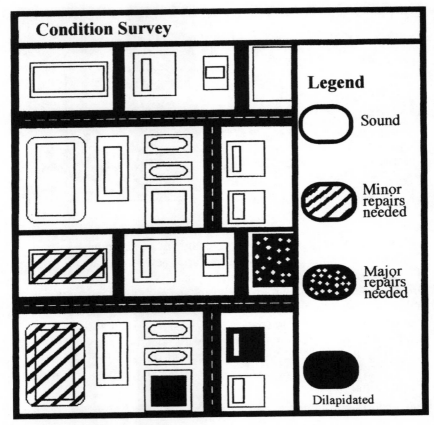

Figure 6.2. Condition Survey Map

- Next, draw a boundary around your group study area. For your fieldwork, go to your assigned section and do a *walk about*. This means take notes on the general condition of the houses. Are they sound? Do they need slight improvements? Or are they dilapidated? Follow the legend that designates the criteria for structural conditions on the condition-survey map, and fill in the correct symbols on your map.

Sound: Overall good condition (roof, good condition; paint, good, no peeling; windows, good, no cracks; no chipped caulking)

Minor repairs needed: Roof in need of minor shingle repairs; some paint chipping; few windows cracked

Major repairs needed: Roof needs total replacement; building needs total paint job; windows need upgrading

Dilapidated: Building unoccupied for long period of time; overall condition poor; does not meet code

• Now go to the assessor's office in city hall and request a printout of the value of the houses on your assigned street. As the values from each group are reported, a comparative analysis can be conducted to determine which areas have affordable houses.

NOTES

1. Elaine Moss, *Land Use Controls in the United States: A Handbook on the Legal Rights of Citizens* (New York: Dial Press, 1977).

2. Rutherford H. Platt, *Land Use Control, Geography, Law, and Public Policy* (Englewood Cliffs, N.J.: Prentice Hall, 1991).

3. Moss, *Land Use Controls*.

4. Jay Stein, *Growth Management: The Planning Challenge of the 1990s* (Newbury Park, Calif.: Sage Publications, 1993).

5. Edward M. Bergman, *Eliminating Exclusionary Zoning: Reconciling Workplace and Residence in Suburban Areas* (Cambridge, Mass.: Ballinger Publishing Co., 1974).

6. Randall G. Arendt, *Growing Greener: Putting Conservation into Local Plans and Ordinances* (Washington, D.C.: Island Press, 1999).

7. Retrieved May 15, 2004, from www.sustainable.doe.gov/codes/agzon.shtml.

8. Retrieved May 11, 2004, from www.co.berks.pa.us/planning/lib/planning/azip.pdf.

9. Andres Duany, Elizabeth Plater-Zyberk, and Jeff Speck, *Suburban Nation: The Rise of Sprawl and the Decline of the American Dream* (New York: North Point Press, 2000).

10. Duany, Plater-Zyberk, and Speck, *Suburban Nation*.

11. Retrieved May 18, 2004, from www.smartgrowthamerica.com.

12. Duany, Plater-Zyberk, and Speck, *Suburban Nation*.

13. U.S. Census Bureau, 1997. TIGER/Line. Washington, D.C. Retrieved May 18, 2004, from www.census.gov/ftp/pub/geo/www/tiger.

14. Retrieved May 19, 2004, from http://themagicalmouse.com/celebration/nytimes971214/article1a.html.

Part III

SUBSPECIALIZED AREAS OF PLANNING

The field of community planning may be broken down into the following specialization areas: land use, environmental planning, urban design and community development, economic development, historic-site preservation and revitalization, transportation planning, and geographic information systems (GIS). For the purposes of this text, land use, economic development, and GIS are not discussed in separate chapters but are incorporated into other chapters. Jobs and research are generally undertaken within these subfields of planning. Of course, the expression "a planner is a generalist with a specialty" still rings true. In many cases the planner is a one-person show. But recently, due to the complexities of planning problems, more planners are purposely taking technically oriented courses in GIS, global positioning system (GPS), economic modeling, and civil engineering.

Chapter 7 includes an overview of site analysis, zoning techniques that are used to protect natural resources, and the environmental-impact statement process. Site-analysis skills are used to determine the most appropriate location for development. Planners who work in the environmental area deal with land-use analysis studies, zoning issues, and environmental assessment reports. Chapter 8 deals with the aspects of urban design and community development. The urban designer decides on the most efficient, aesthetic design for a building, or group of buildings, and places the buildings in the urban fabric of the city. Community development involves developing neighborhood-assessment plans and business and commercial-area plans. A planner working in this area deals primarily with economic trends, demographic projections, housing statistics, and capital-facilities and infrastructure plans to support economic development in the community.

Chapter 9 covers the specialized areas of historic-site preservation and revitalization. Historically, urban renewal and gentrification have been the primary methods to revitalize blighted areas in the United States. Recently, legislation carried out at the local level, such as the Brownfields Act, has changed the planning focus. Brownfields grants are awarded to communities to redevelop contaminated sites. These processes are analyzed to compare the effectiveness of each approach in revitalizing an urban or contaminated area. Chapter 10 presents an overview of transportation planning in the United States and alternative energy sources and outlines the methods planners follow in developing traffic-impact studies. Chapter 11 reinforces how problem-oriented plans are integrated into the comprehensive plan for a community. Finally, all the pieces are together to complete the puzzle for the community.

Chapter Seven

Environmental Planning

Environmental planning is conducted at two levels. One level involves the micro-site scale, or the site analysis of the specific piece of land. The other level involves the macrolevel scale, or regional analysis of the natural resources of the area being studied. Basically, site analysis is the study of the development potential of a parcel of land. As the foremost site planner Ian McHarg emphasizes, our decisions about development must conform to the needs of nature itself.[1] McHarg also stresses that the role of the planner in a site design study is to collect data from several related specialists, including ecologists, geomorphologists, soil scientists, and hydrologists. The process involves determining the existent site characteristics of a parcel of land and how these characteristics should influence what gets built on the site.

FACTORS IN SITE ANALYSIS

The following geographic aspects of a parcel are included in site analysis: soils, topography, microclimate and insolation, hydrology and drainage, hazards, and sounds and smells. The soil factors display the first level of analysis of the development potential of the site. A study of a parcel's soils includes their type and association, fertility, stability, and bearing capacity and the level of topsoil. Whether any topsoil has been dredged or added to the site is a factor in the erosion potential. The characteristics of the soils on the site are directly related to the hydrology and slope factors. For example, when water is withdrawn from an aquifer, or underground water source, soil compresses and compacts. In some cases the soil around the area of extraction caves in and sinks, causing subsidence. This process has created major sinkholes in Florida, where groundwater has been depleted by water-supply withdrawal for development projects.

107

Saltwater intrusion, seawater replacing the depleted underground water, has occurred in areas along the coast of Florida.

The topography of the site directly influences the suitability for development and where infrastructure and development should be located on the site.
Slope is measured either as an angle, a gradient (vertical distance divided by
horizontal distance), or a percentage (vertical distance as a percentage of horizontal distance). Floodplains and marshlands are often associated with flooding, deep unstable soils, sensitive ecological habitats, and fluctuating water
tables that may pose considerable engineering difficulty. The stability of a
slope depends as much on the type of soil as on steepness. Sewage lines are
also particularly sensitive to slope and require a minimum incline for efficient
flow. Drainage of sewers from steep or even moderately steep sites requires
specific engineering solutions such as drainage culverts and pumping and rising mains. Consultation with a hydraulic engineer and knowledge of costs
and difficulties in engineering design must be considered in site-analysis
work.

When development is considered at a site that offers a scenic view, the
analysis should weigh factors such as engineering problems and the impacts
on ecological habitats with the visual advantages of the site. As Kevin Lynch
explains, the most appropriate location for development is not the ridgeline
but the curve on top of the rise of the ridgeline. This location offers the most
efficient placement for utilities and avoids problems that may develop from
exposure to winds or other climatic impacts.[2]

The key factors in determining the microclimate of the site are topography,
insolation, vegetation, atmospheric circulation, and prevailing winds. A
nearby water body tends to moderate temperatures, and tree buffers can be
situated to control climatic factors. The insolation factor is based on the lati-
tude of the site, which determines the position of the sun over the site
throughout the year. Surface materials such as impervious paving surfaces
and roofing materials influence the amount of heat generated at the site from
insolation, and building orientation influences the amount of heat generated
inside the building from insolation. In cold climates the building should be
oriented toward the sun for maximum solar exposure, whereas in hot climates
shielding from solar exposure is more energy efficient. The aspects of the terrain at the site also influence insolation. South-facing slopes in the northern
hemisphere receive more radiation than flat areas or north-facing slopes.
Shadows from high elevation points on the site may also influence the
amount of radiation gained at the site.

Hydrology factors and drainage patterns must be studied to predict erosion
and flood potential at the site. The Federal Emergency Management Agency
(FEMA) produces floodplain maps for the United States. The typical FEMA

floodplain map shows areas flooded by a hundred-year storm (1 percent chance of occurring) and a five-hundred-year storm. Although one can often determine the fifty- and two-hundred-year flood zones from a flood-hazard study and the map, they are not shown on the map series currently produced by FEMA. If you are in a floodplain zone, consult these maps first. Next, study the drainage patterns to develop stormwater management and flooding and erosion controls. Stormwater discharge depends on a number of factors: the intensity and duration of a storm, the extent to which the soil at the site can directly absorb precipitation, and the nature of the vegetation or materials that cover the catchment, or drainage areas.

To map the watersheds in an area, the site must be analyzed and divided into catchment areas. Then the overland flow, or water that cannot be contained on the site, is calculated. The ratio of runoff water to the total volume of water is known as the coefficient of runoff. This can vary from 0.1 or less for a flat site with sandy soil covered with forest and undergrowth to close to 1.0 for urban development on steep slopes. This flow should first be calculated for the undeveloped site, and then for the same event considering the placement of the proposed development. The surplus flow can be stored temporarily on site in a detention basin, which discharges water at a slower rate than it receives it.[3] Another strategy is to direct some part of the overflow to small depressions, channels, or pits where it can directly infiltrate the soil.

In developing a site plan the natural drainage of the site should be preserved as much as possible, and hard surfaces should be minimized to reduce the increased intensity of runoff that accompanies development. Development might be clustered on the site to minimize impervious surfaces, and dense landscaping could be placed to decrease erosion. Generally, only development that can withstand periodic flooding should be located in the floodway.

Besides the hazards related to steep slopes and poor soils, other potential hazards cause concern across the country. Volcanic eruptions may occur in the Northwest United States and northern California. The possibility of eruptions, ashfall, gas discharge, and lava flow that result from volcanic activity must be considered. Since this region and areas south of it are also prone to earthquakes, faults should be mapped and the maps updated regularly. These areas also experience drought and fire.

Planners also need to develop site and evacuation plans for coastal erosion and storm-related events such as hurricanes on the East Coast of the United States, particularly in the Carolinas and Florida. Protective vegetation must be considered for sand dunes and estuarine sites near coastal dunes. Development along canals and coastal wetland areas also must take into consideration the ecological damage that may occur in mangrove vegetation, fish breeding grounds, and wildlife habitats.[4]

Site analysis includes study of sound and odor levels. Levels are measured under varying weather and wind conditions, and preventive measures are recommended to decrease harmful levels. Sound assessments are usually conducted near major highways, railroads, or industrial sites. Similarly, the site planner collects odor data at sites such as a landfill or a natural site such as a swamp, mangrove, or mudflat. The sources of malodors are industrial processes, intensive stock raising, garbage-disposal areas, and sewage treatment plants. The Council of Environmental Quality (CEQ), established under the National Environmental Policy Act (NEPA) of 1969, sets noise and malodor threshold levels, beyond which harmful health effects may occur.

TECHNIQUES OF SITE ANALYSIS

Planners conduct a site analysis to determine what parcels should not be developed and what type of development should be allowed on parcels that are suitable for development. In a land capability analysis, the planner inventories conditions and characteristics of the land including the soil, topography, drainage, climate, and physical geologic factors. The Natural Resource Conservation Service (NRCS) in the United States provides soils maps with tables of associated developmental characteristics for each soil. A site's soils map may be referenced to determine its appropriate development. The planner collects data for an inventory of rivers, lakes, aquifers, marshes, and wetlands on the site and in the region. Then critical areas of environmental concern, which include fragile zones such as wetlands and coastal lands, geologic hazardous zones, or sensitive endangered species and plant habitats, are identified.[5] These areas are unsuitable for development. Since all components of the environment are interconnected, studies of watersheds, air sheds, river barriers, and special habitats should be considered in light of impacts on the region, not just the specific site.

Ian McHarg describes the overlay-mapping technique as an effective method in determining where development should be located. McHarg explains that the soils and water-inventories maps, as well as existent land-use and zoning maps, may be superimposed to show where development should and should not take place. The existent land-use map includes woodlands, agricultural land, and scenic features. The zoning map includes districts for housing and industrial and commercial use. As each inventory map, with shaded areas showing poor suitability, is superimposed on another, the final map shows the unshaded parcels where development may occur. For example, the first map may show soils stability, where poor soils would be considered unsuitable for development. The next map may be a topographic overlay showing shaded areas of steep slopes that should be eliminated from development. The final stage in the process would indicate those parcels that have no development restriction.[6] The GIS program ArcView accomplishes the same type of overlay analysis.

A matrix of land capability may be set up from the results of the overlay process. The matrix is made up of cells for each land parcel and an assigned value of development for several land characteristics, including soil type, slope, and flooding propensity. The matrix indicates the carrying capacity of the land, or the amount of development a parcel can withstand. For some parcels the suitability for development is so low, the parcel should not be developed at all. The carrying capacity indicates the threshold level at which a parcel of land should be protected. To go beyond the threshold level means to go beyond the level at which the parcel of land can support development. Recommendations and policies are based on land-capability value. If a large-scale apartment complex is proposed for a parcel that shows a low suitability due to poor soils and drainage and insufficient capacity of sewer and other infrastructure, problems will more than likely occur.

HOW TO IDENTIFY AND PROTECT NATURAL RESOURCES

When natural resources at a site are endangered, an environmental problem-oriented plan should be developed to promote their regeneration and restoration. The plan should include an inventory of the natural resources in the community and development controls to protect valuable natural resources. Regulations to protect natural resources vary across the country. The protection techniques may fall under federal, state, or county control, as often is the case in the West and Northwest, or under local planning board or conservation-commission control as in home-rule states in New England. Many town officials have recognized this responsibility and the need for development controls to protect valuable natural resources such as groundwater, farmlands, flood-plains, and open space and wetlands.

Groundwater

Groundwater resources are threatened by contamination from many sources, including landfills, septic systems, businesses that generate hazardous wastes, road salts, and gasoline storage tanks. Since state or federal laws may not adequately address regulations for most of these pollutants, planning boards can design regulations such as zoning-overlay districts for aquifer-recharge areas.

The first step in designing a protection strategy is to develop a detailed map of the aquifer-recharge area for municipal wells. This task will generally require assistance from a hydrology consultant or regional planning agency. The extent of the recharge area defines the boundaries of the zoning-overlay district. Useful data sources in this mapping process include U.S. Geologic Survey surficial geology and watershed maps, consultant studies for municipal wells, private-well driller logs, and groundwater-overlay maps from state environmental agencies.

The second step involves evaluating water samples to determine existing and potential groundwater-contamination sources. The final step is designing an aquifer-overlay district that is tailored to the specific needs of the town. An overlay district that delineates the location of the aquifer is superimposed over the community's existing zoning districts. The overlay district establishes additional land-use restrictions above and beyond the existing zoning restrictions. Table 7.1, which is broken down into general land-use zoning districts, shows the most prevalent sources of groundwater contaminants in each land-use category.

In the case of an aquifer-overlay district, the new district is usually established to protect the primary aquifer-recharge area identified in the mapping process. A detailed hydrologic map highlighting the aquifer-overlay district can be adopted as part of the zoning bylaw. New regulations can be adopted to prohibit particularly hazardous land uses, create larger lot sizes in unsewered areas, restrict sand and gravel removal and underground storage tanks, centralize drainage recharge, and allow certain business or industrial uses through a stringent special-permit process. As points of environmental contamination are placed on the problem-oriented-plan map, the relationships between the sources of contamination and the sensitive receptor sites where people are located become clear. The links of points of concern on the map with housing, schools, hospitals, and employment are red flags. Action plans are based on the geographic location of the points of concern in relation to sensitive receptor areas.

Farmland Preservation

The conversion of farmland to nonagricultural uses is an issue of great concern in many states. As a community asset, farmlands provide locally grown produce; contribute to a self-sufficient local economy; protect open space, floodplains, and scenic areas; and help define the character of a community. Local strategies to protect farmlands should be developed by a farmland advisory committee. The committee, made up of farmers and representatives from municipal government and the public, evaluates the agricultural re-

Table 7.1.   Groundwater Contamination Sources

Land Use	Source	Possible Contaminants
Residential	Septic systems	Nitrates, bacteria, viruses, solvent cleaners, household hazardous wastes
	Pesticide spraying on lawns	Toxic chemicals
Agriculture	Manure (storage, spreading)	Nitrates, bacteria, pathogens
	Pesticide spraying on crops	Nutrients, pesticides, biocides
	Slurry run-off	Heavy metals
Business and industry	Manufactuing processes	Hazardous wastes
	Cleaning, degreasing	Oils, bitumen, rubber
	Industrial development, refineries	Metals, microorganics
	Wood treatment works	Biocides
	Breweries, creameries	Nutrient-rich, organic effluents
	Underground storage tanks	Petroleum products
Landfills and junkyards	Solid waste, automobiles	Toxic leachates, solvents
Highways	De-icing salt, storage	Sodium, chloride
	Corrosion of vehicle parts	Metals
	Oils spills, run-off	Carcinogens such as polycyclic aromatics and phenols
Utility and railroad right-of-ways	Pesticide spraying	Toxic chemicals and biocides, especially herbicides
Coastal development	Dredging	Saline intrusion, disposal of bilge waters

Source: Retrieved from www.epa.gov/ebtpages/watewaterpollutants.html.

sources and needs and establishes goals and objectives for farmland preservation. The following techniques may be considered:

- Transfer of development rights (TDR), technical assistance programs, marketing and buy-local programs, farmers markets: TDR allows the transfer of development rights from a prime farmland area to another section of the community where development is more suitable. Technical assistance, buy-local programs, farmers markets, farmstands, and other farm-related revenue enhancements as ancillary uses are all efforts to support local farmers.
- Right-to-farm bylaws: A community bylaw may be developed to create incentives to preserve the farm, including tax abatements, which are reductions

in real estate, income, and inheritance taxes, and protection from nuisance lawsuits.

- Purchase of development rights for prioritized farms: Farm parcels are prioritized based on objective criteria, including soils, type of crops, and proximity to infrastructure. Community officials may apply for local and state funding for the purchase of development rights on priority parcels.
- Land trusts or land banks: Land trusts or banks are established to purchase farmlands that are threatened with development. The trust or bank can sell the development rights of the parcel to the state and resell the farm parcel to a farmer.
- Innovative zoning and creative land development: A zoning bylaw could be developed that requires clustered development on the least-productive parcels of the farm, while retaining the prime farm soils for agricultural use.
- Municipal sewer and water policies: Policies can be adopted to prohibit the extension of sewer and water lines to designated farm districts to prevent development.

Floodplain Management

The protection of floodplains is crucial in minimizing the damaging effects of floods. Floodplains provide a temporary storage area for floodwaters that spill over channels of a river or stream. Once detained, floodwaters can then be slowly released through surface discharge, evaporation, or percolation to groundwater. Unfortunately, many property owners ignore warnings to build in floodplains and develop houses, businesses, and industry along riverbanks or lake fronts. Each structure built in a floodplain incrementally eliminates floodwater storage area and increases the extent and severity of flooding, as well as damage to public and private property.

Nonstructural floodplain management measures, which reduce flooding damage and danger, are in many ways more effective in protecting floodplains than dams and dikes. Techniques such as floodplain zoning and public-land acquisition can help to preserve natural floodwater storage areas and reduce the severity of floods. Flood proofing of structures, flood warning systems, and evacuation plans can help to minimize flood damage and ensure that communities are prepared for floods when they do occur. Finally, purchase and demolition, or retrofitting of *repetitive-loss properties*, is an effective technique. Repetitive-loss properties have had flood damage in multiple storms and the owners have made multiple floodplain insurance claims.

The following techniques are useful tools for planning boards and other planning agencies in developing floodplain-management problem-oriented plans:

- Open space acquisition is an effective technique for ensuring the long-term protection of floodplain areas.
- Model subdivision regulations developed by FEMA that ensure adequate drainage systems can be adopted by the community.
- Floodplain-zoning bylaws can be designed to prevent development within the floodplain and prohibit hazardous land uses, such as landfills, junkyards, or hazardous-waste storage, from floodplain areas. The zoning bylaws can also include stipulations that the development is in conformance with state building code requirements for flood proofing.

Open-Space and Wetlands Protection

Development of an open-space problem-oriented plan is a very effective way to protect open-space parcels and present an action plan for future recreational uses for a community. An open-space plan is required to apply for state or federal open-space land-acquisition funding. Planning boards, working with other town officials or residents, can take a lead role in the development of the plan, which includes natural-resource inventories, recreation and conservation needs, and action strategies for protection. The following open-space-protection techniques should be considered in developing the plan:

- Land acquisition: Funding opportunities for open-space land acquisition at the state and federal levels should be researched for the community.
- Zoning: Traditional large-lot zoning, cluster, or conservation-overlay-district zoning can be effective in preserving open space. For example, large-lot zoning could be implemented in an aquifer-protection area to ensure that septic tanks do not pollute groundwater. It is important to note that unless large-lot zoning requires huge lots, it can actually make sprawl worse instead of solving any problems. Overlay conservation districts may be established to protect natural resources such as prime farmlands, wetlands, floodplains, and aquifer-recharge areas. In an overlay district, additional restrictions on the type and intensity of land use can be adopted that are stricter than the current zoning regulations. Cluster zoning, which groups buildings and preserves open space, may be implemented.
- Subdivision control: Many states have subdivision-control laws that include a requirement for a park in approving a subdivision. The park should be reasonable in size in relation to the entire subdivision, and the developers may be required to meet certain park standards such as playground or recreational use.

ENVIRONMENTAL LEGISLATION
TO PROTECT WATER QUALITY

The first institutions that dealt with water pollution in the United States were created in response to the *sanitary awakening* of the late nineteenth century. Scientists of that era were beginning to clarify the role of contaminated water in transmitting disease. The principal responsibilities for water-pollution control were assumed by the states and local agencies. In 1869 Massachusetts created the Massachusetts Board of Health, which was the first state agency to control water pollution. In the latter part of the nineteenth century, state boards of health administered water-pollution-control programs. The major concern of this period was to control waterborne infectious diseases, typhoid fever, and cholera.

Although effective technology for treating municipal wastewater existed by the late 1870s, only 4 percent of the nation's population had wastes treated as of 1910. By 1939 one-half of the nation's urban population still discharged its waste untreated. Two factors impeded the use of wastewater treatment technology: (1) the prohibitive cost of the large amount of chlorine needed to disinfect the drinking water supplies and (2) the belief that natural waterways could be used as receptors for wastes.

The federal role in water-pollution control came with the Rivers and Harbors Act of 1898, the Public Health Service Act of 1912, and the Oil Pollution Act of 1924, which prohibited oily discharges in coastal waters. During the 1930s and 1940s, debate raged over the federal role in water protection, culminating in the Water Pollution Control Act of 1948. Whether business and industry willingly comply with measures to clean up water in the manufacturing and industrial processes depends to a great extent on the incentives that the government offers. If the laws require installation of costly piping and diversion methods, for example, to keep the water clean, business and industry more than likely will contest the laws. If, however, tax-relief measures, credits, or abatements are issued, business and industry will more likely comply with laws to control water quality.[7]

Table 7.2 lists key federal laws controlling water pollution in the United States, date they were enacted, and primary aspects of each law.

It is interesting to note that at various stages of our history (1940s–1950s), the federal government would add provisions for grant monies or research funding to the legislation. At other stages (1974–1980), more stringent measures, including rigid standards and toxic controls, were added. Recently, EPA enacted the regulation that stormwater permits are now required for stormwater discharges and for one acre or more of land-disturbing activities to control stormwater runoff on most medium and larger urban areas.[8]

Table 7.2. Key Federal Water-Pollution Laws

Year	Law	Primary Water-Control Measures
1948	Water Pollution Control Act	First comprehensive, federal interest in clean water programs
1956	Federal Water Pollution Control Act (FWPCA)	Funding to states for technical assistance Construction grants to municipalities Funding for training programs and research
1965	Water Quality Act	Water quality standards set by state States required to set standards for interstate waters States required to prepare state implementation plans (SIP)[a]
1972	FWPCA Amendments	Increased federal assistance for municipal treatment plant construction Zero discharge of pollution by 1985 National Pollution Discharge Elimination System (NPDES) permits
1974	Safe Drinking Water Act (SDWA)	Standards must be set for drinking water at local level
1976	Toxic Substances Control Act (TSCA)	Regulates production and distribution of toxic substances in water supply systems
1977	Clean Water Act (CWA)	Requires Best Practice Control Technology (BPT) to control conventional pollutants Requires Best Available Technology (BAT) for toxic substances[b] Municipal treatment plants required to meet secondary treatment
1981	Municipal Waste Treatment Construction Grants Amendments	Federal contributions in construction grants reduced
1987	Water Quality Act	Measures to address nonpoint source pollution such as stormwater, runoff from farms, construction sites, and urban areas
1989	State Water Pollution Control Revolving Funds	States contribute matching funds, construction monies repaid to state fund

Source: Retrieved from www.epa.gov/watertrain/cwa.
Notes: a. States are required to prepare SIPs to show methods to meet water quality standards.
b. Both BPT and BAT requirements stipulate enforcement actions for failure to comply.

The amendments to the major water- and air-quality acts, the Clean Water Act and Clean Air Act, are often enacted to lessen the impacts on business and industry. The Safe Drinking Water Act of 1974 made the states responsible for setting standards for drinking water, thus allowing many states to lower the standards. The Clean Air Act Amendments of 1977 relaxed the emission standards for automobiles.

ENVIRONMENTAL LEGISLATION TO PROTECT AIR QUALITY

Air-quality controls follow a historical pattern similar to water-quality controls in the United States. The early efforts to control air pollution were based on *public nuisance* issues. In 1881 the first law regulating smokestacks, the Anti-Smoke Ordinance, in the United States was adopted in Chicago, Illinois. The ordinance was enacted because of harmful levels of dense smoke from smokestacks. The clauses in the ordinance stipulated that emissions were prohibited from stacks. Violators could be fined up to $50.00 per day. Due to Pittsburgh's heavy use of coal and microclimatic factors conducive to temperature inversions, the Pennsylvania city created strict standards for smoke control, initiating the nation's first smoke-control program in 1906.

Throughout the 1940s and into the early 1950s, several cities developed emission standards to limit discharges from particular plants. In Donora, Pennsylvania, in 1948 an episodic, severe photochemical smog event caused the city to develop a citywide air-pollution-control strategy. The event in Donora caused twenty deaths and thousands to become ill from respiratory complications. It was determined that emissions from the steel mills produced the smog.

As is the case with water-quality controls, air-control measures are historically related to the economic factors of the time and the administration in charge. If economic indicators show a strong economy with start-up businesses on an upswing, it is difficult to persuade the administration at the federal and state levels to support costly environmental control measures. At the same time, if the economy is slow, business leaders will often site excessively stringent building codes as a reason for the economic downturn. In either case it is the incentives that are offered that sway support toward quality controls for the environment.

Federal legislation to control air pollution did not surface until the mid 1950s. Table 7.3 lists the key federal laws controlling air pollution in the United States, the date they were enacted, and each law's primary aspects.

Air-pollution laws show a trend for strict controls (1965–1969) and a trend for relaxation of emissions (1977–1979). The establishment of strict controls came during the Nixon era with the introduction of NEPA in 1969, whereas less strict laws were put in place when the Clean Air Act Amendments of 1977 were enacted.[9]

Several environmental problems are linked to acid precipitation. Acidic levels of water bodies alter oxygen content and impact fish and wildlife in New England and Canada. Hathaway Pond on Cape Cod, Massachusetts, for example, was labeled the first dead pond in New England due to acid precipitation.

Table 7.3. Key Federal Air-Pollution Laws

Year	Law	Primary Air-Control Measures
1955	Air Pollution Control Act	Air pollution research funding
1960	Motor Vehicle Exhaust Study Act	Funding for research on vehicle emissions
1963	Clean Air Act (CAA)	Funding for state and local air-pollution-control agencies
		Enforcement process for polluters
1965	Motor Vehicle Air Pollution Control Act	Regulations set for emission levels for cars beginning with 1968 models
1967	Air Quality Act	Federally issued criteria and control methods
		State requirements to meet standards for Air Quality Control Regions (AQCRs) and state implementation plans (SIPs) for nonattainment areas[a]
1970	Clean Air Act Amendments	Set national ambient standards for pollutants[b]
		Transportation management plans
		New point source performance standards set
		Enforcing efficient auto emission standards with new technology
1977	Clean Air Act Amendments	Vehicle inspection programs
		Auto emission requirements relaxed
		Prevention of significant deterioration areas
		Emission offsets for nonattainable areas
1980	Acid Precipitation Act	Research and development for a long-term prevention plan
1990	Clean Air Act Amendments	Air-pollution prevention and control
		Emission standards for moving sources
		Plan requirements for nonattainment areas
		Acid deposition control
		Stratospheric ozone protection

Source: Retrieved from www.epa.gov/region5/defs/html/caa.htm.
Notes: a. Each state is required to submit SIP to EPA that best achieves compliance with National Ambient Air Quality Standards (NAAQS) for that AQCR.
b. The common classes of pollutants covered in the 1970 CAA are sulfur oxides, particulate matter, carbon monoxide, photochemical oxidants, nitrogen oxides, and hydrocarbons.

Another problem is the impact of acid precipitation on vegetation and plant species, especially forests. Many scientists link acid precipitation to the degradation of forests in the Ruhr Valley in Germany and Mount Mansfield in Vermont. Acid precipitation has been found to cause the disintegration of statues and buildings, such as in Florence and Rome, Italy.

ENVIRONMENTAL IMPACT PROCESS

Along with the water- and air-quality controls that were enacted in the late 1960s, the Nixon administration also focused on the development of a national environmental policy. The need for environmental protection came in response to the large-scale urbanization projects being proposed across the country. With the government sponsoring massive infrastructure projects, including major highways, power plants, and bridges to support the city-building trend, the administration believed there was a need to enforce environmental controls on development projects. NEPA was established to force all agencies of the federal government to integrate environmental concerns into planning and decision making. The stipulations that environmental assessments require a multidisciplined approach when considering a variety of alternatives and that all agencies consider the environment in everything they do are perhaps the strongest legacy of NEPA.

Each state is given the authority through NEPA to create its own *little NEPA*.[10] More than half the states have established a state NEPA agency. The environmental-review process, however, varies from state to state. The federal government exempts some projects, which therefore only need some documentation, requires environmental assessments (EAs) for larger projects, and requires environmental-impact statements (EISs) for the largest projects with the greatest environmental impacts. Massachusetts, for example, using similar concepts, has an environmental notification form (ENF), roughly equal to the federal EA, and an environmental-impact report (EIR), roughly equal to the federal EIS.

The stated purpose of NEPA is to

encourage productive and enjoyable harmony between man and his environment; to promote efforts which will prevent or eliminate damage to the environment and biosphere and stimulate the health and welfare of man; to enrich the understanding of the ecological systems and natural resources important to the nation. (Section 2)[11]

The major provisions of the act:

- Declare that each person has a right to a healthful environment, and that it is in part the responsibility of the federal government to ensure that the environment is protected.

- Establish the CEQ, an agency in the executive branch, headed by the president's adviser on the environment. CEQ's responsibility is "to formulate and recommend national policies to promote the improvement of the quality of the environment." Its duties include gathering information, reviewing programs, conducting investigations, and assisting the president in the preparation of an environmental-quality report to be issued annually to the Congress.
- Establish the EIS process. Every federal agency is required to include a statement that protects the environment in any report, legislation, or other major federal actions significantly affecting the quality of the environment. The statement should include a description of the environmental impact of the proposed action, unavoidable adverse effects that would result should the action take place, possible alternatives, and a discussion of short-term versus long-term advantages of the proposal.

EISs are reports that are written to describe the potential environmental impacts of a project. Natural-system-override, or pollution, studies are a major part of an EIS. Basically, pollution occurs when the environment is overloaded with harmful contaminants or excessive elements. The pollution may be toxic, such as from aldicarb (trade name Temik), a carcinogenic tobacco-plant pesticide. Sometimes, the pollution may be a resource out of place, such as the oil spill in Valdez, Alaska. In this case, an overload of a petroleum product—a natural substance formed in pools beneath the earth's surface by carbonaceous action over millions of years—is misplaced in an ecologically sensitive environmental zone. After summarizing and analyzing the impacts on a site, an EIS offers possible alternatives to alleviate the impacts. These alternatives are based on mitigation measures, or changes to the original actions that will create less environmental degradation than the proposed actions.

The EIS process includes four major steps. The first step requires the planning agency or land-use or construction firm to submit the appropriate forms, typically an ENF, to the state environmental protection agency. Based on the analysis contained in the ENF, the secretary of environmental affairs for the state protection agency decides whether an EIS is required. The law requires an EIS whenever an agency proposes to take an action that significantly affects the environment. Each state agency has specific guidelines to follow to determine if the project will have significant impact. The second step involves the preparation of a draft statement. The draft EIS is a preliminary report on the environmental consequences associated with the project. If the state environmental protection agency rules that a statement is not required, the firm may initiate the local development process for approval of the project.

The third step involves the firm or agency sending the draft EIS to all groups with an interest in the proposed project. This process is called scoping. The mailing should include federal agencies, including the CEQ, state and local governments, local business and industry, private citizens, and interest groups such as the Audubon Society or the chamber of commerce. These groups are allowed a specified amount of time, typically forty-five days, to study the draft and respond with comments to the firm. The fourth step involves revising the draft EIS by incorporating the comments received during the scoping process and writing up the final EIS. The final EIS should represent input from the public- and private-agency sectors and include revised mitigations to lessen impacts on the environment and certificates of approval for any permits that may be required during construction.

CONCLUSION

The requirements for an effective site analysis include a comprehensive investigation of the environmental aspects of the site. First, those areas that are environmentally sensitive or fragile, such as wetlands or aquifers, should be protected with a zoning overlay prohibiting development. Second, an extensive study of the problems and hazards of the site should be considered. Mitigation costs and impacts should be weighed against long-term environmental impacts. Third, a map overlay of areas zoned for environmental protection should be superimposed on the areas of topographic hazards and so on to determine suitable areas for building on the site. The final plan is the result of interpreting how the layers of information are related. This study provides the physical layer of information that is needed to make site-analysis decisions for developing environmental problem-oriented plans and writing environmental reports.

> **Discussion Box**
> What is included in an environmental site analysis? What natural resources need to be protected in an environmental protection plan for your community? What specific natural-resource areas that you know of are currently protected in your community? What areas need to be studied and protected for the future?

PLANNING EXERCISE 7: AN ENVIRONMENTAL-PLANNING PROBLEM

For this exercise find a recent newspaper or planning journal article about an environmental-planning problem. Read the article, and then get together with your group and fill in the data under each section.

1. Define the problem. Ask questions to identify areas of concern for this study: What, why, who, where, how, and when? For this exercise collect all the answers to the questions that your group comes up with in the discussion.
2. Articulate the goals and objectives for the plan.
3. Analyze and evaluate. Mark points on a map where specific facilities, transportation nodules, sensitive receptors such as schools, hospitals, or environmental areas of concern are located. Keep asking yourself: What are the areas that should concern us for this study? Draw a circle around the geographic area of concern. Review the alternatives that are presented in the article to solve the environmental problem. What cost-benefit analyses would you run to determine the best alternative for this plan? Evaluate each alternative by weighing the benefits and detriments of each option. What factors influence your decision as to what alternative is the best?
4. Implement action plans. Review the action plans that are discussed in the article. Are the action plans relevant to the planning situation? Do you think they will be effective?
5. Measure results. Is there a monitoring program in place to review the effectiveness of the programs? If not, what would you suggest?

NOTES

1. Ian L. McHarg, *Design with Nature* (Garden City, N.Y.: Natural History Press, 1971).

2. Kevin Lynch and Gary Hack, *Site Planning* (Cambridge, Mass.: MIT Press, 1984).

3. Thomas Dunne and Luna Bergere Leopold, *Water in Environmental Planning* (San Francisco, Calif.: W. H. Freeman, 1978).

4. McHarg, *Design with Nature*.

5. John Simonds, *Landscape Architecture: A Manual of Site Planning and Design* (New York: McGraw-Hill, 1983).

6. McHarg, *Design with Nature*.

7. Retrieved May 19, 2004, from www.epa.gov/epahome/laws.htm.

8. Retrieved May 19, 2004, from www.epa.gov/region5/water/cwa.htm.

9. Retrieved May 19, 2004, from www.epa.gov/region5/defs/html/caa.htm.

10. Rutherford H. Platt, chapter 12 in *Land Use Control, Geography, Law, and Public Policy* (Englewood Cliffs, N.J.: Prentice Hall, 1991).

11. Council on Environmental Quality, *The Fifth Annual Report of the Council on Environmental Quality* (Washington, D.C.: U.S. Government Printing Office, 1976).

Chapter Eight

Urban Design and Community Development

The changes in the land ethic in the United States from the communal sense of the New England village to the mobility of the expansive Western frontier are reflected in our modern settlement patterns. Essentially, the United States swung from pedestrian-friendly villages to high-density, urban-core city patterns, and finally to low-density urban sprawl. However, due to energy and transportation problems, we are now coming full circle and moving back to creating compact, urban villages. As we discussed in chapter 6, smart growth offers many solutions to our suburban woes. But it must be noted that the growth of suburban sprawl and the decline in population density in urban areas are still outpacing the urban village trend. This chapter covers urban-design techniques that support smart growth. We also discuss capital-improvements planning, which determines what capital facilities are needed for the community, as it relates to community-development planning.

ELEMENTS OF URBAN DESIGN

Urban planning deals with the elements of design and the spatial arrangement and circulation patterns around buildings. The urban planner develops inventories of commercial and business centers and social and cultural amenities for residents and tourists and analyzes traffic flows for motor vehicles and pedestrians throughout the area. To be efficient, there should be minimal barriers or conflicts between motor vehicles and bicyclists and pedestrians.

The urban planner maps the location of infrastructure lines and support services and transportation routes. The planner analyzes the setbacks and orientation of the buildings within the context of the circulation patterns around the buildings. The existent infrastructure maps are superimposed on land capability maps to determine the most appropriate places to recommend new development. Next, the planner conducts a needs assessment of what facilities are needed by the community, evaluates the options, and decides which ones are the most effective and at the same time will have the most political support. Finally, the priority projects and circulation studies are integrated into the plan.[1] Overall, the primary concern of the urban planner is carrying out a needs assessment of the residents within the form and function of the block.

Urban designers create plans according to how they want to impact the urban fabric of the area. From a cultural context, the urban designer may be concerned with leaving a legacy or mark on the landscape. This is called self-conscious design, or *high design*. I. M. Pei, for example, certainly left a legacy when he designed the Hancock Building in Boston. In stark contrast to Henry Hobson Richardson's Trinity Church nearby, Pei introduced an ultramodern, geometric design that is out of context with the Romanesque design of the church. The triangular-shaped Transamerica building in San Francisco is another example of a design that stands out in the urban fabric of the city. In some cases the community supports the vision of the architect. Whether or not there is consensus about the design, however, the impact of these projects is evident across skylines in many cities worldwide.

From another standpoint, some creators think of themselves as working with the community to integrate *cross-cultural* designs. Based on their intuition of what they believe the townsfolk want for their community, these designers draw up plans that reflect the ideas the residents have voiced in public forums and neighborhood needs discussions. In Coolidge, Arizona, for example, the urban designer in charge of redeveloping the town square created a Spanish-style, pedestrian mall with low-density, retail corridors serving Mexican foods and handcrafts. The ideas for the form and function of the square came from the residents of the town.

Most of our communities are a mixture of the old and the new, with sections of cultural or historical significance, as well as sections needing revitalization. Over time, change happens in our communities in response to pressure for development. We need to recognize the places of cultural and social value, the places that are worthy of conservation, and the places that need in fill. In fill is adding development that creates new structures that help refine and influence the design and function of the surrounding area. The following design criteria can act as guidelines in implementing new large-scale projects, as well as in-fill development, for urban-design problem-oriented plans:

- The character and amenities of a place make the place distinctive. Places of special character are built around historic, cultural, and social features that draw us to the site. Changes over time, however, may break the links with the past, resulting in an environment that lacks harmony and unity. Creating in-fill design to revitalize an area requires an inventory of the current type and amount of business and residential use, as well as the vacant lots in an area. In-fill design may include office and government, commercial and business, and housing and social services buildings and pocket parks. Planning for amenities involves collecting data on the needs of the population of the surrounding urban area and creating buildings and *pedestrian-friendly* spaces as activity generators. If the demographics indicate a large percentage of young children, a tot lot may draw a substantial number of visitors. If there is a large percentage of elderly in the area, shuffleboard or lawn bowling may draw them. Matching the appropriate activities with the needs of the people creates stimulating social and cultural centers. Kevin Lynch, a renowned urban planner, designed Faneuil Hall in Boston and Baltimore Harborside around the concept of waterfront amenities. Lynch describes these special gathering places for social and cultural events as *nodes*. Keep in mind that dead areas in the urban fabric can be the death knell for pedestrian-friendly areas. For example, Boston City Hall Plaza, so close to Faneuil Hall, is a failure, and Charlotte, North Carolina, is partially ringed by desolate parking lots. What amenities could be created in the urban setting under study? What facilities and services would need to be added to support the amenity?

- The scale, including the height and massing of buildings, is a major factor in creating a unified streetscape. By placing buildings with similar architectural features next to buildings of similar proportion, a sense of unity of scale is created. The massing of a building, its overall bulk and shape, should be a uniform fit within the block. Planners choose in-fill design projects that do not dominate their surroundings and at the same time are not visually lost in the streetscape. Richard Hedman describes the connecting elements of urban design as *visual linkages*.[2] Hedman explains that the building that is out of context must share fundamental characteristics with the surrounding buildings. Does the form and function of the building fit with the rest of the block?

- The surface materials, textures, and decorative features create an architectural theme for the design of an area. In-fill projects should tie together predominant building techniques and features to create consistency in design. If change is desired, color themes and finishes, such as adobe or brick, or roof materials, such as shingle, slate, or tile, can create entirely new visual images for one building or the whole block. Here are some characteristics of surface materials: grass absorbs sound and creates a feeling of softness in an area, wood creates a feeling of natural beauty and even temperature,

Integrating buildings with similar massing and scale creates a uniform effect in a downtown.

and concrete and stone reflect sound and create a feeling of coolness. What overall visual appearance is the main goal of the urban design study? Is the façade of a new building similar to the surrounding buildings? What changes in texture should be made to make a particular urban setting more inviting? Should the texture be changed to make one building stand out? Should the textures be changed to blend in with one another?

- The setback and orientation of buildings can create uniformity with the rest of the block or a sense of procession and movement. Kinetic and sequential techniques are organizing devices that create perceptual images in urban design by creating a series of zones for the viewer. As in photography, the designer adjusts the foreground, middle ground, and background to set up a particular processional flow for the viewer. If foregrounds are eliminated, for example, the viewer gets a sense of the street closing in on itself.[3] This telescopic sense is very strong while standing at the north end of Fifth Avenue in New York City and looking south. Like a canyon effect, the viewer perceives the lines of skyscrapers meeting at a point in the distance. Is the building uniform with the rest of the block? Does the urban space need some variation in the layout?

- Protection from climatic elements and annoyances such as noise and odor create an inviting setting. Design features that protect people from rain and snow, excessive heat and cold, and winds contribute to comfort and safety. Energy-efficient techniques such as the orientation of the building and vegetation buffers add to the comfort level. Anthropometric design is the art of making urban design settings comfortable, such as furniture that is arranged to encourage interaction and walls and stoops that are conducive to sitting. Why do people choose to meet at certain places and not others?

* A security plan for the urban setting should include conceptual drawings showing access to transportation routes for support services, as well as evacuation in case of an emergency. Flow of traffic on arterial roadways, connectors such as bridges, and barriers such as railway lines should be analyzed in relation to efficiency of movement and conflict between vehicles and pedestrians. The landscaping for a design plan should bring open space and recreation into the area, as well as create buffers for highways, airports, and industrial sites. How could circulation be improved in the overall schematics of the movement of people and vehicles? What kinds of services would encourage more pedestrians in the area? What are the natural features of the area? How much park planning is needed for this site? Is the site readily accessible to other parts of the city?

* Orthogonal or geometric form is characteristic of the right-angled grid pattern. The grid pattern, which is based on compass directions, is typical in Southwest cities in the United States. The grid is divided into north, east, south, and west sections with numbered streets and avenues emanating from a center point. Is the urban area a grid pattern? Should certain sections of the city be changed to a grid pattern?

* Axial design consists of a central focus point or centerline, with radiating lines that spread out like spokes on a wheel.[4] Typically, buildings or monuments are organized along the centerline and axes, such as the Mall in Washington, D.C. Piazza Di Pietra, which is located in Vatican City, is a classic example of axial design. The famous square was designed by Giovanni Lorenzo Bernini, who began his work in 1656 and completed the project in 1667. The design of the square features long symmetrical colonnades, a central obelisk, and two identical fountains.[5] Is there any axial design in your urban planning area? Are there components that could be added to capitalize on the axial form?

URBAN-DESIGN PROBLEM-ORIENTED PLAN

The primary goal of urban design is to create a plan that integrates with the physical environment and offers activities for the population surrounding the setting. Creating aesthetic quality by introducing the appropriate design elements makes the plan effective. Sometimes the designers concentrate on order and logic, as in the Mall in Washington, D.C., while in other cases they focus on disharmony and surprise, as in Times Square in New York City or Piccadilly Circus in London. The urban amenities are created by matching up the activities with the physical elements that are part of the setting.

Following the problem-oriented-plan process for urban design we hold forums, ask questions, prioritize issues, and determine the political support for options we might propose. Effective techniques to portray design issues and alternatives include interactive-design charrettes and visualization techniques and three-dimensional computer-generated imagery. The preceding design elements are the tools that can be matched up with the prioritized design concerns from the community. Other technical planning tools used in developing an urban-design problem-oriented plan include commercial-use and vacant-lot inventory and condition-survey mapping.

CAPITAL-IMPROVEMENTS PROGRAM

A capital-improvements program (CIP) is an action plan to guide the construction and acquisition of capital projects. The CIP identifies needed capital projects, estimates their costs, ranks the projects by importance, lists the year each should be started, and determines the best method of payment for each project within the fiscal budget of the community. Capital expenditures may be authorized in the annual operating budget as capital outlays, or they may be adopted in a separate capital budget. A CIP is a form of short-term planning; it must be based on the comprehensive plan and limited to a five-year planning period. Every year the plan should be updated and extended one more year into the future to remain a five-year program.[6]

Capital improvements in a government budget are governmental projects such as municipal buildings, parking lots, cultural institutions, parks, public-private partnerships, such as sports stadiums, and any private project that might be leveraged by public infrastructure improvements. A capital project is the acquisition or improvement of facilities, equipment, or services that are major expenditures and have a useful life of two or more years. The cost of an item and how often it needs to be replaced are the primary criteria used to define a capital project. The Government Finance Officers Association recommends a life span of three years or more for an item to be classified as non-recurring, or not purchased every year.[7] Examples of items usually classified as capital projects include libraries, schools, fire engines, bulldozers, government buildings, treatment plants, landfills, and water and sewer lines. Some *gray area* projects are difficult to classify because they meet only one of the criteria used to identify a capital project. An example would be police cars that cost $15,000 each but need to be replaced yearly because of constant use. Cost qualifies them as capital projects, but annual replacement classifies them as operating expenditures.

A CIP is an important fiscal planning tool that helps a locality replace or repair existing major facilities and meet new capital-improvement needs. The process helps localities select projects where the need is most pressing and identify projects that have a low overall priority. A CIP is a tool for planning future facility needs for a community. It is a detailed plan, usually covering five years, which lists the recommended capital projects for the community. Frequently, the purchase of capital projects will impact the timing, type, location, and density of land uses in a community. The development of a CIP requires a team effort by local officials and citizens. In states with strong county government, a planning commission or county planning agency will oversee the development of a CIP. In home-rule states, localities across the state will adopt a process to develop a CIP.

The CIP includes an inventory of facilities that lists the fixed, capital assets that are owned or leased by the local government. Buildings, parks, parking lots, and other real estate holdings should be shown on a map, as well as vacant and abandoned properties. Requests for capital projects include replacement and expansion or repair of existing facilities and equipment. Data should be collected on the following types of projects: projects completed during the current fiscal year, ongoing projects for which appropriations should continue, and projects to be canceled.[8] Project requests are based on guidelines for eligible capital projects, according to the governing body of the community. The engineering, financial, and planning staff can provide assistance in completing project request forms. Outside agencies and experts such as the planning district commission and appropriate state agencies or private-sector architects, engineers, and contractors may provide valuable data on future capital needs.

A financial analysis is prepared to predict the costs for general operations in the ensuing five years and to assess the availability of funds for approved capital projects. To accomplish this task, revenues and expenditures for the preceding five years are analyzed and historical trends and patterns identified. Projections are based on the historical trends and expectations about future events. To determine net cash flow, subtract operating expenditures from operating revenues. The financial program involves matching the processed capital projects with available financial resources. It also determines the best methods of paying for proposed projects and distributing payments to help maintain stable local tax rates.

The program coordinator reviews the project requests for compliance with the guidelines set by the governing body and feasibility and consistency with the comprehensive plan. All proposed projects should be reviewed by the planning commission and other financial managers and evaluated and ranked for inclusion in the CIP. The planning commission should hold at least one public hearing on the CIP, which may be a joint hearing with the governing body. After the commission has received public input and made any desired modifications, CIP proposals are recommended to the governing body. Before adopting the CIP, the governing body must hold at least one public hearing and make any changes that seem appropriate.

The capital budget is the vehicle for financing the CIP proposals. It is a one-year funding plan for the purchase of capital projects based on the first year of a five-year CIP. The capital budget is adopted in the same way as the operating budget in most states. The CIP and capital budget are updated annually. Steps in the update process include preparing status reports on previously approved projects; revising the financial analysis; identifying, reviewing, and ranking new projects; and reevaluating projects that are in the CIP from previous years. The program coordinator usually assigns the department heads to carry out these functions.

Scheduling of projects is based on their priority and the availability of financing. Programming begins with a summary of the proposed capital projects, scheduling, and financing. Scheduling determines the timing of each project in the five-year program. Highest-priority projects should be scheduled as early as possible, depending on financing and other factors such as phasing or mandates. The most appropriate financing method must be determined for each project proposal by considering the following objectives: maintaining stable tax rates and user charges, maintaining an acceptable balance between debt service and current expenditures, and making judicious use of outside sources of funding. Project scheduling may have to be adjusted after financing methods have been determined. For example, a lower-priority project may be scheduled before a priority project because financing for the higher-priority project is not available or because financing may be lost if the lower-priority project is not begun immediately.

The final phase of the CIP process is implementation. Once the governing body approves the CIP, it can be used as a basis for preparing the capital budget, which should be based on the first year of the CIP. Since the capital budget is enacted in the same manner as is the annual operating budget, the goal should be to adopt the capital and operating budgets at the same time. A monitoring system to review the CIP and capital budget should be established to accommodate any required changes. The financing for capital projects may be complex, and sometimes projects may not be completed on schedule due to delays in bidding procedures, construction, legal activities, or site selection. In addition, entirely new projects may be requested that demand immediate action. As community needs and desires undergo change, so do financial resources and political priorities.

The following case study of the Santa Clara County Strategic Plan is an example of a community that dealt effectively with problem-oriented plans within a regional context.

When planners began investigating the planning issues in Silicon Valley, California, in the early 1990s, they found that the major concern was the homeless population and related problems of the homeless. Due to California's Proposition 13, which limits property tax increases, the residents of the valley feared that low-income people would be without adequate services. The specific planning issues and problems that surfaced at public forums were lack of training for low-income people in high-technology jobs, shortage of affordable housing in the area, and traffic congestion from incoming residents. Based on these planning concerns, the Santa Clara County Strategic Vision Program set out to develop a plan to solve the problems. The goal of the program was to address each specific planning issue and recommend action plans to solve the housing and employment problems. While the planning team dealt with the strategic plans, there was a conscious effort to integrate the plans within the environmental, social, and economic systems of the entire Silicon Valley.

The steering committees that conducted forums to hear public sentiment were made up of more than one hundred community, government, and business leaders. They were divided into groups that addressed a certain area of the research that was needed for the strategic planning. The goals were aligned with strategies from the meetings.

The result of the meetings was a series of reports incorporated into a document, *Vision for Change*. According to this document, future demographic patterns would show increased age and diversity in cultural groups. By 2010, the 1.5 million residents will be an equal mix of Hispanics, whites, and Asians, and many incoming residents will have lower incomes and higher birthrates. Therefore, the strategic plans focused on education, job training, and services for these minorities. For example, the report states that many young people may be unprepared for high-technology jobs because of limited educational opportunities and poor health. But the county's economy depends on the success of its high-tech firms, which in turn depend on the availability of highly skilled workers.

The roundtable on families and children recommended action programs for health and social services and early learning opportunities. It also recommended comprehensive family-support systems that would be organized around after-school, extended activities. Members of the roundtable on the economy suggested lifelong learning programs and the establishment of continuing education to retrain the workforce in high-tech jobs. These suggestions led to tangible results. In 1993 the county United Way and a local foundation formed the Children and Family Collaborative. The collaborative set priorities and allocated funds in accordance with the strategic plan. The Santa Clara Valley Manufacturing Group, a trade organization whose members include large high-tech firms such as Apple Computer and Sun Microsystems, formed Workforce Silicon Valley (WSV). Incorporated as a nonprofit group in 1993, WSV helps educators remain current with the needs of employers and finds county high school students internships and work-related experience. The manufacturing group also organized an advocacy group, the Housing Action Coalition, to push local communities to approve affordable housing schemes. Approximately forty-eight hundred units of moderately priced housing have been approved as a result of the group's efforts.

Housing shortages have also increased homelessness in the valley. Approximately thirteen thousand to twenty thousand residents were homeless at least once during the 1990s, and 43 percent of them were eighteen or younger, according to county figures. These figures prompted the quality-of-life roundtable to deal with the housing issues. It recommended higher-density housing in urban areas and a more flexible transportation system to meet the changing needs of the job force. This group also recommended that county officials manage growth to protect natural resources.

Many of these strategies have been integrated into the county's master plan. A fundamental part of this plan, adopted in December 1994, is compact development. The aim of compact development is to focus growth in existing urban areas, especially along transit corridors and near employment centers, rather than on peripheral hillsides and suburban areas.

In 2001 the Santa Clara County Board of Supervisors approved an updated plan for homelessness for the region. The Santa Clara County California Countywide Five-Year Homelessness Continuum of Care Plan 2001–2006 aims to develop a comprehensive system of affordable housing and support services for homeless people in Santa Clara County. The goal of the program is to end homelessness in the area. Action plans have been developed for outreach, information technology, housing, job training, support services, and overall administration of the county's Continuum of Care System. The action steps include making connections with communities through outreach and information technology, building homes, and creating a successful, stable workforce. Programs have been developed to generate wellness and provide the necessities of life and maintain vitality of the Continuum of Care Plan.[9]

The Santa Clara County Strategic Plan is an example of strategic, integrative planning at work. Each strategic plan was related to the overall regional plan for the valley. In this way the phasing in of the action programs could be correlated with the necessary facilities and support services. The integrative process is effective because cross representation of the community ensures support of implementation of the action programs. For example, job training and retraining in high-tech fields to support the economic base of the region is proactive, or anticipatory, planning. Proactive planning is more effective than reactive planning, in which planners only respond to crises in city and town planning. Preparing the job force in employment skills that are directly related to area business and industry anticipates future needs of the region.

CONCLUSION

Urban design and capital-improvement-facility plans are integral parts of a community-development problem-oriented plan. Building on the elements of urban design, circulation patterns, and capital improvements, the planner shapes the city form.

Discussion Box

What are some of the urban-design or revitalization issues that your downtown is facing? Do you have many empty storefronts? Do you have many vacant lots? What design elements would you choose to revitalize your downtown? What capital facilities does your community need for the future? What principles of smart growth do you think would improve your community? What principles do you think your community would support?

PLANNING EXERCISE 8:
A CENTRAL BUSINESS DISTRICT INVENTORY

This exercise teaches you how to develop an inventory of businesses and vacant buildings for an urban business area. A current inventory is the beginning stage for an effective revitalization plan for a central business district (CBD). Each group will be assigned a section of the CBD for an inventory analysis, and at the end of the data-collection phase each group will present its findings to the class.

A CBD inventory is a list and map showing the type of businesses that are in the downtown, as well as the location of vacant lots and buildings. The data needed for a CBD inventory are current and projected statistics on the businesses by type in the downtown. The sources for the data are the current existing business inventories from the planning department and updated fieldwork. The following steps explain the process in developing a land-use inventory for the CBD:

- Review the most recent inventory and maps of businesses, vacant buildings, and vacant lots in the downtown.
- Conduct fieldwork by first drawing a boundary around your assigned section of the downtown area on the map provided. The *work map* is a blank map showing the footing and placement of the current existent buildings (see the top portion of the existent land-use map). Second, fill in the appropriate symbols of the land-use type as indicated in the legend in the existent land-

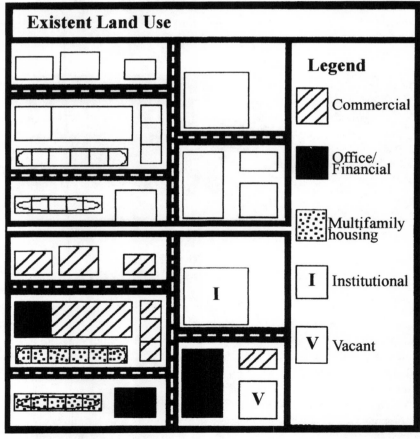

Figure 8.1   Existent Land Use

use map. The bottom map shows the completed updated CBD inventory with the appropriate symbols.

- Finally, note your impressions of the downtown. Does it seem like the businesses are thriving? Are there a lot of vacant lots between buildings? Is there a balanced mix of businesses? What is missing? Informally ask members of the downtown businesses for their opinions about the vitality of the downtown.

NOTES

1. Jon T. Lang, *Urban Design: The American Experience* (New York: Von Nostrand Reinhold, 1994).

2. Richard Hedman, *Fundamentals of Urban Design* (Washington, D.C.: Planners Press, 1984).

3. Ian Bentley, *Urban Transformations: Power, People and Urban Design* (New York: Routledge, 1999).

4. Christopher Alexander, *A New Theory of Urban Design* (New York: Oxford University Press, 1987).

5. Retrieved May 17, 2004, from www.greatbuildings.com/architects/Bernini.html.

6. Charles J. Hoch, Linda C. Dalton, and Frank S. So, eds., *The Practice of Local Government Planning* (Washington, D.C.: International City/County Management Association, 2000).

7. Avrom Bendavid-Val, *Regional and Local Economic Analysis for Practitioners* (New York: Praeger, 1983).

8. Bendavid-Val, *Regional and Local.*

9. Retrieved May 8, 2004, from www.endhomelessness.org/localplans/santaclara.pdf.

Chapter Nine

Historic-Site Preservation and Revitalization

Historic-site preservation is a key factor in revitalization plans for an area. Developing a historic-site-preservation problem-oriented plan involves identifying buildings or cultural or historic sites that meet the criteria for protection. Links between the historic sites should be connected to open space and natural-resource areas in the community and tourist areas. A tool for protecting historic buildings is the adaptive-reuse technique. This tool should be suggested as an option when a building is in good condition and in a good location. Incentives may be offered to encourage developers to rehabilitate a building for a new use, thus protecting the building, as well as creating a new amenity for the municipality. For example, rehabilitating an old mill into boutiques and condos such as was done in Lowell, Massachusetts, addresses the issue of the abandoned building and creates a magnet building for the revitalization plan for a whole block in the city. Adaptive reuse has become a powerful tool for economic stimulation in business improvement districts (BIDs) and empowerment zones. Change can be a positive thing when adaptive reuse is applied to buildings currently bringing down the real estate value and tourist draw for an area.

HISTORIC-SITE PRESERVATION

Federal involvement in historic-site preservation in the United States has been shaped by several major pieces of legislation. The Antiquities Act of 1906 offers protection for prehistoric and historic sites located on federal properties. The Historic Sites Act of 1935 established a national policy of preserving historic properties of national significance for public use and inspiration. The secretary of the interior, acting through the National Park Service, was given the power to survey, document, evaluate, acquire, and preserve archeological and historic sites throughout the country.

The mandate to protect historic sites was expanded with the National Historic Preservation Act of 1966, which called for the preservation of historic properties of state, local, and national significance. The secretary of the interior was authorized to establish the National Register of Historic Places to list districts, sites, buildings, structures, and objects significant in American history, architecture, archeology, engineering, and culture. The secretary also grants funds to assist the states in preparing comprehensive surveys of such properties within their jurisdiction. Programs for matching grants for preservation activities in each of the states, as well as National Trust funding, were also authorized. Title II of the act created the Advisory Council on Historic Preservation to review and advise the president and Congress on federal actions related to preservation. The National Park Service created guidelines for archeological and historic-site preservation that incorporated previous preservation legislation.

The importance of federal participation in preservation activities was further emphasized by Executive Order 11593, signed May 13, 1971, which states that "the federal government shall provide leadership in protecting, restoring and maintaining the historic and cultural environment of the nation."[1] Federal agencies were directed to inventory and nominate historic properties under their jurisdiction that appeared to qualify for the National Register. Specific criteria have been established to guide the states, federal agencies, local governments, the public, and the secretary of interior in evaluating entries for inclusion. The criteria focus on the quality or significance of the site in relation to American history, architecture, archeology, engineering, and culture. Historic significance may be present in districts, sites, buildings, and structures. Objects that possess integrity of location, design, setting, materials, workmanship, feeling, and are associated with events that have made a significant contribution to the broad patterns of our history also qualify for inclusion. Finally, historic sites that are associated with the lives of persons significant in our past or that embody the distinctive characteristics of a type, period, or method of construction that represents the work of a master or possesses high artistic values should be considered.

A historic resource may be an Indian burial ground, a row of sea captains' houses in Newburyport, Massachusetts, Monticello in Virginia, or the Alamo. Natural areas such as seashores that include cultural significance may be protected. The town of Truro on Cape Cod is protected as a national park area. Other natural districts include historic skyline rights such as over Grand Central Station in New York City and historic-ruins protection areas such as the White House ruins in Canyon de Chelly on the Navajo Indian Reservation in

This historic district of Victorian houses protects the integrity of the neighborhood.

Arizona. It may be of value to the nation as a whole or important only to the community in which it is located.

The secretary of the interior is authorized to expand and maintain the National Register of Historic Places. The secretary, in consultation with national historic and archeological associations, establishes and revises criteria for properties to be included on the National Register and for National Historic Landmarks. The secretary provides for the designation and appointment of a state historic preservation officer (SHPO) by the governor of each state to establish a program to locate, inventory, and nominate all properties that appear to qualify for inclusion in the National Register. The SHPO designates a qualified state historic preservation review board and provides for adequate public participation in the review process to recommend and nominate properties to the National Register. After the process is completed and notice is given that the property has been approved, the property is officially registered.[2]

The National Historic Preservation Act Amendments of 1980 require each federal agency to ensure that any registered property is not inadvertently transferred, sold, demolished, substantially altered, or allowed to deteriorate significantly. Once the property is registered, tax provisions go into effect. The Economic Recovery Tax Act of 1981 provides several stipulations for tax credits and savings. The act includes a 25 percent investment tax credit for rehabilitation of historic commercial, industrial, and rental residential buildings that can be combined with a fifteen-year cost-recovery period for the adjusted basis of the historic building.[3]

An Advisory Council on Historic Preservation ensures the proper evaluation of actions involving federal, federally assisted, or federally licensed projects that affect properties listed or determined to be eligible for listing in the National Register. The advisory council is made up of representatives from the public, experts in the disciplines related to historic-site preservation, and heads of the departments of interior, agriculture, and other associated federal agencies.

HISTORIC-SITE PRESERVATION TOOLS

The identification of historic properties provides the data necessary to develop preservation plans. Special zoning overlays and districts can be recommended once the historic area has been delineated, surveyed, and accepted for inclusion in the National Register. Zoning variances, easements, or deed restrictions can be enacted through design guidelines and restrictions when historic sites are threatened with development or demolition. The following tools can be used for historic-site-preservation problem-oriented plans to refurbish buildings:

* Restoration: Restoration involves returning the building to its original condition. It is the most conservative and authentic form of historic preservation. It is also the most costly in terms of obtaining and replacing components of a building with new, authentic materials. Examples of restoration include Old Deerfield, Massachusetts, the restored historic area where the Deerfield Massacre took place in the early 1700s. Old Deerfield includes many of the original homes and cottage-industry buildings and is open for tours. Working museums include Williamsburg, Virginia, and Sturbridge, Massachusetts.
* Rehabilitation and renovation: *Rehabbed*, or renovated, structures are adapted, or changed for safety and maintenance purposes. In some cases the exterior is refaced to the original and the interior is modernized. Unlike restoration, where the buildings return to their original state, rehabbed buildings may be renovated for a different use. Examples of adaptive-reuse buildings are Ghiradelli Square in San Francisco, which is a renovated structure that used to be a chocolate factory and now contains shops and boutiques, and Faneuil Hall in Boston, which used to be a farmers market and now is an area of restaurants and waterfront shops. In New England many of the old abandoned textile mills of the beginning of the twentieth century have been renovated and are now boutiques and

condominiums. The Lowell Mills in Lowell, Massachusetts, is a full-scale renovated project consisting of a museum, condominiums, restaurants, and boutiques. This project was funded as an urban park. Other old mills in Holyoke, Massachusetts, and Manchester, New Hampshire, for example, desperately need renovation.

Stebbins Brassworks factory is a reuse project in which a brass factory was renovated into an office building.

- Replication: When a building or structure has symbolic importance, especially for tourist purposes, planners may want to recommend imitation, or replication. This historic-site-preservation technique requires plank-by-plank imitation of the original. The structures, at least for the exteriors, are authentic reproductions. The interiors may be modernized for comfort and safety. Usually replication is recommended for buildings that represent a historic event or cultural period in the nation's history. The London Bridge in Lake Havasu City, Arizona, with its dramatic connection to the Thames River in Great Britain, is in sharp contrast with the desert surroundings. On the other hand, covered bridges in Vermont, which have been replicated, blend in with the countryside. Mark Twain's lighthouse in New Orleans, Louisiana, is a focal point on the Mississippi River Walk, welcoming visitors to authentic riverboat tours. The purpose of each structure is to recreate a symbol of historic significance and act as a beacon in a tourist area.
- Conservation: Conservation of structures involves preserving what exists to save the building from razing. A planner should recommend conservation when an area is slated for revitalization and a structure that exists has some relevance to the history of the community or some cultural meaning to a certain group of people. If the building is found to be structurally sound, a conservation recommendation could be integrated into the revitalization problem-oriented plan for the area.
- Relocation: Sometimes planners recommend that a building be moved to another area. In this case the character of the building is important to the community in some way, but the area where it currently exists is being razed for a major planning project. This often happens because of major highway construction. In Phoenix, Arizona, in the mid 1980s, the Squaw Peak Highway project took several blocks of the South Phoenix area by eminent domain. Several historic homes and businesses that had relevance to the history and culture of Phoenix were included in these neighborhoods. A decision was made to relocate the historic homes to a designated part of the city that was not going to be affected by the highway. In this way the relocated buildings became a historic block, with a brochure for a walking trail to visit each home. Although the homes are no longer in their characteristic setting, the relocation technique can preserve a piece of the heritage of a city.[4]
- Façades: Saving façades (*façadectomies*) is a tool that preserves the façade although the rest of the building is demolished. Historic-site-preservation supporters usually totally discount this as a preservation tool, but advocates of architectural vibrancy often defend its use if a building cannot otherwise be saved. From a broader perspective, there is much debate over the importance of historic-site preservation versus architectural integrity and vibrancy. It can be argued that architectural compatibility is as important as preserva-

tion, perhaps much more so. For example, the Transamerica building is such a strong anchor because it does not pretend to be an old building, but it provides the same type of focus that an older building can.

URBAN RENEWAL

The first housing act in the United States was a general housing bill introduced in Congress in 1946. It was to be a broad legislative base for a national housing and redevelopment program but failed in Congress. The second bill, the Housing Act of 1949, extended and broadened private-housing programs of the Federal Housing Administration. The goals of the Housing Act were to eliminate substandard and blighted areas, stimulate housing production and community development, provide a decent home for every American family, support public-housing programs, implement urban development plans by awarding loans for land acquisition, and issue subsidies to lower land costs.[5] The underlying priorities of the Housing Act were to rebuild our cities, clear up physical decay and blight, and set up government assistance programs with planning administrators. The rationale behind the Housing Act was to remove the heavy demands on taxpayers for the cost of maintaining obsolete cities.

Congress intended to eliminate blighted areas by sponsoring programs to clean up and revitalize urban neighborhoods. It was a public action against slums, and the programs that were designed and implemented to eradicate slums were large scale and widespread. Incentive programs to develop new housing projects, as well as social and cultural centers, were instituted. The focus of the legislation was on providing housing units for low-income families. Since the demographics of the major cities showed that most poor in the inner cities were black, it was understood that urban renewal would serve an overwhelming majority of black people. Much of the literature concerning city revitalization during this era focuses on the theory that in many cities officials were biased when they declared areas blighted. Many urban theorists and sociologists believed that city officials would target black neighborhoods and label them *grant renewal areas*. By doing this, the blighted areas would become revitalization areas, and the minorities who lived in these areas would be relocated.

The following steps describe the urban-renewal process:

1. Land acquisition: The area that is declared blighted and slated for urban renewal is taken by eminent domain.
2. Relocation: The law requires that residents in areas that are deemed urban-renewal areas must be relocated satisfactorily. The residents by law are to

be relocated to comparable housing in their neighborhood or another part of the city if the urban-renewal project does not provide enough housing units. A renewal project in the West End of Boston, for example, displaced thousands of people during the 1950s. Unfortunately, displaced Italians did not find their new housing suitable and desperately missed the culture of their old neighborhood. They missed the closeness of the community and the respect they had for their homes that they displayed each year when they placed a geranium on their *stoops*, small front porches, to usher in summer. Many sociologists, foremost among them Herbert Gans who studied the Italians in the West End, have researched displaced groups. Since the pride and association of extended families and friends are interwoven into the lives of these people, the findings of the sociologists in many cases indicate discontent with the breakdown of cultural ties and bonds resulting from relocation.[6]

3. Site clearance: The site of an urban-renewal project is completely razed— the buildings demolished and the landscaping cleared. Infrastructure lines, such as water and sewer, are mapped and noted. Dredging and movement of soil to eliminate slopes is carried out across the site.

4. Site improvements and supporting facilities: At this stage the existent infrastructure lines are compared with the lines needed for the new project. Upgraded lines, extensions, and new lines are constructed. A plan for utility needs and support services for the new project is implemented.

5. Disposition of improved land: When the infrastructure is in place to support the incoming project, a request for proposals (RFP) is made. Contractors reply to RFPs to receive consideration in a competition for the contract to develop. The contractors bid, or submit a breakdown of expenses, detailing how much each part of a job would cost. For example, developers itemize their costs for materials, labor, and added expenses. The government awards the contract to the contractor with the winning proposal.

6. New construction: The final stage in the urban-renewal process involves the construction of the project. All the construction projects are redevelopment. The timing of the project will depend on the federal awarding of the grants.[7]

Whatever the intent of Congress, the final outcome of many urban-renewal projects was not what was originally foreseen. Urban planners who have studied the impacts of urban-renewal projects have concluded that urban renewal to a great extent has failed in what it started out to do, which was to stimulate housing production and community development. Many sociologists and urban planners believe that the serious social-welfare issues, including drug and crime problems, are directly related to the high-rise projects that have been built. With high levels of unemployment contributing to behavior problems, there is also a great need to develop job training programs as components of community-development problem-oriented plans.

In 1954 there was a shift from redevelopment and clearance to rehabilitation. The 1960 Housing Act included a provision for the rehabilitation of housing projects. Local agencies could purchase individual dwelling units and remodel and sell them to private owners. Each project was limited to fifty units or not more than 2 percent of the total units in any renewal project. The 1960 Housing Act included a new planning component called the Workable Program. This program called for local agencies to develop an action plan for renewal that included an overall community program for the removal of slums and blight. The Workable Program specifically outlined codes and ordinances and a comprehensive community plan that were required to receive a grant. The codes and ordinances section outlined required building standards to prevent the deterioration of housing. Standards for construction included structural strength, fire-safety materials, and proper plumbing, electrical, and heating installations. Other standards included regulations to prevent overcrowding and provisions for basic sanitary facilities, lighting, and ventilation.

There were several planning requirements under the Workable Program. The first requirement was for a plan projecting future land-use needs. The plan would show the location and extent of areas to be used for residential, commercial, and industrial purposes. The second requirement was for a thoroughfare plan that would provide for a system of existing and proposed major streets. The third requirement was for a community-facilities plan that would show the location and type of current and proposed schools, recreation areas, and public facilities.

The fourth requirement was for a public-improvements program that would have recommendations for future public facilities. The fifth requirement was for a zoning ordinance and map, in which the zoning districts would be clearly marked according to the use of land. Finally, the Workable Program required a subdivision regulation plan. This plan would detail standards for adequate lot sizes and arrangements, utilities, and street improvements.

Essentially, the Workable Program added a neighborhood-analysis component that was missing up until 1960. The focus of the neighborhood analysis is to assess the needs of neighborhoods according to the demographics of the residents. The demographic statistics, which are broken down into age, gender, and ethnic groupings, show population trends from which neighborhood needs may be predicted. A steady increase in the elderly, for example, would indicate to the planner that housing and facilities to support the elderly need to be developed.

The neighborhood analysis is a thorough, overall assessment of the neighborhood. The stipulations in a neighborhood plan include:

• Delineation of residential areas into neighborhoods: Determine neighborhood boundaries by holding focus sessions and asking the residents where they live, shop, and play. Where are the edges of the neighborhood? What groups are included within the boundaries? Develop a point map, and it will be clear how to draw the boundaries for the neighborhood.
• Determination of location, extent, and intensity of blight: Based on statistics of poverty levels and the number of units below code, the most blighted areas are earmarked for funding for rehabilitation.
• Analysis of needed upgrades and projected maintenance costs: A condition survey, which includes criteria to evaluate housing and buildings, shows units needing immediate repair and those that might need slight improvement. A unit not meeting code, for example, indicates a need for an itemized cost list for necessary plumbing and electrical work. The condition survey enables the planners to set a schedule indicating the order in which the projects should be developed. The timing of the development can be related to infrastructure improvements and the extension of utility lines.
• Recommendations for actions required to meet neighborhood needs: This part of the plan includes specific actions for code enforcement, public improvements, conservation, clearance, and rehabilitation.[8]

The 1960 Housing Act set up an administrative organization for local government departments and agencies to become involved in planning. The act required communities to set up interdepartmental committees to oversee the enforcement of housing and neighborhood plans. The act also required enforcement of codes for appropriate financing and technical assistance for developing housing plans. The capital outlay expenditures, distributed over a five- to six-year period, fall under a fiscal program coordinated by the planners. The Housing Act also includes two parts that relate directly to the residents of the neighborhood under study. One part includes relocation assistance for housing for displaced families. Another part of the act stipulates that citizen participation is required in the planning process. Public hearings and forums have to be held or funding will not be awarded.

In 1965 all housing agencies consolidated within the Department of Housing and Urban Development (HUD). With this new federal-level administration of housing programs came a national impetus to create large-scale renewal projects. President Lyndon Johnson enacted the Model Cities and Metropolitan Development Act in 1966. The purpose of the Model Cities program was to create and fund demonstration programs in thirteen specified cities, which would become examples for other cities to follow.[9] Programs related to social services, education, urban land use and development, and employment were coordinated under the federal umbrella. Unfortunately, several major problems arose in the distribution of funds for these programs. Due to the massive infusion of monies, many cases involving fraud and embezzlement occurred. Accusations were made that contracts and funds were distributed illegally and unethically, and in some cases the thoroughness and completion of jobs were contested.

Another problem that has developed over the years with HUD funding is the allegations of political favoritism. In several cities, politicians and city officials have been indicted for awarding funds to political favorites, rather than the lowest or most reliable bidder in the construction industry in the area. Finally, the scale of HUD projects has become a major problem. It is very difficult to coordinate specific programs from a central office in Washington. Continuous monitoring of program objectives and implementation strategies must occur at the local level. Because of the problems that have occurred with HUD and the federal urban-renewal program, recent trends indicate that lawmakers and planners favor problem-oriented, strategic grants for revitalization and housing plans.

Community Development Block Grants (CDBGs) are awarded for a small, focused plan such as a façade study that would provide funds for a street section to renovate the exterior of the buildings. For entitlement cities, the central cities of metropolitan statistical areas, and most cities over fifty thousand, large pots of CDBG monies come to communities to spend with a huge amount of discretion. The money may be spent for housing, jobs, infrastructure, and public services, as long as the programs primarily benefit low- and moderate-income residents. CDBGs are essentially the only competitive grants for smaller communities. The funds must be obtained from the community's respective state under the small-cities program. Title VIII under the CDBG program is funding that is awarded for housing for the elderly. A more extensive discussion of CDBGs is in chapter 11.

In 1993 the Clinton administration created Home Ownership for People Everywhere (HOPE) VI, which was established under HUD to eradicate severely distressed public housing. Since its inception, $5.4 billion has been allocated to 114 cities nationwide to replace dilapidated housing with new neighborhoods. In the 1990s the Boston Housing Authority (BHA), for example, received $79.9 million to transform the crime-ridden, blighted Roxbury developments of Mission Main and Orchard Park into affordable apartments. These projects acted as a catalyst for the revitalization of nearby Dudley Square, where new shops, an office building, and the $30 million Orchard Gardens K–8 school have recently been built.

In terms of urban-design patterns, site designers have been turning to several innovative techniques to create affordable housing in the early 2000s. Affordable-housing techniques include (1) zero lot line, which eliminates backyard and side-yard space; (2) cluster development, which places houses in dense groups leaving open space in another part of the development; (3) planned-unit development (PUD), which is clustered development on a larger scale with some mixed commercial, recreational, or office use; (4) rural farm housing, which is cooperative housing where more than one family share a house; (5) manufactured housing, which is housing mass produced in sections and shipped to the site for construction; and (6) transit-oriented development and general increases in urban density.

GENTRIFICATION

Gentrification is the process of rehabilitating a neighborhood by upgrading the existent housing and other building stock. From the outset it must be emphasized that gentrification usually has negative connotations among urban planners and residents. Investment in low-income areas and rehabilitation are often seen as improvements, but once poor people are displaced *gentrification* denotes harmful effects.

Unlike urban renewal, in the gentrification process houses and buildings are renovated rather than razed. Urban renewal is redevelopment, whereas gentrification is rehabilitation. There are two primary factors considered in the decision to gentrify, or redevelop, an area. The first factor is location. Favorable-location characteristics for gentrification include easy accessibility to main transportation routes, the availability of support services such as shopping and banking, and nearness to institutional facilities, cultural centers, and amenities. Since city residents want to be part of the pulse of the city and near amenities, they generally support improving an area through gentrification.[10] Two classic examples of gentrification are Beacon Hill in Boston and Knob Hill in San Francisco. In both cases the gentrified section is a coveted, centrally located area that offers access to the most acclaimed cultural activities.

The second factor in gentrification is the condition of the housing stock. The housing stock needs to be in good condition to undergo gentrification. Gentrification is rehabilitation rather than new building as in redevelopment. The decision to gentrify an area is based on the potential for upgrading the existent housing stock and, in many cases, following strict historic-site-preservation techniques to maintain the historic integrity of the neighborhood.[11]

Gentrification in some cases upgrades an area to the extent that lower-income residents can no longer afford to live and shop in the area.

The intent of gentrification, which is to improve and rehabilitate an area, may have damaging effects on the original residents. When housing and facilities are upgraded, rents in gentrified areas escalate to pay for the improvements. Many people are forced to move because they cannot afford the higher rents. As in urban renewal, the displaced residents suffer an unplanned, unwanted move to another part of the city. As real estate values escalate, the increasing stature of the neighborhood becomes known across the region.

This cycle continues as more financially elite move into the area, and the reputation of the gentrified area becomes more and more prestigious.

BROWNFIELDS

The Brownfields Prevention Initiative was established under the Resource Conservation and Recovery Act (RCRA) in June 1998. Much of the focus of brownfields programs, even those funded with federal money, is for brownfields that are not necessarily in the RCRA system. Many states have their own brownfields programs, both in terms of regulating contamination and funding reuse.

The primary goal of the Brownfields Prevention Initiative is to encourage clean up and long-term sustainable reuse of potential brownfield sites through redevelopment into productive commercial or residential sites or greenspace. A brownfield site is a parcel of land in which redevelopment or reuse is prohibited by the presence or possible presence of a hazardous substance, pollution, or contamination. The Environmental Protection Agency (EPA) is promoting the reuse of industrial sites rather than using valuable farmland or other *greenfields* for economic development. The Brownfields Prevention Initiative benefits a community in the following ways: contaminated areas are cleaned up; areas blighted by brownfields are revitalized; greenfields that otherwise would be developed are preserved; and the overall greenspace in the community is maintained, and in some cases increased.

The mission of the Brownfields Prevention Initiative under the EPA is to empower communities and other interested stakeholders to work together in an efficient manner to prevent, assess, safely clean up, and reuse brownfields in a sustainable manner. The initiative provides that eligible entities may apply for grants through EPA regional offices and that the EPA establish a competitive system for awarding grants. The applicants that earn the highest ratings receive awards. Grants cover funding to inventory, assess, and organize community involvement related to a brownfield site. Revolving loan-fund grants provide funding to carry out cleanup activities at a brownfield site.[12]

The planning process for brownfield cleanups requires a team approach, with representatives of the community on the planning committee. Consensus is reached on what options would serve the community, and the committee carries out and monitors the action plans. Site redevelopment for brownfields includes industrial reuse, commercial development, or wildlife habitat restoration. In January 2002 President George W. Bush signed into law the Brownfields Revitalization Act, which authorizes annual funds for brownfields grants, including cleanup of low-risk petroleum contamination. The 2002 Brownfields Revitalization Act expanded the use of federal brownfields grants to petroleum-contaminated sites for the first time. In the past sites could be mixed waste but not just petroleum. The act provides funds for cleanup for the first time. In the past funds were for assessments only. More importantly, the act provides a safety net for certain innocent purchases of contaminated properties and properties down gradient from contaminated sites.

CASE STUDY: WASHINGTON, D.C.

The Historic Division of Washington, D.C., assists in applying for a D.C. building permit for any building that may be designated a historic property. The Historic Preservation Review Board, under the city's preservation law, determines whether changes to historic landmarks and historic districts are appropriate. The Revitalization Division of the Office of Planning has four major goals: revitalize neighborhoods, restore economic health, create a world-class waterfront, and encourage a diverse and dynamic downtown.

The Revitalization Division focuses on the areas of neighborhood strategic-planning and economic-revitalization planning. The goal of the neighborhood strategic planning team is to assist District residents and businesses to develop action plans to preserve historic properties for each of the thirty-nine neighborhood clusters in the District. They follow the problem-oriented plan approach. First, neighborhood priorities are identified. Next, a needs assessment is conducted, and the action plans are drawn up to meet the needs of the neighborhoods. Neighborhood-planning coordinators work with the neighborhood groups to develop targeted revitalization efforts, which will fit into the revitalization master plan for the whole city.

The goal of the economic-revitalization team is to develop strategies for economic development. The team works with focus groups to identify needs, explain alternatives, and integrate innovative renovation and restoration techniques into the final designs. The economic revitalization planners have worked on the following projects: the Anacostia Waterfront Initiative, the Georgia Avenue Revitalization Plan, the East of the River Revitalization Plan, and the Downtown Action Plan. The Planning and Design Information Technical (PDIT) division provides statistical data, computer-aided design (CAD), maps, graphic designs, and multimedia to the Office of Planning and other District agencies.

CONCLUSION

The main point of this chapter is to show that the housing programs that planners have dealt with in the past in the United States have drawbacks. When planning for the future, historic-site-preservation problem-oriented plans that focus on a strategic area of study will be more effective in rehabilitating an area. The most effective way to plan for diverse communities is to consider what facilities are needed in the future by all the groups in a neighborhood.

Discussion Box

Do you have many historic properties or a historic district in your community? Are there historic sites that you think should be investigated for historic inclusion? Develop an inventory of old buildings, mills, and historic sites in your community and think about the tools you could use to rehabilitate or redevelop the area.

PLANNING EXERCISE 9: A REDEVELOPMENT PLANNING PROBLEM

Each group will be given a *work map* of a small section of the college downtown. We will be repeating the process that we followed in developing a condition survey in planning exercise 6. This time the buildings are commercial, industrial, multifamily, institutional, and vacant. The following steps are involved in a condition survey for the downtown:

- First, review the zoning for your designated area and identify the specifics about this zoning district in the zoning ordinance for the community. What is its zone designation? What are the dimensions and so on for this zone?
- Now note the condition of the downtown. Are the buildings sound? Are slight improvements needed? Or are the buildings dilapidated? Are there any historic buildings? Follow the legend that designates the criteria for structural conditions in planning exercise 6, and fill in the appropriate symbols on the *work map:*
  - Sound: Overall good condition (roof, good condition; paint, good, no peeling; windows, good, no cracks; no chipped caulking)
  - Minor repairs needed: Roof in need of minor shingle repairs; some paint chipping; few windows cracked
  - Major repairs needed: Roof needs total replacement; building needs total paint job; windows need upgrading
  - Dilapidated: Building unoccupied for long period of time; overall condition poor; does not meet code
- Now go to the assessor's office in city hall and request a printout of the value of the buildings on your assigned block. A comparison of the values

from each group shows which parts of the CBD may offer more incentives for redevelopment due to lower real estate value and taxes.

NOTES

1. Retrieved May 10, 2004, from www.gpoaccess.gov/fr.

2. Retrieved May 16, 2004, from www2.cr.nps.gov/laws/NHPA1966.htm.

3. Fritz W. Wagner, Timothy E. Joder, and Anthony J. Mumphrey, *Urban Revitalization: Policies and Programs* (Thousand Oaks, Calif.: Sage Publications, 1995).

4. John Pierson and Joan Smith, *Rebuilding Community: Policy and Practice in Urban Regeneration* (New York: Palgrave, 2001).

5. Pierson and Smith, *Rebuilding Community*.

6. Herbert Gans, *The Urban Villagers: Group and Class in the Life of Italian-Americans* (New York: Free Press of Glencoe, 1962).

7. Fritz W. Wagner, Timothy E. Joder, and Anthony J. Mumphrey, *Urban Revitalization: Policies and Programs* (Thousand Oaks, Calif.: Sage Publications, 1995).

8. Lawrence J. Vale, *Reclaiming Public Housing: A Half Century of Struggle in Three Public Neighborhoods* (Cambridge, Mass.: Harvard University Press, 2002).

9. Alexander Von Hoffman, *House by House Block by Block: The Rebirth of America's Urban Neighborhoods* (New York: Oxford University Press, 2003).

10. Sean Zielenbach, *The Art of Revitalization: Improving Conditions in Distressed Inner-City Neighborhoods* (New York: Garland, 2000).

11. Zielenbach, *Art of Revitalization*.

12. Charles Bartsch and Elizabeth Collaton, *Brownfields: Cleaning and Reusing Contaminated Properties* (Westport, Conn.: Praeger, 1997). Also see www.epa.gov/superfund/ (retrieved May 17, 2004) and www.epa.gov/correctiveaction (retrieved May 18, 2004).

Chapter Ten

Transportation and Energy Planning

There is a direct relationship between transportation networks and the development of the surrounding land. The interstate highway is a prime example of a massive transportation system impacting the development patterns across our nation. The sprouting of subdivision after subdivision followed the construction of the interstate in the mid 1950s. In the West entire suburban areas such as San Jose, California, were built near highways. With the addition of beltways and loops around major cities, many small towns turned into sprawled communities with uncontrolled development. Environmental impacts of roadways on nearby wetlands, vegetation, and wildlife habitats must be considered in developing a transportation plan. Other considerations include socioeconomic impacts on neighborhoods, schools, and business districts.

The primary components of a transportation plan include transportation management and traffic impact studies, as well as analysis of transit and land-use links. Considering the air pollution and traffic problems we now face due to our dependence on the automobile, changes in energy policy need to be introduced at the federal and state levels. Along with the problems caused by automobiles, air traffic has increased and home heating and cooling needs grown. With the depletion of fossil fuels, which are currently our main source of energy, alternative energy policies and plans should be considered.

HISTORICAL HIGHLIGHTS OF TRANSPORTATION

Over the course of the twentieth century the United States evolved from a nation dependent on its harbors and main European trade routes to a nation connected by advanced technological computer-assisted transport networks.

From hub cities that acted as gateways to specific regions of the country, the country was transformed into one super network of connecting interstate and beltway routes and air routes. The four eras of transportation in the United States are local transport, trans-Appalachian, railroad dominance, and the present era of competition.[1]

The era of local transport in the early 1800s was marked by local sustainable agriculture in which farm products and other goods were distributed by road and a network of small canals throughout cities in the New England and Appalachian areas. Many major Corps of Engineer projects expanded and deepened waterways from the 1930s to the postwar period. The Ohio, Mississippi, and the Illinois Waterways linked up with the American Manufacturing Belt, providing a transport route for bulk materials. During the trans-Appalachian transport era several cities, including Baltimore, New York, Philadelphia, and Washington, D.C., were competing to gain access to the Ohio area by road or canal. Baltimore did gain access with its National Road. New York, however, gained the most efficient, least expensive access with the completion of the Erie Canal in 1825.[2] The Erie Canal developed into a major trunk line and helped establish New York as the major port among the east coast cities.

The era of railroad dominance lasted approximately from the Civil War to World War I. During this course of massive railroad expansion, the canals were losing their dominance and actually became feeder lines to the rail trunk lines.[3] While interconnections were taking place between the eastern seaboard and the Midwest, railways began to be opened to the West. The first intercontinental link was constructed in 1869. In the early 1900s electrification of rail was instituted, creating major intercity and regional passenger service. With the diffusion of the Industrial Revolution, the railways were expanded to support the influx of manufacturing plants. The railroads stayed competitive into the present day by entering the age of technological advancement and developing automated freight-handling and shipping methods. Rail continues to provide rapid, low-cost distribution for medium- and long-haul freight. Contrary to Europe and other parts of the world, however, rail is not a primary mode of passenger travel in the United States. Although Amtrak has expanded rail service for passengers along the New York and Chicago corridors, generally these lines fail to lure enough passengers to achieve a competitive advantage over airlines. The subway has fared much better than the train as a primary mode for mass transit in many major cities in the United States. In Boston, for example, where the first subway line in America was laid one hundred years ago, residents depend on the subway for transportation. The Boston subway has grown to 64 miles of subway and trolley lines with a total of more than one thousand route miles, including commuter trains and buses.[4]

Since World War I, there has been an era of competition over what mode of transportation would dominate. After the war the advancement of technology, truck transport, inland waterways, the private auto, and finally air transport transformed transportation networks in the United States. The primary impact of the highway was to allow truck traffic to compete with rail. Trucks basically changed the distribution and shipment of goods by providing short-haul transport. In the 1920s the private automobile became the primary mover of short-haul passenger traffic, eliminating the short-haul electric urban trains.

Rail, however, held its own against this competition because long hauls were still cheaper by rail. A well-connected airline system was created during the postwar period. High-density markets for air traffic rapidly developed in the New York–Chicago and New York–Los Angeles areas. Jet services also expanded throughout the late 1950s to the early 1960s. Air traffic has expanded to include nodes for international travel, such as Chicago's O'Hare International Airport, and nodes for regional travel as in Phoenix, where several carriers serve the southwestern states. Daily commuter and economy airlines such as Southwest Airlines have become popular. Service on the eastern seaboard, for example, includes daily routes to cities in Georgia, Florida, and the Carolinas from the northeastern cities, with Atlanta as the hub.

Americans have evolved over our history to a general dependence on the private auto for commuting to work and making short, leisure trips.[5] For long trips, Americans have overwhelmingly chosen air transport. There is a direct relationship between the popular mode of transportation and the life-style of the people. With the continual growth of the suburbs, the use of mass transit has decreased in many areas of the country.[6] Arguably, the suburbanization of jobs and the increase in commuters who do not commute within or into the central cities make any high-volume transit system difficult to implement in many areas.

TRANSPORTATION PROBLEM-ORIENTED PLAN

The transportation planner is concerned with spatial organization. In developing a transportation plan for an area, the planner must take into consideration the aspects of site analysis that we covered in chapter 7, as well as transportation routes. The transportation and land-use overlay maps for an area should be analyzed and integrated into a circulation plan for a town. One impacts the other, and an ongoing study should be conducted of how new roads, bridges, or airstrips may affect the environment.

The transportation planner studies transportation as an aspect of the organization of an area. The concept of organization of an area is a study of the *fit* of the transportation paths with the topography of the site. The pathways of transportation are the circulation patterns showing the movement of vehicles and people. The topography of the site includes the environmental constraints that are present. To discover whether the transportation layer fits efficiently over the topographical layer, the planner needs to conduct a spatial-analysis study. There are two primary focus areas involved in a spatial-analysis study: spatial structures that are formed by transportation modes and how certain transportation networks developed in certain areas.[7]

The spatial structures are the central areas where each mode of transportation is accessible. A mode of transportation describes a particular method of travel or transport of goods. There may be one primary mode or several modes. In major cities such as New York, for example, there is a multimodal transportation network. This means that people from outlying suburbs such as Westchester County travel by auto to the commuter train station, by train, and then possibly by subway or taxi to their place of work. The train stations are spatial structures at each point along the journey into the city. Subway stations are also main spatial structures to access a particular line connecting to the place of employment. Points to flag a taxi are obviously organized haphazardly, especially in New York City. This spatial organization is linear access. The overlay map of transportation networks across a city would show the spatial structures that house the major modes of transportation.

The second aspect of a spatial-analysis study involves investigating why and how certain modes of transportation developed along the lines that they did. The topography of the area should be considered in the network patterns for circulation. Clusters of population should also be considered in planning transportation routes. Overall, the transportation planner is concerned with (1) the centers, or nodes, of transportation; (2) the flows, or linkages, that tie together the nodes; (3) the intensities of the flows and linkages; and (4) the relationships between the transportation network and the inner city, peripheral areas, and rural countryside. The planner studies and analyzes these four areas as components of an entire system. Two questions should be asked: What relationships exist among the first three factors? What problems exist due to the relationships?

A transportation system is a network, and stress in one part of the system pushes users throughout the network, with repercussions elsewhere. Improvements to roads may sometimes induce new traffic, as people give up mass transit and drive farther, quickly leaving roads just as congested as they were before the improvements. The following are basic transportation-management concepts that determine circulation patterns in an area:

- Street design: Street-design patterns at the local level include the gridiron, or geometric block, design; the organic design; the cul-de-sac, or circular, hammer-head, turn-around, or loop street; and the continuous circular pattern with no through traffic. Street-design patterns at the regional level include minor arterial and collector streets, secondary roads, and freeways and expressways that provide continuous movement with limited access.

- The right-of-way: The U.S. government established a public roads system to ensure *the safety and welfare of the people*. By claiming the right of sovereignty, major routes have come to be known as public routes, or post roads. Up to one-third of most urban communities are public routes.
- Linkages: Linkages are the routes and pathways, or connections, between transportation lines. The study of linkages involves identifying and evaluating the connections between where people live and employment sites and services offered in a city. How effective are the linkages in terms of transporting people and goods to major sites across the city and outlying areas?
- Nodes: The nodes are the centers of transportation access and social and cultural interaction.
- Trunk lines: The trunk lines represent the main lines of transportation in a region and include major arterials such as throughways, railways, and navigable waterways. Overlay maps of trunk-line networks can be studied to determine aspects of flows and densities of traffic. First, the main trunk lines are identified and then the feeder lines. Feeder lines are the minor arterial lines that lead into the main trunk lines. Both the trunk and feeder lines are mapped to show the spatial organization of the entire system.
- Bridge lines: Bridge lines are linkages that connect or cross over two major transportation systems. An example of a bridge line is the Richmond, Fredericksburg, and Potomac line, which carries rail traffic between the southern railroads and the railroads to the northeast. This rail line, most of which converges on Richmond, has connections in the Potomac Yard in Washington.
- Gateway: A gateway city acts as a major entryway or central focal area for transportation routes. These cities are major *pass-through* cities, with bulk materials passing through to reach another area of the country. Boston, for example, is a gateway city to the other parts of New England and Canada. Called a hub city because of the various spokes of transportation lines that emanate from the central district, Boston serves as a distribution center for the whole northeast region of the United States and Canada. Boston's hub areas are the harbor point, where bulk goods are shipped in from all over the country and overseas, and the rail points, where goods are freighted from the mid-Atlantic states.
- Transportation-demand management (TDM): Transportation-demand management is the art of modifying travel behavior, in most cases to avoid more expensive expansion of the transportation system. TDM strategies that have

been proved effective include on-site employee-transportation coordination, parking-management provisions, and alternative work schedules.

- Transportation-management associations (TMAs): A TMA is made up of representatives from business associations, employers, building-management companies, landowners, and developers. The objectives of TMAs are to solve common problems such as traffic congestion, air pollution, and parking problems.
- Trip-reduction ordinances (TROs): A TRO is a municipal, county, or state regulation that requires developers and employers to participate in implementation plans to improve traffic flow. The primary goal of TROs is to mitigate existing traffic congestion by introducing mass transit and programs such as ridesharing and flexible work hours to reduce the number of solo drivers. Some ordinances include stipulations to improve air quality standards and reduce energy consumption through conservation techniques.
- Traffic mitigation measures: Traffic mitigation measures are changes that are made to lessen impacts of traffic flow. The primary goal of these initiatives is to reduce peak-hour traffic demand by encouraging the use of alternative transportation modes.[8]

Traffic-Impact Studies

Traffic-impact studies are site-specific arterial and intersection studies that form the basis for transportation problem-oriented plans. The structural elements of the plan include the roads, bridges, rail and subway lines, and airspace. The management of transportation includes the establishment of TDM and TRO policies. The overall goals of a traffic-impact study are to (1) make recommendations for short- and long-range planning for site access; (2) describe off-site improvements needed to accommodate site and nonsite traffic and on-site circulation; (3) describe and evaluate the interface between the on-site circulation and off-site traffic; and (4) assist developers and property owners in making critical land-use site-planning decisions regarding traffic and transportation issues.[9] These goals represent the guidelines that local governmental agencies need to follow in implementing a traffic study. The specific objectives of the traffic-impact study are to identify the contribution a particular site makes to roadway-system traffic loads (traffic impacts) and to recommend roadway improvements. The recommendations that come from the traffic study must be integrated into the local and regional transportation plans to ensure efficient circulation patterns across the region.

Transportation agencies across the country vary in their interpretation of what criteria should trigger an impact study. Some agencies have established strict guidelines and conduct many impact studies, whereas other agencies have weaker criteria that demand fewer impact studies. The following criteria have been approved by the Institute of Transportation Engineers (ITE) to trigger a traffic-impact study:[10]

- When development will generate a specified number of peak-hour trips
- When development will generate a specified number of daily trips
- When a specified amount of acreage is being rezoned
- When development contains a specified number of dwelling units or amount of square footage
- When development will occur in a sensitive area
- When financial assessments are required and the extent of impact must be determined

It is difficult to assign specific threshold quantities, or levels that should be met, for the first four criteria. Overall study requirements should be related to the intensity of the traffic problems in the area. For example, a study should be conducted if trip-generation data during peak hours indicate levels beyond the threshold for an area.

Generally, a traffic-impact study should be conducted when a proposed development will generate one hundred or more additional peak direction (inbound or outbound) trips to or from the site. This number is calculated by determining how many new employees, shoppers, or clients will be traveling to or from the site each day.[11] In some cases, however, levels of less than one hundred vehicles should trigger a study. Usually, these cases are based on local safety issues of the traffic count. The following specific local conditions should trigger a study:

- Existence of any current traffic problems, such as a hazardous intersection. *Hazardous* is defined as unsafe due to accident counts, line-of-sight problems, or traffic signal problems.
- The current or projected level of service (LOS) of intersections or highways adjacent to the development will be significantly impacted. The LOS is the grade given to an intersection or roadway segment. The rating scale ranges from A to F and is based on the efficiency of the intersection. For an intersection, for example, an A rating means little waiting and a B or C means waits of one light or more. A D rating means a long wait through several light changes, and an F rating means a jammed intersection.
- Adjacent neighborhoods or business districts may be impacted. Data may indicate that added traffic from a new development may cause congestion in a neighborhood near the proposed development. In many cases neighborhood associations protest a proposed development.

- The capability of the adjacent existent or planned highway system may be inadequate to handle the projected traffic. Layers of traffic data should be collected to show the existent level with overlays of the proposed trip generations from the new development. The existent level of traffic flow is the current measurement. The proposed level is the estimated number of vehicles from the new development.

The ITE publishes a manual[12] that lists the projected levels of trip generation for various projects. For example, fast-food restaurants would generate high numbers of trips to and from the new project, whereas a nursing home would generate moderate inbound and few outbound trips. The estimated number of trips is based on the type and size of the proposed project. Whether a housing subdivision or doctor's office, assigned daily trips are estimated for each use. The transportation planner can refer to the tables to predict the estimated number of trips for the new project. The journey to work (from home) is the largest single factor in traffic generation, and critical data showing commuting patterns is available from the U.S. Census Bureau.

The scope and extent of the traffic-impact study will depend on the scale of the new development and the population and transportation network of the area. Superimposing the layers of information on the proposed development over the layers of information on the existent conditions will determine the scope.

Steps in a Traffic-Impact Study

The ITE publishes guidelines and traffic engineering statistics for transportation planners. It has developed a process for a traffic-impact study.

1. Define the Problem

Hold forums to identify issues of concern, prioritize issues, and define the problem areas. Where are the transportation and traffic issues in the community?

2. Articulate the Goals and Objectives

What end results does the community want in regards to traffic flow and transportation-management issues? Develop specific objectives to meet these goals.

3. Analyze and Evaluate

First, traffic is measured by conducting traffic counts to determine the existent traffic conditions. Traffic counts involve collecting numbers of vehicles for average and peak hours of intersections and roadways. Traffic counts can be gathered by manual count or by electronic cable. Data are collected on hazardous conditions, including the intersections and arterial roads that are unsafe due to improper road or bridge construction, poor line-of-sight or visibility factors, or improper traffic signal conditions. Data are collected from police departments on the number of accidents, collisions, and fatalities at an intersection or roadway.

Next, data showing predicted traffic impacts of the proposed project are gathered. Trip-generation and trip-distribution counts are based on the type and size of the project. Estimating trip generation and trip distribution involves using computer modeling programs that predict the number of trips based on the type of services in the zones across the area. Demographic statistics, including the income levels, racial breakdown, and location of housing, are used to predict what trips will be taken by what groups of people to the various zones.

Mathematical models can be set up to predict how trips will be distributed between alternative routes from the same origin to the distribution point. This is called trip assignment. Models can also predict the usage of more than one mode of transportation, or a modal split. A modal split means that more than one mode of transportation is used to travel from the point of origin to the point of destination under study. For example, private-auto and bus routes may be distributed across the area being studied. In this case the mathematical model would show the percentages of people using the two modes of transportation, based on the demographic data and proximity to services. Relationships between the clusters of population and the services available are considered in this equation.

Circulation patterns that will be generated by the project are also presented. It is useful to generate a map of the circulation patterns that shows traffic counts. Finally, data are collected on planned highway improvements. The data layer showing highway improvements is superimposed over the layers of data showing estimated trip distribution, hazardous areas, and proposed development impacts. This step allows the timing of road improvements to correspond with the construction phases of the new development.

The data from the existent conditions are mapped on the base map. The other data layers, including trip distribution and trip assignment from the new project, are mapped and superimposed over this base map. A circle is drawn around the planning area, and the areas of the community that are currently impacted by traffic problems are indicated. Consider the regional implications when identifying how traffic situations are related across an area.

Tests are run to determine the feasibility of each alternative. The data include expenditures for infrastructure to support the projected transportation lines, new highways or bridges, and other transportation-related services such as signage, tollbooths, or bus or rail stations. These costs are weighed against revenues available and projected grants or awards that may be received from federal or state programs. Since transportation and land use are integrally related, a new highway, bridge, or rail line will ultimately impact the surrounding land. A traffic-impact study must take into consideration the aspects of the environment that may be affected by the new development or expanded transportation lines. The database of information that is collected during this step in the traffic study includes delineation of wetlands in the study area, soil conditions and drainage patterns of water bodies in the area, and topographic features such as slope and geomorphology of the area. This data layer shows the environmentally sensitive, or fragile, areas that are included in the transportation-study area. When the traffic-data layer is superimposed over the environmental layer, the areas that should be protected are visible. New highway construction should not occur in these areas.

The alternatives are then evaluated, and one is chosen. This involves weighing the costs of the proposed transportation improvements against the savings in safety and economic development.

4. Implement Action Plans

After the data at each step are synthesized and analyzed, the traffic-impact study can be prepared. The preparation involves writing up the analysis for each database, reviewing the findings, and drawing conclusions about the traffic impacts. When this part of the study is completed, it can be circulated for comments from the public and city officials. After revisions are made based on the comments, the final traffic study can be implemented. The planner needs to constantly assess the political obstacles that might be encountered if a particular project is recommended. For example, there are typically several land-use issues involved in a highway-expansion project. One issue is rezoning. Since highway projects require vast amounts of land, many of the parcels included in the project may need to be rezoned. To create a highway corridor, the parcels would have to be rezoned as business or commercial or urban. The residents of the community, the business leaders, and the city officials usually have differing opinions in terms of the actions that should be taken. In fact highway rerouting is almost always a political quagmire. The planner needs to be able to sort out who will support and who will oppose each political scenario and prepare documents and materials for the most efficient plan.

5. Measure Results

A monitoring system should be put in place to annually review the traffic-impact study. Of particular concern are the updated data on traffic counts,

LOS, and police and safety data on intersections. The TDM strategies should be annually reviewed to ensure that the programs are accomplishing the goals of the plan.

ENERGY PLANNING

Americans use more energy per capita than any other country, and statistics show that we are the most wasteful country. The United States is home to 4 percent of the world's population, yet consumes 26 percent of the world's energy. It is the world's largest energy producer, consumer, and net importer. It ranks eleventh worldwide in reserves of oil, first in coal, and sixth in natural gas. The United States uses about seventeen million barrels of oil every day, and fossil fuels account for nearly 80 percent of the country's energy. It takes the equivalent of seven gallons of gasoline per day for every man, woman, and child to maintain the current economic level. Coal is used to produce close to 60 percent of the electrical power in the United States and accounts for 22 percent of the overall energy consumption. Natural gas accounts for roughly 23 percent of the United States energy usage.[13]

The United States imports one-third of all the oil used in the world every day, and one-seventh of the oil used in the world every day is used on American highways. Traffic congestion in the United States is primarily attributable to the private automobile. Statistics show that since 1945 automobile numbers have grown by more than 450 percent. In the United States in 1945, with the population at 133 million, there were a total of 25 million passenger cars. In 1986 with the population at 242 million, there were 136 million cars. This translates to one car per 1.8 people. At the same time, our use of public transportation has decreased from its 1945 peak to one-eighth of the 1945 level today.[14]

Along with traffic and congestion problems, our dependence on the private automobile has caused air pollution and high numbers of accidental injury and death. Due to our suburban sprawl land-use patterns, these problems will continue unless we consider alternative energy sources for our energy demands.

RENEWABLE ENERGY SOURCES

Amory Lovins argues that we should replace our current petroleum and nuclear energy sources with alternative sources.[15] Lovins describes alternative sources such as solar, hydropower, and wind as *soft energy paths*. The *hard energy paths* are the petroleum and nuclear sources we now use. The alternative sources decentralize the use of energy by replacing a central grid system with energy sources at small sites. This type of energy source and distribution can transform how we impact the environment.

Lovins relates the practice of homeostasis, the balance between humans and nature, to the energy-source dilemma we now face. He states that we have a crisis because we depend on nonrenewable energy sources. He defines non-renewable energy sources as sources that are finite—once used, they cannot be replenished as an energy source. The nonrenewable energy sources are the fossil fuels. They include coal, oil, natural gas, oil shale, and tar sands. Formed millions of years ago, fossil fuels are the organic carbonaceous remains of plant and animal matter. These energy reserves exist in underground pockets. Fossil fuels are a chemical source of potential energy; potential energy releases its energy when activated. Once extracted from the earth, however, only voids remain.

Renewable energy sources, on the other hand, have no finite limit. These energy sources, such as solar, wind, water, geothermal, and wood, replenish themselves. Since all these forms of energy derive from solar or terrestrial processes that occur on a universal or geologic time scale, we can assume a limitless supply of energy with respect to human time.

The political climate regarding environmental controls and natural-resource conservation influences the energy policy of a nation. Over the past several decades, politicians have sponsored bills to open up Western lands to mineral and other natural-resource development and to strengthen development incentives for business and industry. Offshore drilling for oil on the West Coast, timber cutting in the Pacific Northwest, and strip mining in the West have led to much debate in Congress. Environmentalists claim that the Clean Air and Clean Water Acts have been weakened. They also voice concern that the fight to redefine wetlands and private property rights currently being waged in the early 2000s will change land-use practice dramatically by 2010.

Besides the depletion of finite oil and gas reserves, there are several other problems with our reliance on fossil fuels. Private-automobile use is the primary cause of the air pollution we are experiencing throughout the country. Smog is at hazardous levels in many Western cities. In many cases smog events, dangerous levels of sulfur dioxide and nitrogen oxides, are precipitated by temperature inversion. Temperature inversion occurs, particularly in cities surrounded by mountains such as Phoenix and Denver, when a layer of cool air is trapped against the surface of the earth below a layer of warm air. The lower layer of cold air cannot rise and neither can the auto-exhaust pollutants it holds. Mixing sunlight and warm temperatures with the trapped pollutants produces smog. In the eastern part of the country, ground ozone is a major air pollution problem. The culprit is the burning of fossil fuel in automobile engines. Carbon dioxide, a combustion product of fossil fuel, and ozone, a product of NOx (another fossil fuel combustion product) and sunlight, are both greenhouse gases, but carbon dioxide doesn't contribute to ozone, except that it leads to a warmer atmosphere, which is conducive to ozone production. The by-products from manufacturing plants coupled with the meteorological conditions in the Northeast create excess levels of ozone, a hazardous air pollutant.

Along with air pollution, the problem of global warming has been associated with the combustion of fossil, or carbon, fuels. According to most scientists, the build-up of carbon dioxide in the atmosphere has been linked to the problem of temperature increases across the earth. Scientists speculate that the increase in temperature across the globe may be the cause of higher water levels, particularly along the continental coasts, and ecological changes in species habitats, including water bodies and forests.

Amory and L. Hunter Lovins argue that another problem with fossil fuels is the highly centralized grid system that is required by electricity.[16] Electricity distribution systems are highly capital intensive and inflexible in energy delivery. They also have long transport distances between energy source and energy plant. Basically, this means that electrical grids, with substations along the way, are set up in a rigid pattern across the country. The primary fuel sources, for example, oil and gas fields and coal and uranium mines, are far away from consumers and energy plants. For example, New England is far from petroleum sources. The electrical system is very capital intensive and inefficient because of the long distances between energy production and consumer. Recent major blackouts affecting large swathes of the country have occurred because of failures in the grid system.

Alternatives to the fossil fuels we use today may be set up locally. Since renewable energy sources can be harnessed at the local level, they are decentralized energy systems and do not require a hard-energy-path grid system.

• Solar energy: Radiant energy from the sun drives the earth. The atmosphere, ocean currents, the hydrologic cycle, and biological systems depend on the sun. Solar energy is renewable because the supply of energy from the sun is inexhaustible. Solar energy is very efficient, clean, and continually replaced. Solar energy is electromagnetic energy and is created when hydrogen atoms fuse to form helium. The sun emits ultraviolet rays, and at any given place the amount of incoming solar radiation is called insolation. The insolation factor depends on the angle at which the sun's rays strike the earth and the number of daylight hours. Other meteorologic factors such as the amount of water vapor present and cloud cover affect the insolation factor. This factor is a primary determinant in the design and orientation of solar buildings.

Passive solar energy involves harnessing the rays of the sun without mechanical means. The building envelope itself may act as a passive solar collector. In this case the orientation, or placement, of the building in relation to the sun is critical. For example, Minneapolis, Minnesota, in the northern latitudes of the Northern Hemisphere, has a severe winter and cold climate, and buildings there should face south. A southerly exposure, with glazing, or windows, on the south side of the house, provides passive solar heat for the building on winter days when temperatures are low and the sun shines. The north side should not have as many windows, to block winds and shield from storms. In the summer months in this climate, the building should be shaded by deciduous trees or should have overhangs positioned to block the rays of the sun. In Phoenix, Arizona, with an arid and hot climate, the building should be shaded from the sun. In this case the south side of the house should have minimal glazing, with overhangs to cover the windows.

Active solar energy applications include mechanized parts such as solar collectors or heating units. Solar collectors are rectangular units that include copper piping or other heat-collector elements with a glazed cover. Basically, a solar collector acts as a storage and distribution mechanism to transfer heated water to a piping system that distributes the water throughout a building. The solar principle is the process of trapping the rays of the sun and transforming them to electromagnetic energy on the surface of the earth. Solar energy is transferred from a building's collection site to other parts of the building. Solar heating units include mechanized parts that collect ultraviolet rays from the sun and transform the rays into solar energy or heating or cooling for a building.

Unlike electricity, which wastes 40 percent of its energy, solar energy is very efficient. It is also very clean, unlike coal, which emits sulfurous gases when burned. The problems with adopting and building solar systems are long periods of cloudy weather when a back-up system is needed and the expense of the units. Since solar energy has not been a priority in national energy-planning strategies, research and development funding to design solar applications has been minimal.

• Hydropower: The amount of water available to harness for power depends on the climate of the region and the size of the watershed feeding the reservoir. The higher the flow and vertical drop of the water, the higher the velocity for generating power. Hydropower is harnessed by water wheels or turbines. Hydropower is very efficient and renewable. The main problems with hydropower are related to the availability of a source such as a river to dam and a reservoir's relatively short life due to silt build-up. Dams also cause problems in areas where they disrupt species habitat. Fish and other watershed species may be disturbed by dams. Salmon runs in the reaches of the Connecticut River in western Massachusetts, for example, have been disturbed by dams in the Turner's Falls area.

- Tidal energy: Harnessing the forces of tides is less efficient than harnessing the potential energy of water with hydropower. Since the power has to be captured near the interface of the water with the land, this type of energy source is difficult to decentralize. The current state of the technology makes it useful only for short strips of oceanfront near large tides, such as a small village along the northern British coast.
- Wind power: Wind, captured by wind energy conversion systems (WECSs), usually windmills, is a very efficient, clean, and renewable energy source in climates with strong winds and predictable wind patterns. Meteorologic factors, including temperature, amount of moisture, and humidity, influence the type and duration of winds in a microclimate. These factors relate to the amount of solar energy that falls on a region. One major problem with wind is its unpredictability. During periods of no wind, a back-up system for electrical power is needed. Another problem with wind is the size of the windmill needed to collect the wind energy. In many communities WECSs have been voted down due to aesthetic considerations. The public and town officials often object to the size and ugliness of the windmills. In many cases the argument against windmills is similar to the argument against satellite dishes. Petitions against these structures often claim that the structures are unsightly and mar scenic views, thus impacting the aesthetics of the area. Nantucket is currently embroiled in a battle against a company that wants to build a large windmill project in Nantucket Sound off the coast of Cape Cod.
- Geothermal energy: The heat from natural hot springs is directly used to heat homes and businesses or converted to electrical energy.
- Biomass: Biofuel is a renewable source of energy that is formed by directly combusting organic matter or converting it into a usable gas. Using a thermal or fermentation process, organic material can be transformed into methane that may be used as an energy source. The carbonaceous elements are broken down in the process of fermentation, and the energy released is harnessed and converted to heat. The problem with biofuel production is that it requires high temperatures and pressures or corrosive chemicals to activate the conversion process. Direct incineration (heating of organic wastes) and direct gasification (producing pipeline gas and methane) can have harmful impacts on the environment. Conversion of a biofuel such as

natural gas to methanol consists of treatment with carbon monoxide and steam under pressure, distillation, and acid treatments, which may also impact the environment. The fermentation process to convert biomass into ethanol has fewer environmental effects.

Wood is the primary biomass product used worldwide. Wood is one of the most abundant, useful natural resources. Trees, which are renewable, cover more than 30 percent of the earth's land surface. Although it can take fifty to one hundred years for trees to reach maturity, forest management is very effective in wood production. As mature trees are trimmed and young growth is planted, the woodlands are replenished. The United States has 30 percent of its land area in forests (750 million acres). Two-thirds of the forests are commercial forests producing at least 20 cubic feet of wood per acre per year. The energy plantation concept, where large lots of trees are used in electricity-generating plants nearby, is practiced in several areas worldwide. Widely available, wood is a clean-burning energy source when proper wood products are used and the incinerator or stove is efficient.

• Nuclear power: Fission reactions split an atomic nucleus into usually two fragments of comparable mass, releasing approximately one hundred million to several hundred million electron volts of energy. Uranium is used as the mineral source in the fission process. A nuclear reactor is any of several devices in which a chain reaction is initiated and controlled, with the consequent production of heat, typically used for power generation. The nuclear reactor also produces neutrons and fission products, which may be used for a variety of experimental purposes. A breeder reactor is a nuclear reactor that produces more fissionable material than it consumes.

Nuclear power is not in widespread use around the world, nor is it uniformly spread across countries. Some regions of the world depend on nuclear more than others. France, Great Britain, and Japan have relatively large numbers of nuclear reactors. Russia has large oil reserves on its own territory, yet it has built many reactors. If the political situation is tenuous between a nation and the Middle East such as in Israel, there will be more of a dependency on nuclear or an alternative energy source. In the United States some regions have more of a concentration of nuclear power plants, such as Phoenix, Arizona, where a cluster of nuclear towers is located just outside the city limits in Glendale. The political climate and feelings about the safety of nuclear power often influence voters to vote down proposals for nuclear plants. The disposal of nuclear waste is another issue that influences voters. Spent fuel rods, the residue of the fission process, are radioactive and must be disposed of properly. The radioactive waste could be intercepted and used to make bombs by terrorists. For this reason activists against nuclear energy often protest the development of nuclear power plants.[17]

Fusion involves a nuclear reaction in which nuclei combine to form more massive nuclei with the simultaneous release of energy. A fusion process's energy output comes principally from fusion reactions of light nuclei, such as hydrogen isotopes. Because of the extremely high temperatures required, fusion is a long way from becoming an energy source for power plants. In 1989 Utah scientists announced that they had discovered a cold fusion process, but other scientists have never been able to definitively replicate their results. Many scientists theorize that a breakthrough in producing this form of nuclear energy could revolutionize the production and distribution of energy by offering limitless energy without the hazards of radioactive waste disposal.

CASE STUDY: THE BIG DIG IN BOSTON

Running through the heart of downtown Boston, the Central Artery was designed in the 1950s to carry 75,000 cars each day. But some 190,000 cars jammed the artery daily by the early 1990s. Logan Airport, the tenth busiest in the country and only one mile from downtown Boston, had constant back ups due to heavy traffic on the Central Artery. For these reasons the dream of the Big Dig, the largest transportation project in the United States, began to take shape during this time.

The new Central Artery, the Big Dig Project, was completed in May 2003. It is an eight- to ten-lane underground expressway, allowing an increase of traffic flow through the city. The Third Harbor Tunnel, which is beneath Boston Harbor, runs between Logan Airport and South Boston. The tunnel carries 18,000 vehicles a day directly from South Boston to the airport. The final portion of the project is an extension artery that goes up and over the Charles River, linking up with I-93, Route 1 (Tobin Bridge), and Storrow Drive.

Many problems developed during the construction of the Big Dig. Already the most expensive, most controversial transportation project in the United States, the costs of the project tripled over the course of construction. Businesses and industry in the construction area lost millions in revenues, and in some cases their livelihoods, over the course of the project. Contractors also faced serious environmental problems during construction. While digging the tunnels under the harbor, workers encountered problems with species-habitat disturbances, water-quality contamination, and rodents. The environmental mitigations ordered for this project were extensive.

CONCLUSION

Alternative energy sources are available, efficient, and clean. The main obstacle to widespread adoption of alternative energies is related to the lack of support by the government. A national energy policy that focuses on the development of alternative energy sources could be the solution for our energy needs for the future.

> **Discussion Box**
> Do you have traffic problems in your community? What tools do you think you could use in developing a transportation plan for your community? Do you think the United States should consider energy alternatives for the future?

PLANNING EXERCISE 10: A TRAFFIC-PLANNING PROBLEM

Read a transportation-planning or traffic-impact study article from the newspaper or a planning journal. With your group answer the following questions:

- What is the history of the project?
- Explain the transportation management or traffic problems in terms of transportation-demand management, energy-conservation measures, public-transportation initiatives, traffic calming, LOS, and hazardous intersections. Discuss how land-use issues relate to the transportation problem.
- Describe the various aspects of the traffic-impact study. Discuss the major environmental impacts of the project, eminent domain issues that may impact surrounding residents or businesses, and open-space or park issues that may impact the region.
- What alternatives did the traffic engineers come up with for this project?
- What is the preferred alternative for the project? Why?
- Discuss why the political implications of this project should be considered.

NOTES

1. Carlos A. Schwantes, *Going Places: Transportation Redefines the Twentieth-Century West* (Bloomington: Indiana University Press, 2003).
2. Schwantes, *Going Places*.

3. John Edward Clark, *Railroads in the Civil War: The Impact of Management on Victory and Defeat* (Baton Rouge: Louisiana University Press, 2001).

4. Boston's subway, called the Tremont Street Subway, opened on September 1, 1897, and cost $4.4 million to build. Opening with Park Street and Boylston Street stations, the Boston subway system was the world's second electric subway, following a similar service in Budapest, Hungary.

5. Henry Moon, *The Interstate Highway System* (Washington, D.C.: Association of American Geographers, 1994).

6. Robert J. Dilger, *American Transportation Policy* (Westport, Conn.: Praeger, 2003).

7. Kenneth John Button and David A. Hensher, *Handbook of Transport Systems and Traffic Control* (Amsterdam, N.Y.: Pergamon, 2001).

8. Button and Hensher, *Handbook of Transport*.

9. C. Jotin Khisty and B. Kent Lall, *Transportation Engineering: An Introduction* (Upper Saddle River, N.J.: Prentice Hall, 2003).

10. Institute of Transportation Engineers, *Trip Generation Manual*, 7th ed. (Washington, D.C.: Institute of Transportation Engineers, 1997).

11. Wolfgang Homburger, *Residential Street Design and Traffic Control/* Institute of Transportation Engineers (Englewood Cliffs, N.J.: Prentice Hall, 1989). Institute of Transportation Engineers and Wolfgang S. Homburger, *Transportation and Traffic Engineering Handbook*, 2nd ed. (Englewood Cliffs, N.J.: Prentice Hall College Div., 1982).

12. Institute of Transportation Engineers, *Trip Generation Manual*.

13. Retrieved May 16, 2004. from www.solcomhouse.com/fossilfuels.htm.

14. Toni Marzotto, Vicky Moshier Burnor, and Gordon Scott Bonham, *The Evolution of Public Policy, Cars and the Environment* (Boulder, Colo.: Lynne Rienner Publishers, 2000).

15. Amory B. Lovins and Hugh Nash, *The Energy Controversy: Soft Path Questions and Answers* (San Francisco, Calif.: Friends of the Earth, 1979).

16. Amory B. Lovins and L. Hunter Lovins, *Brittle Power: Energy Strategy for National Security* (Andover, Mass.: Brick House Publishing Company, 1982).

17. Amory B. Lovins and L. Hunter Lovins, *Energy/War, Breaking the Nuclear Link* (New York: Harper & Row, 1981).

Chapter Eleven

Tying It All Together: The Integrative Problem-Oriented Approach

Throughout this text the main purpose has been to teach us to re-think the way we solve problems. Considering the complexity of the issues we are dealing with today and the extent of globalization across the earth, more than ever we need to plan with an integrative perspective. We need to integrate content from different areas into specific problem-oriented plans and integrate the problem-oriented plans into the comprehensive plan for the community and the region. There are several related themes that tie the chapters together and work to teach us to think in an integrative way. One theme is the *crossover*, or cross-disciplinary, nature of planning problems. We need to learn to identify the crossover areas for a particular planning problem and refer to the specific chapters for the theories and data that we need. Although each chapter in the text is self-contained, it is also tied to the big picture of planning.

A second theme is the *interconnectedness of it all*. To solve complex planning problems, we need to study how one planning issue may be related, or interconnected, to another. The interconnections that we discover in our planning study direct us to the solutions for the problems. Although each chapter deals with a different planning concept, the thinking process to solve the problems is the same. The third theme is *anticipating chain reactions*. Throughout the text there are many examples of actions that, in turn, caused other actions and reactions. Whether the chapter involves a site-analysis problem such as steep slope or an economic problem such as insufficient revenues for a capital project, we have constantly been required to anticipate future events.

As we confront planning problems, we need to ask the right questions and look for the right data. When we ask questions, it will trigger a response to look for related data, to consider interconnections, and to recommend solutions to the problem based on these connections. Fortunately, the problem-oriented plan approach teaches us to integrate content and ideas at both the local and global levels. It is an effective approach because we are fitting interdisciplinary plans into an overall plan. It guarantees that the big picture is made up of interconnecting parts, which in turn create an integrated whole. The geographic information system (GIS) software that we use in planning practice is effective in solving problems. The significance of grant-proposal writing and private partnerships are also integral to the problem-oriented process in today's political and fiscal climate.

METHODS IN PLANNING PRACTICE

GIS programs are valuable in planning, because the focus is on the integration of material from the physical, social, and economic layers of information that we have covered. With a GIS program a planner can enter and retrieve data and query the program to analyze data layers.[1] The technical analysis that the software program generates is used to formulate recommendations for action plans. In this way a GIS program actually replicates the problem-solving process in planning.

GIS programs can generate layers of geographic data, including types of soil, slope, and other geographic attributes. Database layers showing land and water resources such as aquifers, infrastructure, and location of population and economic activity may be generated. The GIS computer programs can be queried to produce databases concerning zoning, ownership, parcel deed restrictions, and other land-use data information.[2]

The purpose of GIS programs is to make planning more efficient by coming up with multifaceted solutions to problems. GIS technology provides capability for (1) generating efficient and effective views of databases that describe land records; (2) integrating land-use data to minimize duplication; and (3) manipulating land-use records to show changes in ownership.[3] This whole layer of information is a land-records-modernization program. Once the program is established for a city or town, government officials and planning boards have access to the database. It is a database that may be shared and used according to the needs of each city department.

The GIS program sets up a land information system (LIS) program from which analysis programs may be run. When the analysis program is queried, the GIS program will spatially arrange the data across the base layer of data. For example, the software program ArcView can generate a map showing which parcels are prone to flooding in a designated area. ArcView analyzes the relationship between meteorological, soil-condition, drainage, and water-table factors and flooding attributes to display the parcels that are prone to flooding.[4]

GIS programs analyze the relationships among layers of data and display the results in map, or graphic, form. The layers of data may be related geographic or land-use records information. If, for example, a developer needed information on the existent floodplain in a proposed subdivision, a GIS query could be generated. The two categories, floodplains and ownership, could be analyzed. The display map generated by the GIS program would combine the two layers to show the parcels in the floodplain and their ownership.

GIS programs have the capability to link locational and attribute data for objects; relate data across layers, by point-in-polygon or polygon overlay; and support topological data structures to facilitate data editing and routing applications. Basically, these three functions distribute the data across layers and automatically interpret and display the results. GIS programs place the data points within a geometric space. The layers of data are transformed into a resultant layer that we can use to solve our problem. Municipal officials, as well as planners, recognize the value in this type of programming. Public works departments, for example, frequently need maps that show types of soils, existent sewer lines, projected sewer lines, and proposed subdivisions. Mapping current infrastructure over soil and drainage layers helps to determine the location for future infrastructure sites.

The GIS process is essentially the overlay mapping process that Ian McHarg first used. As we discussed in chapter 7, McHarg's process of determining site suitability for development involved superimposing one map over another until the areas suitable for development showed through. GIS programs accomplish the same tasks, with much more technical precision. The other major advantage of GIS programs is that the data is stored permanently. A database that is created for one project may be used again for another. A different set of criteria may be analyzed by querying the GIS program. GIS analyzes various scenarios by manipulating the databases.

The GIS program works like the integrative approach we have been discussing throughout the text. GIS technology provides the tools to collect and analyze land-use data that can be integrated to address complex planning problems. The following steps are involved in the GIS process:

- The first step in the GIS process involves digitizing map boundaries. The geographic site is divided into quadrants and each point on the site has a pair of coordinates relative to the origin of the quadrant. A digitizer, or automated instrument, is used to register points along geographic boundaries. Each point on the paper map is interpolated into the software program for storage, creating a computer map. In this way the boundary points are permanently recorded and may be called up to generate maps. The scale of the map varies depending on the type and scope of the planning problem or topic under study.

- The second step involves data entry that the computer stores. One method of data entry involves land-use suitability mapping. Analytically, this is conducted by partitioning land into polygons or grid cells to facilitate overlay of physical and locational characteristics of land. The other method of entering data is through analysis of parcels expressed as attributes of points in geographic space.
- The third step involves querying the computer to generate maps showing certain data layers or querying to perform specific analysis on the stored data. Either grid- or vector-format data can be used for this type of analysis. Since it usually requires weighted variables, grid-format data is usually chosen. Grid format handles weighted variables more easily than vector format. The scale of the study area also determines how the data are compiled in the program. If a regional study area is the focus, *between-parcel* analysis is conducted. On the other hand, if more detail is required of one parcel, a *within-parcel* analysis is conducted.[5]

The GIS process clearly shows a parallel with the integrative thinking process that is the focus of this text. GIS programs filter and analyze data and generate various alternatives based on the databases. In the final stage of decision making, GIS programs can run cost-benefit analyses to determine the most cost-effective alternatives for problem-oriented plans.[6]

FUNDING THE PLANS

Fiscal-policy analysis is the process in which planners estimate and evaluate the economic and financial consequences of future programs. Proposed projects and zoning changes are evaluated with cost-benefit-analysis programs. For example, city officials may request an analysis of the potential impacts of instituting a local income and sales tax in their city instead of a property tax. The fiscal programs, which are usually set up to analyze periods of five to six years, are related to the community-development problem-oriented plan.

After the budget has been approved by the city council, planners need to assess the fiscal allocations. The planners should prepare a list of projects covered within the budget allocations, as we discussed in chapter 8. A scope of work for each project should be prepared. Also, a phased schedule of the construction process should be prepared. Another list consisting of projects not covered in the budget should be made. The unfunded projects should be prioritized in terms of the immediacy of the development of the project. The following questions should be asked: What projects will not be funded for this year and probably not in the near future? What is the priority of each unfunded project? What groups will the projects serve? What are the social and economic impacts of each project? Is the project a single building or is it part of a major regional district plan?

Maps showing the infrastructure and utilities in the area of each project should be prepared. Conceptual drawings of the proposed projects should also be designed, to show the impacts of the projects on the area. City officials, local boards, and neighborhood groups should be consulted about the unfunded projects. After this process is completed, the planners should begin matching up the high-priority projects with available grants. Throughout the text and lab manual we have covered many innovative, effective techniques to carry out our ideas. We have learned about new zoning tools, community-development plans that are effective in revitalizing neighborhoods, and capital-improvements programs (CIPs) that can direct us in shaping the development of our downtowns. But the big question is, in today's fiscal environment where will the funding come from?[7]

Community Development Block Grants (CDBGs) originated in the Housing and Community Development Act of 1974. The act includes specific sections on neighborhood-needs assessment and rehabilitation. The goal of the act was to provide funds for specific activities, including sewage treatment, recreation, housing, and to bring blighted areas up to code. One of the nation's largest grant programs, the grants are targeted to specific projects with clear objectives; therefore, action plans are directly related to the planning issue at hand. CDBGs provide eligible metropolitan cities and urban counties, entitlement communities, with annual direct grants to revitalize neighborhoods, expand affordable housing, and provide economic opportunities for low- and moderate-income persons. The projects are chosen by citizens to prevent or eliminate slums or blight or meet other urgent community-development needs. The CDBG Entitlement Communities Program provides federal assistance to almost one thousand of the largest localities in the country. Block by block, whole downtown areas may be revitalized through CDBGs.

The CDBG program allocates funds based on the higher result of two formulas. One formula uses the presence of overcrowded housing in the locality, its population, and the poverty rate in its calculation. The second uses housing age, population growth, and poverty rate.

The CDBG guidelines stipulate that the monies must be used for acquisition of real property, public facilities improvements, parks and playgrounds, neighborhood facilities, waste disposal and treatment plants, and rehabilitation services. The act also requires each community to outline its housing needs in a consolidated plan that includes an assessment of barriers to fair housing and is updated every five years.

Section 8 is a legislative act in which governmental rent subsidies are issued to qualified low-income people. Rent subsidies were very widespread during the 1970s but were drastically cut beginning with the Reagan years. With the recession throughout the late 1980s and the increasing distrust of governmental controls, much less funding has been appropriated to Section 8 and other federal programs. Because of less support of federal governmental control, a recent trend to create private-public partnerships has been evident. Home ownership partnerships (HOP) is a program of partnerships between private interests, such as a local business, and a public agency, often a housing authority. It is one of the strongest options in funding housing programs for the next century. The partnership works to improve neighborhood housing by setting up programs with local banks in the community. The Neighborhood Services Program, for example, sets up a revolving loan fund. Other banking programs include mortgage subsidies and lower interest rates to qualified buyers. The Federal Housing Authority (FHA) also oversees a renter subsidy and permanent financing programs.

The grant-proposal writer has to show how the goals of the housing program will be met. One requirement is to project population and employment numbers to approximate future housing need. Another requirement is to provide an analysis of the market dynamics of the area housing industry. Citizens, particularly minorities, should be involved in devising proposed facilities and activities. In 1977 Congress expanded the scope of community-development efforts through additional funding under Urban Development Action Grants (UDAGs). These grants, which are extremely competitive, are also awarded based on poverty, age of housing stock, and demographics. Similar to CDBGs, the emphasis of the UDAGs is on rehabilitation and preservation. These grants are low-interest loans that are awarded to remediable blighted areas of cities. Urban-homesteading programs, which transfer deeds of housing in disrepair for minimal cost, and sweat-equity programs, which deed housing to owners who agree to do the repairs and construction themselves, have also been successful in creating housing for low-income people. The intent of these programs is to preserve the cultural and ethnic neighborhoods of the inner cities.

Federal housing programs have been slashed dramatically over the past several decades. Since the 1980s and continuing into the 2000s, revelations of scandals have surfaced over improper allocations of funds by the Department of Housing and Urban Development (HUD). Programs that have survived the reorganization of HUD include revolving-loan-fund programs and guaranteed loans for housing improvements. Inclusionary zoning, which we covered in chapter 6, has also become a strong tool. Inclusionary zoning creates mandatory zoning laws that encourage all types and price levels of housing in a community. Density bonus, giving a developer more units if low-income housing is included in the plan, has also been used extensively. Both of these tools encourage integration of housing types.

A computer search using keyword descriptors is the most efficient way to find grants applicable to your particular project. University libraries usually offer bibliographic searches by computer. After compiling a list of grants to pursue, the planner can obtain the supplementary materials required to submit the grant proposal. The following guidelines are helpful in discovering sources for grants:

- University libraries have general directories, foundation directories, and U.S. government sources.
- Books and pamphlets provide information on grantsmanship, proposal writing, and computer search services.
- Off-campus information centers provide information on associated grants makers of particular state and regional funding resource centers.
- Use the following keywords for community-planning searches: urban planning, city planning, regional planning, environmental planning, community development, and sociology. Private foundations that frequently award grants for planning projects are the ARCO Foundation and Standard Oil Company of Ohio (SOHIO). Federal agencies usually awarding planning grants are the Environmental Protection Agency (EPA), National Trust for Historic Preservation, Schools of Advanced International Studies, United Nations Development Program, Department of Energy, American Association for the Advancement of Science, Department of Agriculture, and National Institute of Environmental Health Sciences.

INTEGRATING THE PROBLEM-ORIENTED PLANS INTO THE COMPREHENSIVE PLAN

To complete the whole planning picture, our last task is to fit together all our problem-oriented plans into the comprehensive plan. We won't be effective unless we develop plans that stand on their own to solve specific problems but also fit into an overall plan for the community and the region. Things come crashing down when we don't pay attention to the whole picture. First, let's pull out from the text all the different kinds of plans with which we have been working. The following chapters introduce a specific type of plan: chapter 6 describes growth-management plans; chapter 7 discusses environmental and site-analysis plans; chapter 8 centers on urban-design and community-development plans; chapter 9 discusses historic-site-preservation and revitalization plans; and chapter 10 deals with transportation plans. In each case a specific issue for the community is addressed.

The problem-oriented plans are the puzzle pieces; the comprehensive plan is the big puzzle for the community. But each community in turn must be in line with the bioregion. For example, if a computer-technology research and development center is planned for an abandoned mill in a community, the community and the surrounding area should think about support services and ancillary projects that would support the facility and accompanying development. The professionals and families that would be drawn to the area would need housing, school placement, and recreational and social services. Transportation facilities, as well as hospitals and other health-related services, would have to be reevaluated. Traffic and pollution impacts on the region should be identified and plans for circulation improvements implemented. The issues that are addressed are the pieces of the puzzle of the comprehensive plan. The pieces of the puzzle are a good fit when the planning issues at the local level are connected to the environmental, socioeconomic, and transportation systems throughout the bioregion.

The following case study exemplifies the opportunity model in community planning. Faced with the worst blight in the country in the early 1980s, the people of the Dudley Street neighborhood in Boston banded together to solve their problems.

CASE STUDY: DUDLEY STREET
NEIGHBORHOOD INITIATIVE

The Dudley Street Neighborhood Initiative (DSNI) is an innovative, nonprofit community-based planning organization dedicated to rebuilding the Dudley Street neighborhood of Boston. The DSNI looks for opportunities for grants and partnerships with businesses and matches up funding with the needs of the community. The Dudley neighborhood is located in the Roxbury–North Dorchester section of Boston, less than two miles from downtown. It is one of the poorest neighborhoods in Boston. The ethnic breakdown of the 5,455 people in the neighborhood is 37 percent African American, 29 percent Latino, 25 percent Cape Verdean, and 7 percent white. The per capita income is $7,600, compared with $16,000 for the city of Boston as a whole. The median family income is $20,848, and the unemployment rate is 16 percent. Approximately 32 percent of the population falls below the poverty level.[8]

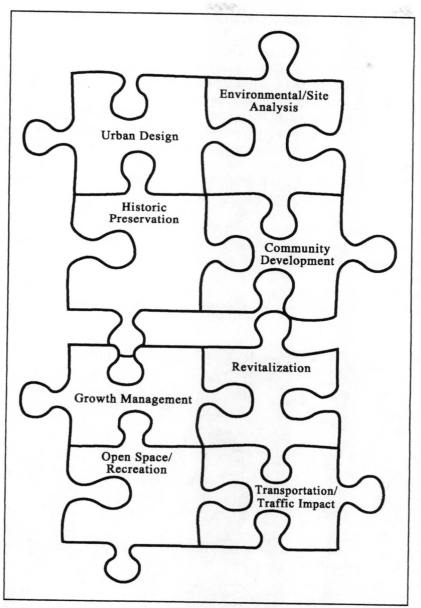

Figure 11.1.   Comprehensive Plan: The Interlocking Pieces

The Dudley Street area was one of the most blighted inner-city parcels in the nation in the early 1980s. When the DSNI was conceived in 1984, nearly one-third of the neighborhood was vacant and scarred after years of arson, dumping, and lack of investment. When planners first approached the Dudley Street neighborhood with a plan to revitalize the area, the residents balked at the plan and asked why no members of the community had been involved in the planning process. In response to the sentiment of the residents, the planners redesigned the planning structure. A new advisory board made up of the diverse ethnic groups in the area was formed, and the community took charge of developing their own revitalization plan.

The people of Dudley Street turned urban planning on its head by successfully championing what was then a novel idea: the community itself needs to be in charge of the planning process. The mission of DSNI is to empower Dudley residents to organize, plan for, create, and control a vibrant, diverse, and high-quality neighborhood in collaboration with community partners. The primary goals of DSNI are

• Economic power: develop initiatives to stimulate the local economy, increase employment opportunities, attract investors, and increase home and business ownership

Dudley Street business and mixed-use in-fill projects have contributed to the revitalization efforts.

- Environmental justice: enhance sustainable development through brownfields reclamation, provide for safer environments through strict lead-removal programs, and maintain a community greenhouse, gardens, and pocket parks
- Resident empowerment: promote leadership-training programs and support community-planning initiatives
- Children, youth, and families: provide access to educational programs and services including health care, child care, recreation, and other ancillary support services

The DSNI now has more than three thousand members, including youth, elders, and representatives from business, nonprofit, and religious organizations. Members also include representatives from several Community Development Corporations (CDCs). The main governing board is a twenty-nine-member board of directors elected by the community. Reflecting its multicultural membership, the board is made up of African Americans, Latinos, Cape Verdeans, and whites. The group is trilingual, and all committee meetings are conducted in Spanish, Cape Verdean Creole, and English.

The board of directors develops strategies to ensure that the local residents benefit from economic divestiture, home-ownership and business-grant

The DSNI continues to develop vacant lots into affordable housing in the Dudley Triangle. *The view is to the west, with Boston in the background.*

programs, and environmental programs to clean up the area. The board works with the residents to reach consensus and publicize their shared vision through a communitywide planning process. In 1987 the group developed a Comprehensive Revitalization Plan. This plan was updated in 1996. The planning committee included more than 180 representatives from various organizations. The goals of the 1996 plan focus on a commitment to create an *urban village* and to develop new programs to promote economic vitality.

The proposed projects for Dudley Street should be evaluated in terms of the *fit* with the CIP for the area. Projects should meet a need and not duplicate services. At the same time, the revitalization plan can incorporate development that would support existing functions in the surrounding area. With downtown Boston so close, the DSNI will be considering potential links to major Boston redevelopment projects that may have economic benefits for Dudley Street.

As the DSNI confronted each crisis, from serious drug and crime to shortages of affordable housing and lack of educational facilities, the neighborhood association took it upon itself to solve its own problems. As specific problems were addressed and integrated into the giant problem puzzle, the community developed a sense of cohesiveness. The community continues to work to meet the social and economic needs of the residents, while searching for opportunities to merge with the vibrant Boston scene.

CONCLUSION

This last chapter has tied together the aspects of problem-oriented planning with the grants that are now available for planning. With the changing political scene, we need to be creative in developing integrated plans for our communities. We need to identify the connections between planning issues and how to integrate these connections in problem-oriented plans. If we follow the integrative process, the local plans will fit into the comprehensive plan. This will make grant-proposal writing and funding fall into place. Clearly, this is the route we have to follow to accomplish our future planning goals.

Discussion Box
Does your community have a GIS program? What grants has your community received for urban revitalization, community development, or housing? Can you think of areas for which your community should apply for grants?

Learning Challenge: Databases and Tools in Subspecialized Areas
Analyze the prioritized issues of concern in your community, and decide what data you need from the specialized areas to address urban and environmental problems. Select practical tools that are compatible with the data and apply them to the problems in your community. Think about where you might want to work and practice in the planning arena.

PLANNING EXERCISE 11: A HOMETOWN PLANNING PROBLEM

For the final project presentation you will give a concise, informative presentation about your hometown or the community where the college is located. The final presentation is a profile of your community and an overview of a planning problem that the community is currently facing. The presentation comprises a *general profile* of the community, including historical highlights, demographics, and an overview of the zoning for the community. The *specific application* includes a discussion of a regional planning problem in the community. The planning problem may involve land-use, environmental, urban-design and community-development, economic-development, or transportation issues.

You need to collect data and maps concerning your topic from the planning department, local planning boards, and the regional planning agency or county planning commission. Specific data about demographics for your community may be gathered from websites (U.S. Census Bureau and area universities) and state agencies (yourstate.gov). Other related sources for data include federal data (EPA, HUD, and Department of Transportation [DOT]) and state agency data (your state environmental agency, state office of community development, and state historic commission).

Follow these steps for the final presentation:

- Choose your hometown or college town and the regional planning problem.
- Review the zoning ordinance, land-use and zoning maps, and GIS maps that you collected in planning exercise 1.
- Evaluate the maps and choose the most appropriate zoning map for a base map for the display board for your presentation. Choose the zoning map with the most updated information and the most appropriate scale and clarity for presentation.
- If you don't have a colored GIS map, color the base map. Land-use mapping colors such as green (forest, agricultural land), blue (water bodies),

brown (topographic features, such as contour lines), and white (open space) should be used in your graphic design. Choose a different color for each zoning district on your base map. For example, if you have large areas of single-family residential zoning, you should leave those areas white. However, if your community is built out with high-density areas, you need to clearly distinguish the districts. For example, if the downtown area consists of a dense central business core with surrounding multifamily districts, use crosshatch or checkerboard patterns to indicate the different zones.

• Make an overlay that focuses on your planning topic for your presentation. For example, if you are showing the number of subdivisions that have been built in your community over the past ten years, make an overlay that depicts the location of each subdivision with circles. In this case a chart showing the year of construction, the number of units, and the assessed and market values for each development is an effective presentation technique. Make the overlay with tracing paper or Mylar to fit over the base map. Make a border around the overlay; give it a title and legend with bold, legible letters and symbols; and put a north arrow on the overlay. Tape the overlay along the top of the base map to *line up* the overlay during the presentation.

NOTES

1. Jonathan Raper, *Multidimensional Geographic Information Science* (New York: Taylor & Francis, 2000).

2. Harvey J. Miller and Jiawei Han, *Geographic Data Mining and Knowledge Discovery* (New York: Taylor & Francis, 2001).

3. David M. Theobald, *GIS Concepts and ArcView Methods* (Fort Collins, Colo.: Conservation Planning Technologies, 2001).

4. Theobald, *GIS Concepts*. Also John Grimson Lyon, *GIS for Water Resources and Watershed Management* (London: Taylor & Francis, 2003).

5. Theobald, *GIS Concepts*. Also David B. Kidner, Gary Higgs, and Sean White, *Socio-Economic Applications of Geographic Information Science* New York: Taylor & Francis, 2003).

6. Ian Bateman, Andrew A. Lovett, and Julii S. Brainard, *Applied Environmental Economics: A GIS Approach to Cost-Benefit Analysis* (Cambridge: Cambridge University Press, 2003).

7. David G. Bauer, *The "How To" Grants Manual: Successful Grantseeking Techniques for Obtaining Public and Private Grants* (Phoenix, Ariz.: Oryx Press, 1999).

8. Retrieved May 19, 2004, from www.dsni.org/.

Glossary

build-out A projected view of a community in which all parcels are developed according to current zoning.

capital-improvements program (CIP) A six-year comprehensive statement of the objectives of capital programs with cost estimates and proposed construction schedules for specific projects.

charrette A focal group, focus session, or workshop in which community teams work together with municipal officials, interested citizens, and developers to determine the main issues of concern in a community.

city planning The term coined in the early 1900s to describe the field in which planners work to solve urban and inner-city problems. Theorists argue whether the field is a physical science or a social science or a combination of both.

community A grouping of neighborhoods and villages, the population of which may range from twenty-three thousand to thirty thousand in suburban areas and up to forty thousand in corridor communities.

comprehensive plan Twenty-year, long-range plan that encompasses all the major areas of planning, including land use, transportation and circulation, utilities and infrastructure, parks and recreation, natural systems, demographics, and economic systems.

density The number of dwelling units or persons per acre of land, usually expressed in units per gross acre. Single-family detached dwellings usually range from less than 1 to 6 per acre on a single lot. Townhouses usually range from 6 to 12 per acre and are attached in a row.

easement A contractual agreement to gain temporary or permanent use of or access through a property, usually for public facilities and access ways.

environmental impact statement (EIS) A technical document that is prepared by a federal agency that is proposing a development project. It outlines impacts of the project that may significantly affect the quality of the environment and discusses mitigations and actions to lessen impacts.

Euclidean zoning A traditional zone in which certain types of land uses with specific regulations are permitted. Based on the *Village of Euclid v Ambler Realty Company* court case.

gentrification The revitalization of an area by renovating existent buildings and structures.

geographic information systems (GIS) An organized collection of computer hardware and software and geographic data designed to collect, store, update, manipulate, analyze, and display all forms of geographically referenced information.

historic site An individual historic resource that is significant in American history, architecture, archeology, or culture and is so designated on the National Register of Historic Places.

in-fill development Development that takes place on vacant or underutilized parcels in an area that currently has access to urban services.

infrastructure The services such as roads, water, and sewer lines that support the development and operational needs of a community.

land use The types of buildings and activities existing in an area or on a specific site.

master plan A plan that guides development for a special jurisdictional area such as a downtown or airport district. The plan covers policy statements, goals, standards, maps, and pertinent data relative to past trends and future needs. Topics typically covered include population, housing, economics, social patterns, land use, water resources, transportation, and public facilities.

metropolitan centers Areas of the county with a high concentration of land uses, including government service or major employment, major educational complexes, and high-intensity commercial uses, that attract employers and customers from the region.

mixed-use zoning Zoning that permits a combination of uses within a single development, for example, permitted combinations of residential, office, and commercial uses.

nonattainment area A geographic area in which the level of a regulated air pollutant is higher than the level allowed by federal standards.

nonconforming structure Any structure that is not in conformance with a requirement of the zone in which it is located provided that the requirement was adopted after the structure was lawfully erected.

nonconforming use A use that is prohibited by, or does not conform to, the zoning ordinance. Nonconforming uses are generally ones that were allowed under the original zoning but have not been allowed since the land was rezoned or the law changed. The use in some cases may continue subject to limitations.

open space Areas of land not covered by structures, driveways, or parking lots. Open space may include homeowner-association common areas, parks, lakes, streams, and ponds.

pedestrian-oriented design Land-use activities that are designed and arranged in a way that emphasizes travel on foot rather than by car. Elements include compact, mixed-use development patterns with facilities and design that enhance the environment for pedestrians in terms of safety, walking distances, comfort, and the visual appeal of the surroundings.

planning commission *Planning commission* is a legal term that refers to the official governmental body that directs the comprehensive planning process for a community. This body may be called the planning and zoning commission, planning commission, or planning board. It is typically a local board of volunteer members who guide the development of the comprehensive plan, revise the zoning ordinances, and approve and disapprove new subdivision plans.

pollution The presence of matter or energy whose nature, location, or quantity produces undesirable environmental effects. Point-source pollution is a stationary source of large individual emission, generally of an industrial nature. In water pollution, a point source is a stationary source of wastewater discharge into a stream, such as from a factory or sewage treatment plant. Non-point-source pollution is generated by diffuse land-use activities rather than from an identifiable facility. It is conveyed to waterways through natural processes, such as rainfall, stormwater runoff, or groundwater infiltration.

preliminary subdivision plan The preliminary detailed drawing to scale of a tract of land, depicting its proposed division into lots, blocks, streets, alleys, or other designated areas within a proposed subdivision.

regional planning Sometimes defined as intergovernmental planning, regional planning evolved into regulating development from a bioregional perspective. Rather than being planning for specific towns and cities, regional planning is based on crossing over jurisdictional boundaries to solve planning problems.

smart growth Neotraditional, New Town type of redevelopment that is based on specific criteria that focus on pedestrian-friendly, accessible, high-density growth.

stakeholders Stakeholders include residents, politicians, city officials, and developers who have a vested interest in the comprehensive plan that is developed for a community. The stakeholders may have economic interests, business ventures, or specific interests in public facilities or activities.

state implementation plan (SIP) A plan developed by a state in response to air and water pollution levels that exceed specific criteria. The plan details programs to lessen the pollution levels.

stormwater management The collection, conveyance, storage, treatment, and disposal of stormwater runoff in a manner to prevent accelerated channel erosion, increased flood damage, and degradation of water quality.

subdivision The division by plat or deed of a piece of property into two or more lots, plots, sites, tracts, parcels, or other land divisions.

subdivision regulations Laws or regulations for the division of any land, lot, or parcel into two or more lots, including the provision of streets and other public facilities.

transfer of development rights (TDR) A growth-management tool used to protect designated rural and environmentally sensitive areas by allowing development rights to be transferred to properties in other parts of the county.

transportation-demand management (TDM) Techniques used to increase the efficiency of the existing transportation system through conservation programs such as ride sharing, bus and transit fare subsidies, and flexible work schedules.

urban design The blending of architecture, landscaping, and city planning concepts to make an urban area accessible, attractive, and functional.

urban renewal The redevelopment of an urban area that has been deemed blighted.

visioning Defining the future goals and aspirations of a community through public participation.

zoning The classification of land by types of uses, densities, and intensities permitted and prohibited in a district. Zoning is the regulation of existing and future land uses.

zoning district An area designated for a specific type of land use, based on certain density or intensity of development standards.

zoning map The official map showing the location of the zoning districts in a community.

Bibliography

Alexander, Christopher. *A New Theory of Urban Design*. New York: Oxford University Press, 1987.

Alonso, William. *Journal of the American Institute of Planners* (May 1971): 169–173.

Arendt, Randall G. *Conservation Design for Subdivisions: A Practical Guide to Creating Open Space Networks*. Washington, D.C.: Island Press, 1996.

———. *Growing Greener: Putting Conservation into Local Plans and Ordinances*. Washington, D.C.: Island Press, 1999.

Babcock, Richard F., Charles L. Siemon, et al. *The Zoning Game Revisited*. Boston, Mass.: Oelgeschlager Gunn & Hain, 1985.

Baerwald, John Edward, and Institute of Traffic Engineers. *Traffic Engineering Handbook*. Washington, D.C.: Institute of Traffic Engineers, 1965.

Bartsch, Charles, and Elizabeth Collaton. *Brownfields: Cleaning and Reusing Contaminated Properties*. Westport, Conn.: Praeger, 1997.

Bateman, Ian, Andrew A. Lovett, and Julii S. Brainard. *Applied Environmental Economics: A GIS Approach to Cost-Benefit Analysis*. Cambridge: Cambridge University Press, 2003.

Bauer, David G. *The "How To" Grants Manual: Successful Grantseeking Techniques for Obtaining Public and Private Grants*. Phoenix, Ariz.: Oryx Press, 1999.

Bendavid-Val, Avrom. *Regional and Local Economic Analysis for Practitioners*. New York: Praeger, 1983.

Benfield, F. Kaid, Jutka Terris, et al. *Solving Sprawl: Models of Smart Growth in Communities Across America*. New York: Natural Resources Defense Council, 2001.

Bentley, Ian. *Urban Transformations: Power, People and Urban Design*. New York: Routledge, 1999.

Bergman, Edward M. *Eliminating Exclusionary Zoning: Reconciling Workplace and Residence in Suburban Areas*. Cambridge, Mass.: Ballinger Publishing Co., 1974.

Branch, Melville C. *Planning Aspects and Applications*. New York: J. Wiley & Sons, 1966.

———. Continuous City Planning: Integrating Municipal Management and City Planning. New York: Wiley-Interscience, 1981.

———. Comprehensive Planning. Chicago: American Planning Association, 1985.

Braybrooke, David, and Charles E. Lindblom. A Strategy of Decision: Policy Evaluation as a Social Process. New York: The Free Press, 1963.

Bressi, Todd W., and Seaside Institute. The Seaside Debates: A Critique of the New Urbanism. London: Rizzoli Troika, 2002.

Button, Kenneth John, and David A. Hensher. Handbook of Transport Systems and Traffic Control. New York: Pergamon, 2001.

Calthorpe, Peter. The Next American Metropolis. New York: Princeton Architectural Press, Inc., 1993.

Clark, John E. Railroads in the Civil War: The Impact of Management on Victory and Defeat. Baton Rouge: Louisiana State University Press, 2001.

Council on Environmental Quality. The Fifth Annual Report of the Council on Environmental Quality. Washington, D.C.: U.S. Government Printing Office, 1976.

de Blij, H. J., and Peter O. Muller. Geography: Realms, Regions, and Concepts. New York: J. Wiley & Sons, 2002.

Dewey, John, Sarah Catherine Brooks, et al. The Relation of Theory to Practice in the Education of Teachers. Chicago: University of Chicago, 1904.

Dewey, John, Addison Webster Moore, et al. Creative Intelligence: Essays in the Pragmatic Attitude. New York: H. Holt and Company, 1917.

Dilger, Robert Jay. American Transportation Policy. Westport, Conn.: Praeger, 2003.

Duany, Andres, Elizabeth Plater-Zyberk, and Jeff Speck. Suburban Nation: The Rise of Sprawl and the Decline of the American Dream. New York: North Point Press, 2000.

Duch, Barbara, Susan E. Groh, and Deborah E. Allen, eds. The Power of Problem-Based Learning. Sterling, Va.: Stylus, 2001.

Dunne, Thomas, and Luna Bergere Leopold. Water in Environmental Planning. San Francisco: W. H. Freeman, 1978.

El-Khoury, Rodolphe, and Edward Robbins. Shaping the City: Studies in History, Theory and Urban Design. New York: Routledge, 2004.

Etzioni, Amitai. "Mixed-Scanning: A Third Approach to Decision-Making," in A Reader in Planning Theory, edited by Andreas Faludi. Oxford: Pergamon Press, 1973.

Falconer, Allan, Joyce Foresman, et al. A System for Survival: GIS and Sustainable Development. Redlands, Calif.: ESRI Press, 2002.

Faludi, Andreas, ed. A Reader in Planning Theory. Oxford: Pergamon Press, 1973.

Fisher, Irving D. Frederick Law Olmsted and the City Planning Movement in the United States. Ann Arbor, Mich.: UMI Research Press, 1986.

Friedmann, John. The Spatial Structure of Economic Development in the Tennessee Valley: A Study in Regional Planning. Chicago: University of Chicago Press, 1955.

———. Planning in the Public Domain: From Knowledge to Action. Princeton, N.J.: Princeton University Press, 1987.

Friedmann, John, and William Alonso. Regional Policy: Readings in Theory and Applications. Cambridge, Mass.: MIT Press, 1975.

Gans, Herbert J. *The Urban Villagers: Group and Class in the Life of Italian-Americans*. New York: Free Press of Glencoe, 1962.

Gaus, John. *The Education of Planners*. Cambridge, Mass.: Harvard Graduate School of Design, 1943.

Getis, Arthur, Judith Getis, and Jerome Fellmann. *Introduction to Geography*, 2nd ed. Dubuque, Iowa: Wm. C. Brown Publishers, 1981.

Hayden, Dolores. *Redesigning the American Dream: The Future of Housing, Work, and Family Life*. New York: W. W. Norton, 2002.

——— . *Building Suburbia: Green Fields and Urban Growth, 1820–2000*. New York: Pantheon Books, 2003.

Hedman, Richard. *Fundamentals of Urban Design*. Washington, D.C.: Planners Press, 1984.

Hoch, Charles J., Linda C. Dalton, and Frank S. So, eds. *The Practice of Local Government Planning*. Washington, D.C.: International City/County Management Association, 2000.

Homburger, Wolfgang. *Residential Street Design and Traffic Control/ Institute of Transportation Engineers*. Englewood Cliffs, N.J.: Prentice Hall, 1989.

Howard, Ebenezer, and Frederic James Osborne. *Garden Cities of To-morrow*. London: Faber and Faber, 1945.

Institute of Transportation Engineers. *Trip Generation Manual*, 7th ed. Washington, D.C.: Institute of Transportation Engineers, 1997.

Institute of Transportation Engineers and Wolfgang S. Homburger. *Transportation and Traffic Engineering Handbook*, 2nd ed. Englewood Cliffs, N.J.: Prentice Hall College Div., 1982.

Jacobs, Heidi, ed. *Interdisciplinary Curriculum Design and Implementation*. Alexandria, Va.: Edwards Brothers, 1989.

Jones, Mark Wilson. *Principles of Roman Architecture*. New Haven, Conn.: Yale University Press, 2000.

Kaiser, Edward J., David R. Godschalk, and F. Stuart Chapin, Jr. *Urban Land Use Planning*, 4th ed. Urbana: University of Illinois Press, 1995.

Kelly, Eric D., and Barbara Becker. *Community Planning: An Introduction to the Comprehensive Plan*. Washington, D.C.: Island Press, 2000.

Kendig, Lane. *Performance Zoning*. Washington, D.C.: American Planning Association, 1980.

Khisty, C. Jotin, and B. Kent Lall. *Transportation Engineering: An Introduction*. Upper Saddle River, N.J.: Prentice Hall, 2003.

Kidner, David B., Gary Higgs, and Sean White. *Socio-economic Applications of Geographic Information Science*. New York: Taylor & Francis, 2003.

Krumholz, Norman, and John Froester. *Making Equity Planning Work: Leadership in the Public Sector*. Philadelphia, Pa.: Temple University Press, 1990.

Lang, Jon T. *Urban Design: The American Experience*. New York: Von Nostrand Reinhold, 1994.

Levy, John. *Contemporary Urban Planning*. Upper Saddle River, N.J.: Prentice Hall, 2003.

Lindblom, Charles E. "The Science of 'Muddling Through,'" in *A Reader in Planning Theory*, Part III, edited by Andreas Faludi. Oxford: Pergamon Press, 1973. Reprinted by permission of the *Public Administration Review*, Spring 1959.

Listokin, David. *Land Use Controls: Present Problems and Future Reform.* New Brunswick, N.J.: Center for Urban Policy Research, Rutgers University, 1974.

———. *Energy/War, Breaking the Nuclear Link.* New York: Harper & Row, 1981.

Lovins, Amory B., and L. Hunter Lovins. *Brittle Power: Energy Strategy for National Security.* Andover, Mass.: Brick House Publishing Co., 1982.

Lovins, Amory B., and Hugh Nash. *The Energy Controversy: Soft Path Questions and Answers.* San Francisco: Friends of the Earth, 1979.

Lynch, Kevin. *Managing the Sense of a Region.* Urbana: University of Illinois Press, 1979.

Lynch, Kevin, and Gary Hack. *Site Planning.* Cambridge, Mass.: MIT Press, 1984.

Lyon, John Grimson. *GIS for Water Resources and Watershed Management.* London: Taylor & Francis, 2003.

Marzotto, Toni, Vicky Moshier Burnor, and Gordon Scott Bonham. *The Evolution of Public Policy: Cars and the Environment.* Boulder, Colo.: Lynne Rienner Publishers, 2000.

McHarg, Ian L. *Design with Nature.* Garden City, N.Y.: Natural History Press, 1971.

Mellier, Scott Goodin. *American City Planning Since 1890.* Los Angeles: University of California Press, 1969.

Meyerson, Martin, and Edward C. Banfield. *Politics, Planning, and the Public Interest.* Glencoe, Ill.: The Free Press, 1955.

Miller, Harvey J., and Jiawei Han. *Geographic Data Mining and Knowledge Discovery.* New York: Taylor & Francis, 2001.

Moon, Henry. *The Interstate Highway System.* Washington, D.C.: Association of American Geographers, 1994.

Mumford, Lewis. "The Fourth Migration," *Survey LIV* (May 1, 1925): 130–133.

———. *The City in History.* San Diego, Calif.: Harcourt Brace & Company, 1961.

Natural Resources Defense Council and Elaine Moss. *Land Use Controls in the United States: A Handbook on the Legal Rights of Citizens.* New York: Dial Press, 1977.

Nelson, Robert H. *Zoning and Property Rights: An Analysis of the American System of Land-Use Regulation.* Cambridge, Mass.: MIT Press, 1977.

Newell, William. *Interdisciplinary Undergraduate Programs—A Directory.* Chicago: Planners Press, 1986.

Olmsted, Frederick Law. *The Years of Olmsted, Vaux and Company, 1865–1874.* Baltimore, Md.: Johns Hopkins University Press, 1992.

Perloff, Harvey S. *Education for Planning: City, State and Regional.* Baltimore, Md.: Johns Hopkins University Press, 1957.

———. *Planning and the Urban Community: Essays on Urbanism and City Planning.* Pittsburgh, Pa.: Carnegie Institute of Technology and University of Pittsburgh Press, 1961.

Peterson, Jon A. *The Birth of City Planning in the United States, 1840–1917.* Baltimore, Md.: Johns Hopkins University Press, 2003.

Pierson, John, and Joan Smith. *Rebuilding Community: Policy and Practice in Urban Regeneration.* New York: Palgrave, 2001.

Platt, Rutherford H. *Land Use Control: Geography, Law, and Public Policy.* Englewood Cliffs, N.J.: Prentice Hall, 1991.

Raper, Jonathan. *Multidimensional Geographic Information Science.* New York: Taylor & Francis, 2000.

Rodgers, Joseph Lee. *Environmental Impact Assessment, Growth Management, and the Comprehensive Plan.* Cambridge, Mass.: Ballinger Publishing Co., 1976.

Schwantes, Carlos. *Going Places: Transportation Redefines the Twentieth-Century West.* Bloomington: Indiana University Press, 2003.

Seelig, Michael. "A Redefinition of the School's Role." *Journal of the American Planning Association* (September 1972): 178–184.

Sherif, Muzafer, and Carolyn W. Sherif. *Interdisciplinary Relationships in the Social Sciences.* Chicago: Aldine, 1969.

Simonds, John Ormsbee. *Landscape Architecture: A Manual of Site Planning and Design.* New York: McGraw-Hill, 1983.

So, Frank S. *The Practice of Local Government Planning.* Washington, D.C.: American Planning Association by the International City Management Association, 1979.

So, Frank S., Irving Hand, and Bruce McDowell. *The Practice of State and Regional Planning.* Chicago: American Planning Association, 1986.

Stein, Jay M. *Growth Management: The Planning Challenge of the 1990's.* Newbury Park, Calif.: Sage Publications, 1993.

Susskind, Lawrence. *Guide to Graduate Education in Urban and Regional Planning.* East Lansing, Mich.: East Lansing Association of Collegiate Schools of Planning, 1974.

Sutcliffe, Anthony. *The Rise of Modern Urban Planning 1800–1914.* New York: St. Martin's Press, 1980.

Theobald, David M. *GIS Concepts and ArcView Methods.* Fort Collins, Colo.: Conservation Planning Technologies, 2001.

U.S. Census Bureau. TIGER/Line. Washington, D.C. www.census.gov/ftp/pub/geo/www/tiger.

Vale, Lawrence J. *Reclaiming Public Housing: A Half Century of Struggle in Three Public Neighborhoods.* Cambridge, Mass.: Harvard University Press, 2002.

Von Hoffman, Alexander. *House by House, Block by Block: The Rebirth of America's Urban Neighborhoods.* New York: Oxford University Press, 2003.

Wagner, Fritz W., Timothy E. Joder, and Anthony J. Mumphrey. *Urban Revitalization: Policies and Programs.* Thousand Oaks, Calif.: Sage Publications, 1995.

Zielenbach, Sean. *The Art of Revitalization: Improving Conditions in Distressed Inner-City Neighborhoods.* New York: Garland, 2000.

Index

Index

About the Author

By combining her passion for teaching with an avid interest in the environment, **Stephanie B. Kelly** has made a career of educating preschoolers through college students about environmental protection. While organizing energy conservation workshops for community groups in the 1970s, Professor Kelly decided to make her avocation her vocation. She earned her master's in environmental planning and worked as a city planner in Phoenix, while her husband, who is a physician, worked on the Salt River Indian Reservation. With a focus on problem solving, her primary goal is to teach students how to link practical applications to real-world situations. It is the driving force in her professional and community service work.

In the early 1980s Kelly returned to New England to enter a doctorate program and work as a regional planner. She has served as professor and coordinator of the Regional Planning Program at Westfield State College since 1986. She teaches courses in geography, community planning, site-location analysis, and legal issues in zoning and planning. As internship coordinator, she places students in land-use, community development, environmental engineering, and transportation positions. She has developed numerous open-space and affordable housing plans and published many planning articles. Her research includes growth management and resource allocation planning and environmental impact analysis. Twice selected as a Fulbright scholar, she conducted environmental research in Brazil, Ecuador, and Peru. Kelly and her husband consulted on the community needs assessment and developed a strategic plan for a medical clinic in Barra Mansa, Brazil. She has taught abroad at the University of New England in Armidale, New South Wales, Australia, and the University of Barra Mansa in Barra Mansa, Brazil. Kelly is a long-distance runner and has run the Boston Marathon, as well as other races, in support of multiple sclerosis. She resides in Northampton, Massachusetts.